FERRARA

FERRARA

THE STYLE OF A RENAISSANCE DESPOTISM

WERNER L. GUNDERSHEIMER

1973 PRINCETON UNIVERSITY PRESS
PRINCETON, NEW JERSEY

FOR KAREN

54055

ACKNOWLEDGMENTS

The subject of this book was first proposed to me in 1958, by Professor Richard M. Douglas, as a possible topic for an undergraduate honors thesis at Amherst College. Though many other concerns intervened, I was finally able to take up his suggestion some years later, and I remain grateful to him for having alerted me to some of the intriguing problems of the northern Italian city-states, and to Ferrara in particular.

The research for this study was begun in the supportive environment of the Society of Fellows of Harvard University. I am indebted to the Senior Fellows for the many great benefits of my three-year term in the Society, but above all for their generosity in permitting me to spend nearly a year of that time in Italian libraries and archives. Grants-in-aid from the American Philosophical Society and the Faculty Research Funds of the University of Pennsylvania advanced the project during several recent summers. The actual writing took place in the ideal, and idyllic, setting of the Institute for Advanced Study in Princeton, New Jersey during 1970-71, while I was a member of the School of Historical Studies.

Despite this catalogue of obligations, my principal debts are intellectual. The wisdom, patience, and generosity of Felix Gilbert deserve special mention. Other friends and colleagues who have helped me by offering information, suggestions, criticisms, and new ideas are Max Ascoli, Sergio Bertelli, Malcolm Campbell, Jack P. Greene, Lewis Lockwood, Millard Meiss, Bruno Paccagnella, Antonio Rotondò, Nicolai Rubinstein, Donald Weinstein, and Fred Weinstein.

Margaret Van Sant deserves a special word of thanks for typing the manuscript and its revisions. My editor, George Robinson, has improved it by bringing to it his taste, tact, and keenness.

Philadelphia
November, 1972

CONTENTS

ILLUSTRATIONS

(between pages 116 and 117)

1. Alberto d'Este, Marquess of Ferrara
2. Niccolò d'Este, Marquess of Ferrara
3. Leonello d'Este, Marquess of Ferrara
4. Borso d'Este, Marquess, then Duke, of Ferrara
5. Borso d'Este in triumph
6. Giovanni Blanchini presenting his *Astrological Tables* to Emperor Frederick III
7. Bartolommeo Pendaglia, merchant of Ferrara
8. Ludovico Carbone
9. Ercole I d'Este, Duke of Ferrara, Modena, and Reggio
10. St. Martin dividing his cloak
11. Ercole d'Este receiving a book from its author
12. Ercole I d'Este
13. Ercole d'Este as a Christian prince
14. Eleanora d'Aragona, Duchess of Ferrara
15. The Roverella Altarpiece (detail)
16. Covered stairway in the courtyard of the municipal building of Ferrara
17. View of the Palace of Belriguardo
18. Niccolò da Correggio
19. Planimetric view of Ferrara, 1499

ABBREVIATIONS

AAM	*Atti e Memorie dell'Accademia di Scienze, Lettere ed Arti in Modena*
ACSF	Archivio Communale Storico di Ferrara
AE	*Atti e Memorie della Deputazione Provinciale di Storia Patria per l'Emilia e la Romagna*
AF	*Atti e Memorie della Deputazione Ferrarese di Storia Patria*
AM	*Atti e Memorie della Deputazione di Storia Patria per le antiche Provincie Modenesi*
AMP	*Atti e Memorie delle RR. Deputazione di Storia Patria per le Provincie Modenesi e Parmensi*
AMR	*Atti e Memorie della R. Deputazione di Storia Patria per le provincie di Romagna*
Ant. Est.	Ludovico Antonio Muratori, *Antichità Estensi ed Italiane*, 2 vols. Modena 1717 and 1742.
ASE	Archivio Segreto Estense
ASF	Archivio di Stato, Ferrara
ASI	*Archivio Storico Italiano*
ASM	Archivio di Stato, Modena
ASL	*Archivio Storico Lombardo*
BAV	Biblioteca Apostolica Vaticana
BEM	Biblioteca Estense, Modena
BHR	*Bibliothèque d'Humanisme et Renaissance*
DF	*Diario Ferrarese dall'anno 1409 sino al 1502 di autori incerti*, ed. G. Pardi, in *Rerum Italicarum Scriptores*, rev. ed. vol. XXIV, pt. VII, Bologna, 1928.
EHR	*English Historical Review*
GSLI	*Giornale Storico della Letteratura Italiana*

Iter	Paul Oskar Kristeller, *Iter Italicum: A Finding List of Uncatalogued or Incompletely Catalogued Humanistic Manuscripts of the Renaissance in Italian and other Libraries,* 2 vols., Leiden, 1963-67.
JHI	*Journal of the History of Ideas*
JWCI	*Journal of the Warburg and Courtauld Institutes*
RIS	L. A. Muratori, *Rerum Italicarum Scriptores ab anno Aerae Christianae quingentesimo ad millesimum quingentesimum* . . . 25 vols., Milan, 1723-51. New edition, ed. G. Carducci, V. Fiorini, P. Fedele, Bologna, 1900-
RSI	*Rivista Storica Italiana*
TRHS	*Transactions of the Royal Historical Society*
Zambotti, *Diario*	*Diario ferrarese dall'anno 1476 sino al 1504,* ed. G. Pardi. Appendice al Diario ferrarese di autori incerti, Bologna, 1934-36.

FERRARA

INTRODUCTION

For many reasons, some of which are presented for the first time here, Ferrara is one of the most interesting and important of the Italian despotic states. Among the first to escape from the freedom of the representative but chaotic communal politics of the late Middle Ages, the principal city of the Po delta opted for despotism in the middle of the thirteenth century. Though some of its citizens had second thoughts about this decision, especially during the first fifty years or so of the Este hegemony, the relationship between the Ferrarese *popolo* and their Estense *signori* rested upon a solid foundation of consent. The Estensi strengthened and built upon this foundation over the following centuries, and created and maintained the scaffolding of a social and political structure that endured without interruption in Ferrara until 1597, and in Modena until the Napoleonic invasion. But it is important to understand that the essential elements of the Este state were introduced at the very beginning. My views on the consensual character of the signory should not be taken to mean that I believe the Estensi and their circle were not aristocrats who exploited the *popolo* systematically and energetically. On the contrary, they behaved as most governments have always behaved, and as many still do.

But the Ferrarese were willing to be so exploited or, to put it differently, they were prepared to accept such exploitation as the price for particular forms of security which they urgently needed. One of the principal reasons for the continuing success of the Este was their more or less consistent ability to recognize and provide for this demand in many areas of Ferrarese life. Thus, their grip on power only became tenuous when forces beyond their control threatened or compromised their ability to fulfill their part of an implicit social contract existing between themselves and the Ferrarese people. Flood, famine, plague, and war posed dangers to their rule greater by an order of magnitude than the effects of their taxes and extravagances. It was at such critical flashpoints of danger—and only at such moments—that the Estensi found it necessary to use force, the last resort of all rulers who desire at all costs to stay in power. Even at times of crisis, the use of force was relatively rare, and I believe that this is not merely a function of the threat of superior power over a cowed and subservient populace, but the product of a consensual relationship that had to be flagrantly undermined or compromised to produce anything even vaguely resembling organized social unrest.

The maintenance of such stability is itself a significant feat in the tormented history of Italian politics in the fourteenth and fifteenth centuries. By solving the problem of political stability, the Estense *signoria* made it possible for the Ferrarese to get on with the tasks of land reclamation, flood control, agricultural production, and urban construction, all of which had particular urgency in their situation. To turn this around, it might even be argued that the Ferrarese, perhaps more than other Italians, could not afford the luxury of prolonged social upheaval, because of the economic and geographical imperatives of their lives. Their conscious escape from freedom was perhaps also a deliberate step toward the mastery of their natural and human milieu, and toward an emerging sense of control upon which significant political and cultural achievements would have to be built.

In a sense then, I see the Estensi in almost Burckhardtian terms, as accomplished rulers who practiced statecraft as an art (which is now an archaic way of saying that they were adroit monarchical politicians rather than tyrants pure and simple). But they may also be seen as the liberators of the Ferrarese from a servitude deeper and more terrible than the rule of a reasonably well-disposed monarch. For the Estensi came increasingly to patronize not only artists and men of letters, scientists and physicians, but also engineers and hydraulic experts, shipbuilders and architects, and all the other kinds of specialists upon whom an increasingly complex, urban community depends. Both materially and intellectually, they aided in a process in which a poor agrarian population, subject to the vagaries of a treacherous climate, a capricious river, and a tumultuous political world, gradually achieved a more harmonious and masterful relationship with its surroundings, developed more reliable economic arrangements, and committed itself to a relatively unoppressive and dependable though certainly self-interested political regime. If there were Machiavellians before Machiavelli, it is also fair to say that there were enlightened despots before the Enlightenment, and that the Estensi have a solid claim to be placed in that category.

The major part of this book deals with the regimes of the four greatest princes of the House of Este—Niccolò III and his three sons, Leonello, Borso, and Ercole I, who succeeded him in that order. As a group, these four men ruled over eleven decades of Ferrarese history, spanning the entire fifteenth century. Each cultivated some of the interests and concerns of his predecessors, and each undertook new departures. Though other aspects of their reigns will be treated at length, especially topics relating to administrative and social institutions, the most interesting and important kinds of changes occurred in the areas of literature, scholarship, and the arts. Here it will emerge that in a society as small and as centralized as the court of Ferrara, the interests and the personality of the head of state had a determining influence on the concerns and achievements of artists and men of knowledge; and I suggest in particular the precise ways in which this affected the developing cultural life of the Ferrarese court from 1441 to 1500.

In fact my search for an understanding of the unique achievements of Ferrarese culture has led me into a rather far-ranging and detailed analysis not only of the reigns but also of the personalities and interests of the individual *marchesi* and of the cultivated societies that they fostered (or in some cases tolerated) at their court. Some of the sources upon which I have drawn in those parts of the book that deal with artistic and cultural matters appear here for the first time, though others are already well known to scholars. I have tried to be explicit about my debts, often extensive, to the many scholars who have contributed to our knowledge of particular aspects of Ferrarese cultural and artistic history. It has been especially difficult to limit discussion of some of the new sources which I have been lucky enough to find so that they would fit within the scale of the book as a whole, and still contribute what they have to offer to its general interpretive thrust. In the interests of maintaining some sort of proportion, I have deliberately limited discussion and quotation of some of these manuscripts. In particular, the *De triumphis religionis* of Giovanni Sabadino degli Arienti is a work which requires and deserves more extended discussion, and which will appear as a separate volume, entitled *Art and Life at the Court of Ercole I d'Este,* in the *Travaux d'Humanisme et Renaissance.*

Many of the literary sources for Ferrara—particularly the writings of court humanists such as Arienti—are alien to contemporary tastes and sympathies. Their language is windy and fancy, their praise of rulers effusive and cloying. Here, perhaps, a cautionary note should therefore be sounded. Scholars have always been skeptical, and with good reason, of the lavish praise heaped upon Renaissance rulers by the humanists who surrounded them. These self-serving *epigoni* of the ancient rhetors, with their inflated comparisons of the merest princeling with Augustus or Alexander, certainly do not inspire confidence. Yet we have been much less cautious about accepting the sometimes comparably extravagant or inflated rhetoric of those humanists who surrounded the powerful men of the republics. It is at least arguable that they may have had an equally great interest in maintaining the *status quo,* and that their own political thought reflected the facts that they had careers to build, wives to support, and investments to safeguard. Can we be certain that their ideals were invariably higher and their achievements always superior to those of their counterparts elsewhere? Some of these considerations may seem a bit crass, and there is no doubt that a deep sense of conviction lies behind the libertarian rhetoric of the Florentine chancellors and other humanists in republican states. But there can also be no doubt that this conviction and commitment coincides very nicely with their own private interests, as it does at the courts, and that the values and concerns of republican governments, as measured by their behavior, often differed very little from those of the despots, whose humanists perhaps deserve equal credence or skepticism. In all times and places, the claims and the rhetoric of governmental spokesmen and highly-placed apologists must be taken with extreme caution, even when they are not professional rhetoricians. There is, I would venture, little if any evidence that the Florentines' sense of moral superiority was based on any criteria that could command widespread assent, then or now. Florence's civic propaganda, whether republican, Medicean, or Savonarolan, is freighted with a parochial chauvinism, a fact that was not lost even on Dante. And it is doubtful, to put it mildly, whether the Ferrarese, or the Milanese for that matter, ever inflicted the kinds of hardships on their client states that the Florentines imposed on Pisa and Arezzo, or the Venetians on Ferrara.

More generally it can and should be said that regardless of the constitutional arrangements under which Italians lived in the fourteenth and fifteenth centuries, they were almost invariably ruled by an aristocratic élite, whether of birth or wealth, and that these élites usually showed a primary commitment toward their own interests and values. To believe otherwise not only goes against the evidence, but flies in the face of common sense. Without denying the enormous impact of humanist thought on political ideology and civic behavior, one may suggest that some scholarly interpretations of humanist political ideology have tended to accept at their face-value statements that may also be considered in the light of existing circumstances to have been politically useful, and perhaps even self-serving. In the Florentine case, for example, there remains at least the possibility that republican rhetoric was used—though perhaps not consciously—to further the goals of an expansionist territorial state. In some respects, the resonances of this scholarly debate have a familiar ring to modern ears, despite the obviously and radically different circumstances.

In some ways it has required an unusual act of will to pursue these studies with the traditional professional detachment. To choose to spend years in the study of a relatively little-known, medium-sized Renaissance despotism in a period when many of the best Renaissance scholars of one's own and immediately past generations have devoted their energies to illuminating the history of its greatest republic, Florence, has sometimes seemed an idiosyncratic and perhaps somewhat marginal undertaking. And indeed, I have neither wished nor been able to divorce my own sympathies entirely from those of the scholars working on Florentine history, at least some of whom like myself find a special attraction in the study of the Arno city in these times, when democratic assumptions and representative institutions are undergoing fundamental challenges from every side. In fact, perhaps the most important and distinctive achievement of Renaissance historical scholarship since World War II has been an outgrowth of this affinity—it is the fundamental archival research which has provided the groundwork for a major new synthesis of the history of Florence.

The history of Ferrara and the other so-called tyrant courts has not fared nearly so well, which is attributable in part to these republican preferences of Western European and particularly American historians, especially after the great global conflicts of this century. But it also reflects the greater glories of the Florentine achievement in many fields, and the particular pleasures and benefits of working in the city of Michelangelo, Machiavelli, and the Medici. Florence's pre-eminence is well deserved, but it has produced some imbalance in our understanding of *Quattrocento* culture. Although some of the non-republican city-states have begun to receive increased attention in the last decade (and have never been entirely neglected by local historians and antiquarians writing in Italian regional journals) none has been studied in sufficient depth, and over a long enough time span. However, we now have such important works— produced by British scholars—as those of D. P. Waley on Orvieto, J. K. Hyde on Padua, and J. Larner on the despotisms of the Romagna, and work is proceeding apace on Urbino as well. There has also been a renewed concern with the processes of political and institutional change in Italy from the thirteenth century onward, and this has served to refocus interest on the "problem of the despots," which is really the problem of why all the medieval republics sooner or later collapsed.

The fact that the despotisms have tended to attract fewer serious students than the republics makes any attempt at scholarly synthesis hazardous. The case of Ferrara is perhaps typical. Here, there is hardly even a tradition in relation to which one's own views can be expressed. To the best of my knowledge this is the first book on the history of Ferrara to be written by an American, and only the third in English. The other two were written almost three-quarters of a century ago, and they show their age. In the last half-century the only comparable work is a crude little Marxist tract published in Italian nearly twenty years ago. (Recently, Luciano Chiappini has published a useful family history of the Estensi, from the "beginning" to the nineteenth century, but his work is broader in chronological scope, less analytical in intent, and altogether different in focus from serious scholarship on the Renaissance period.) This for the city that produced—to mention only a few—those remarkable princes Leonello, Borso, and Ercole d'Este, those sublime poets Boiardo, Ariosto, and Tasso, those splendid painters Tura, Cossa, and Roberti, those magnificent scholars Guarino, Leoniceno, and Calcagnini, those superb women Eleanora, Isabella, and Lucrezia.

Fools rush in where angels fear to tread. There are hundreds of thousands of documents in the Archivio di Stato in Modena which no one has ever studied, and which it would take a large team of very busy scholars many years to read and interpret. I have made occasional use of this great treasure-house for information on various specific topics, but for many subjects it remains a mine that has hardly been worked. There are humanistic manuscripts bearing on Ferrarese culture in libraries throughout the world, and it will be some time before they can be completely collated into a usable checklist. In many respects, the administrative, economic, and social history of the Este state remains to be written, and one can rely only on a small series of old and dated studies—quite limited in scope—on which to base some tentative generalizations or speculations. The same is true for political and diplomatic history, though to a lesser degree.

These are wide and discouraging gaps, and no one is more conscious of how much remains to be done than I. Yet what is immediately needed, at least in my judgment, even more than another monograph dealing with a single aspect of the history of Ferrara, is an audacious attempt at synthesis, which would bring together the scattered and uneven results of monographic scholarship over the years, and would amplify this with new findings from other sources, as a basis for further research and debate. That, in any case, is what I am offering here; and my research has been guided by a primary interest in discovering the ways in which Renaissance despots used their powers, in the broadest sense, as rulers of men, as wielders of the fisc, as builders of dynasties and empires, and as patrons of the arts and letters.

Though this essay is devoted to Ferrara, readers will recognize implications both for the history of Renaissance despotisms and republics. Many of these are spelled out in the text, which can be read without reference to the notes. In the notes, however, I have tried to take up many of the vexing and provocative issues that have engaged scholars in the fields concerned, by way of providing necessary bibliography and offering further explanation and discussion. The bibliographical references are cited either as sources or as points of departure for further reading or debate. They are not intended to be exhaustive, and the absence of a particular work should not imply that it is unknown to the author.

In both the text and the notes I have tried to focus on a single overriding topic—what I call the style of a Renaissance despotism. There are those who will be irritated by each of the three operative words in that phrase, for they are all words that have proven themselves sturdily resistant to precise and consistent usage. But the resources of both the language and the author are limited, and the best I can do here is to try to be quite clear about the senses in which these terms are to be used in this book. I use the term "despotism" to mean monarchy, not tyranny. That is to say that the term is intended here in the traditional Greek sense, to be non-normative, and to imply neither approval nor condemnation. The word *Renaissance* is used in a purely chronological sense, to denote the period roughly bounded by the years 1300 and 1600 in Western Europe, though in this book it is used almost entirely in relation to the fifteenth century. The word *style* presents greater problems and has more serious implications for my purposes: I use it very broadly to refer to the way the Estensi did things in all fields, for in my research I have tried to establish whether or not there were particular methods, procedures, and concerns which carry over from one reign to another and from one field of signorial activity to another. It is this problem, more than any other, that forms the unifying thread for discussion of such disparate subjects as hydraulic projects, administrative innovations, religious piety, education, and musical and artistic patronage.

I Origins of Renaissance Ferrara

The rise of the Este family to hereditary lordship over Ferrara and a vast hinterland is inextricably related to the growth and development of the city as a major political and cultural center. For nearly three centuries, men of the house of Este ruled Ferrara. Soon after they arrived, it became a place to be reckoned with, a town that could enforce its laws, maintain its walls, defend its boundaries, collect its revenues, attract and entertain its distinguished visitors and sojourners, and send forth its own emissaries—political, cultural, religious, and scientific—to the courts and academies of Europe. And when in 1598 the Este left, and Ferrara reverted to direct papal rule, it quickly resumed its role as the dreary provincial backwater it had been before their arrival. Unable even to live on its past (for what the Estensi could not take along to Modena the papal governors soon destroyed), its population dwindled, its university hibernated, and weeds grew in the streets. Such tribute as it collected took the form of poetic nostalgia from Goethe, Browning, and Carducci.[1]

[1] There is no systematic study considering reflections of Renaissance Ferrara in later European literature, though such a work would be useful. It would have to take account not only of such key works as Goethe's *Tasso*, Browning's "My Last Duchess," and Carducci's "Alla Città di Ferrara," but also of more passing references to the city or members of the Este family, such as those by William Butler Yeats, in the poem "To a Wealthy Man who Promised a Second Subscription to the Dublin Municipal Gallery if it were Proved the People Wanted Pictures." An interesting conspectus of the general literary impact of Ferrarese culture has, however, been offered in a brief essay by G. Getto, "La Corte Estense di Ferrara," *Letteratura e critica nel tempo* (Milan, 1954), 219-40. Getto's main point is that by analyzing the poems of Boiardo, Ariosto, and Tasso, it would be possible to develop a synthetic understanding of the courtly life of Ferrara. See some comments on this view in my article, "Toward a

This study intersects a lengthy continuum. In concentrating on the period beginning with Leonello d'Este's accession in 1441 and ending with the death of Duke Ercole I in 1505, it deals closely with only about one-fifth of the period of Este rule. But that does not demand apology, for ours is a central period, both chronologically and developmentally. It was the period in which Ferrara made many of its most distinctive literary and artistic contributions, elaborated its most effective and characteristic political forms and social organizations, and, above all, perfected what I call the style of a Renaissance despotism.[2] If one can really begin to understand the dynamics of these sixty-four years of Ferrarese history by analyzing what they reveal about the structural strengths and weaknesses of Ferrara's political, economic, social, and cultural institutions, one will have implicitly shed some light on what went before and came afterward. But by the same token, it is obviously impossible to acquire such understanding without frequent reference to times and places outside this special focus. In particular, it is important to review now the unique elements in Ferrara's transition from commune to signory in the thirteenth century, because the particular form that this change took helps in essential ways to explain the configurations of the *Quattrocento* city-state.

Despite extensive investigation, the origins of Ferrara remain obscure. Because of the nature of the marshy terrain of the Po delta, the archaeological record has suffered greatly, but it is clear that the region of which Ferrara became the natural center had already been inhabited,

Reinterpretation of the Renaissance in Ferrara," *BHR,* xxx (1968), 274-76 (hereafter "Toward a Reinterpretation").

[2] The preface and conclusion of this book specify the kinds of concerns which I subsume under the category of despotic style. I have also dealt with this question in "Toward a Reinterpretation," esp. on pp. 279-81.

though probably sparsely, since ancient times.[3] Food abounded. Cereal grains flourished in the fertile, well-watered soil. So did fruit trees and the vine, though the wine tended to be more abundant than delectable. The branches of the Po—one of which flowed by the site of the future city along its southern edge—teemed with a wide variety of fish, and the enormous tidal ponds of Commachio pullulated with the spawning Atlantic eels for which they are still known today, and with the natural predators that sought them there. In the copses, thickets, and woods dividing marsh and cultivated land lived game of all sorts, from thrushes and warblers to huge herons and eagles, from weasels and foxes to stag and boar. And of course, insects were everywhere, especially the mosquito, playing its traditional Mediterranean role in controlling the human population.[4] The climate of the region was, and remains, Medi-

[3] For the early development of Ferrara, see G. Righini, "Come si è formata la città di Ferrara," *AF*, n.s., xiv (1955), 55-96, which should be supplemented by the study by O. Vehse, "Le Origini della storia di Ferrara," *AF*, n.s. xviii (1957), 1-149, and the survey by A. Ostoja, "Ferrara nella sviluppo storico della regione," *Ferrara Viva* ii and iii (1960-61). All of these articles cite the extensive earlier literature on the subject, which is also covered in the able study by L. Chiappini, *Gli Estensi* (Varese, 1967), which also has the best recent bibliography on the history of Ferrara and the Estensi (pp. 511-52). In the following pages, I shall often refer the reader to Chiappini's competent narrative both for more detailed and factual treatment of political and diplomatic events than will be found here and for more systematic bibliographical references. This book, in contrast, seeks to focus discussion on developments that are particularly revealing for an understanding of the general character of the signorial regime of the *Quattrocento*.

[4] On the impact of mosquitoes on the life of Ferrara and the Po delta, it is worth consulting the anonymous fifteenth-century poems published by L. Frati, "Sonetti satirici contra Ferrara in un codice Bentivolesco del Secolo XV," *GSLI*, ix (1887), 215-37. These sonnets are perhaps the work of Antonio Cammelli ("Il Pistoia"). They frequently use rhyme schemes in which Ferrara may be rhymed with *zanzare*. The sonnets were

terranean in summer, and almost southern Baltic in winter. When the sun beats down on that low, flat land, humidity presses in everywhere, and the sky appears almost white through an aqueous haze. In the cold season, the counterpart of haze is fog, the syrupy ground-fog of Emilia that blots out everything until, for a brief stretch at noon, the sun may transform the miasma from cotton to gauze, or until the piercing Alpine winds disperse it over the Adriatic.

The first settlements in the region appear to have been those of lake- and river-dwelling peoples. The Museo Archeologico Spina, which is primarily devoted to artifacts of later origin, also preserves two impressive dugout canoes that may be assigned to the pre-Etruscan settlement. The site at Spina, near the present Commachio, demonstrated the existence of an important Hellenistic commercial center at a place near the sea, later submerged beneath a tidal pond. During the barbarian invasions the territories around Ferrara, which had never attracted much Roman interest, became a refuge for inland peoples who found themselves in the path of the invaders. Some have speculated that the name Ferrara is a corruption (*via* the Latin Ferraria, or Feraria) of a Roman outpost called Forum Alienum. That village, or what was left of it, came under the dominion of the Exarchate of Ravenna in 575. It is quite certain that by the year 750, the essential village, consisting perhaps of not more than a hundred houses, a few small churches, and possibly some fortified towers, was situated at its permanent location on the newly formed Po di Volano, and the first reference to it by name occurs in a document of the Lombard King Astulf, which scholars have dated to 753 or 754.[5] There is no evidence of any major growth over the

---

written in 1494, a time when Ferrarese collaboration with the French had brought her reputation in much of Italy to its nadir.

[5] *Encyclopaedia Brittanica,* 11th ed., vol. 10, (New York, 1910), 282, art. "Ferrara," author not given.

next three centuries, though there are indications that drainage of the surrounding marshes was initiated, with a view to eventual further expansion of the tiny nucleus. Having passed through the hands of the Byzantine Exarchs, Ferrara became a possession of the King of the Lombards for a time, and was then confiscated by Charlemagne and given to the papacy. Subsequently, it was conferred as a fief upon a nephew of the German Emperor Otto I, Tedaldo, Count of Modena and Canossa.

Like many other towns in Lombardy and Emilia, Ferrara took advantage of the political confusion of the Guelf-Ghibelline struggle to establish a *de facto* liberty from both papal and imperial control. In 1101, Tedaldo's illustrious grand-daughter, Matilda of Tuscany, besieged the city and re-established imperial authority.[6] By that time, the town had already adopted a communal form of government, but one in which the great feudal families of the region continued to play a role commensurate with their real power. Of these, the Adelardi were pre-eminent, both as feudatories and as the principal office-holders within the commune. Muratori observes that although they lacked princely title and prerogatives, they nevertheless acted like princes because of their wealth and nobility.[7] When Guglielmo died in 1146, his entire estate passed into the hands of his brother, Adelardo, the last of the Adelardi. About the year 1185, the family's entire inheritance appeared to devolve

[6] See N. Duff, *Matilda of Tuscany* (London, 1909), 19, 27, 198; and esp. L. A. Muratori, *Ant.Est.*, I, 16-26, 226, *et al.*

[7] *Ant. Est.*, I, 354: "Fu la Famiglia de gli Adelardi, chiamata anche da alcuni della Marchesella, a'suoi giorni la più potente e riguardevole di Ferrara, in guisa che quantunque le mancassero Titoli e Stati Principeschi, tuttavia per le sue richezze e per la sua Nobiltà, faceva la figura di Principe." For the most authoritative discussion of Muratori as an historian see S. Bertelli, *Erudizione e storia in Ludovico Antonio Muratori* (Naples, 1960).

upon the young Azzo d'Este (son of Obizzo I), by virtue of his newly arranged engagement to Marchesella, Adelardo's daughter.

Suddenly, a member of the most distinguished family in northeastern Italy would be first among equals in the Ferrarese feudal aristocracy. Obizzo, the first of the Estensi to bear the title of Marchese, owed his son's imminent good fortune at least in part to the intercession of the Bishop of Ravenna, who had had the girl kidnapped for safekeeping, so that she could make a safe Guelf match, acceptable to Rome.

Who were the Estensi, these powerful newcomers on the scene of Ferrarese government, and how were they received? The oldest and most prestigious noble family north of Florence and east of Milan, the Estensi were of Lombard origin, for early documents identify them as such, and they observed Lombard customary laws of succession and inheritance. Though they settled north of Tuscany, they were descended from the Obertenghi, those great feudal lords of the ninth and tenth centuries who controlled almost the whole Tuscan *contado,* and parts of Liguria and Lombardy. Their strong tradition of service to the Holy Roman Emperors led, throughout the middle ages, to a vast series of feudal grants and titles, which formed the basis for the family's political and economic fortunes in their Paduan domains. Their name derives from their castle at Este, in the Eugenaean hills southwest of Padua, though their activities always encompassed a much broader sphere. By the late eleventh century, for example, the Estensi had established close marital ties with some of the princely houses of the Welfs.[8]

[8] The origins and development of the Estensi have received extensive scholarly attention. Muratori's work is of course basic, but much additional research now supplements his findings. For more detailed discussion of

Like many other great medieval institutions, important noble families often tried to cultivate an image of even greater antiquity than they could legitimately trace, and sought to imbed their claims of princely precedence in the amber of a mythic past. The Estensi typify this tendency. Chroniclers in the late thirteenth and early fourteenth centuries thought they were descended from Trojan princes, a popular derivation which Ariosto immortalized and the great Muratori debunked with obvious relish.[9] Other early historians, failing to realize that the Lombard tribal origins of the Obertenghi clearly denoted a Germanic past, held that the Estensi were originally settlers from Carolingian France. This was the view of Pope Pius II, and it appears to have been shared by Borso d'Este himself, and a host of *Quattrocento* authorities. Though somewhat wide of the mark, it commands interest as the earliest attempt to de-mythologize the origins of the family by providing a historically plausible account of their early presence and power in central Italy. In the 1560's, the myth-makers were still at their old games, as appears from the fact that court historians such as Giovanni Battista Pigna, among others,

---

the earliest period see now ch. II of Chiappini's *Gli Estensi,* and his bibliography, pp. 514-17. For relations between the Estensi and the Hanoverians see A. Lazzari, "La dinastia regnante in Inghilterra deriva da un ramo di Casa d'Este," *Attraverso la storia di Ferrara: Profili e scorci, AF,* n.s., x (1954), 427-29.

[9] *Ant.Est.,* I, 68: "Dichiamola però ben presto: questo Marto Principe Troiano, e assediatore di Milano, e questo discendere da lui la Casa d'Este, sono sogni, son favole. La malattia è vecchia." Muratori goes on to say that even the Romans suffered from the same delusions of Trojan origins, more recently put forward by the French. He also takes Ariosto to task for propagating the myth, and disdainfully dismisses the latter's views, suggesting that they are perhaps acceptable for poets, "ma da gli storici, e da gli amanti della Verità nè pur degnate d'un guardo." After a survey of the literature he introduces his own view of the German origins of the family (see his ch. X).

claimed that the Estensi were descended from a noble family of republican Rome.[10]

The notions that we call myths and Muratori debunked as "dreams" were taken with perfect seriousness by the men of the medieval towns. And so, the imposition of one of the most ancient and powerful European families on the stage of Ferrarese internal politics brought an unusual sense of uncertainty to Guelfs and Ghibellines alike for, though the Estensi ruled many of their territories under imperial grants, they fully recognized papal sovereignty over Ferrara. The imperial faction in Ferrara at the dawn of the thirteenth century had as leaders the Torelli family, less ancient but no less vigorous than the Adelardi had been before their demise. The history of Ferrara from 1187 to 1264 can best be viewed as a relentless struggle for power between Estensi and Torelli, the latter acting with increasing desperation from a solid local base, the former inexorably strengthening their position through international support, superior wealth and power, and canny political maneuvers within the town.

By the year 1200, Ferrara was beginning to be worth a struggle. Over the preceding two centuries, the city had shared fully in the remarkable commercial and demographic expansion of the Italian towns. Though lacking the major

[10] It is evident that the mythification of family origins by the Estensi in Ferrara is analogous to a similar process used to justify the sovereignty and establish the antiquity of Renaissance republics. Such a process for Florence is analyzed in the important study of N. Rubinstein, "The Beginnings of Political Thought in Florence," *JWCI*, v (1942), 198-227. Correspondingly, the challenging and eventual refutation of such myths is an essential step in the development of historical consciousness in European societies. Muratori represents an advanced stage in that process. For its earlier development, see now D. R. Kelley, *Foundations of Modern Historical Scholarship* (New York, 1970); and D. Weinstein, "The Myth of Florence," in *Florentine Studies,* ed. N. Rubinstein (London and Evanston, 1968), 15-42.

industries, mineral resources, and financial institutions developed elsewhere, it was able to benefit from a good location, astride the north-south land routes from Venice to Bologna, the Romagna, and Tuscany, and the east-west water route connecting the cities of the Lombard plain and the northwestern interior with the Adriatic. The increasing volume of transported goods and services provided revenue in the form of tolls and customs duties. In good years, the region could yield a grain surplus, and parts of the delta produced an acceptable grade of salt. The noble families—the Trotti, Turchi, Costabili, and many others—derived a comfortable level of income from their lands, and maintained the customary towers in the town. Riccobaldo—if indeed he was the author of the *Chronica Parva Ferrariensis* (*R.I.S.,* VIII, 483)—counted thirty-two of them around 1200 but none have survived. In brief that is how one has to think of Ferrara around the year 1200: a growing city, living off the produce of the land, producing such new marks of prosperity as an increasing array of impressive civil and ecclesiastical buildings and public works, a proud, new cathedral (begun May 8, 1135), good walls, and claiming also the mixed blessing of its natural defenses of water and swampland, and the usual factious nobility.

The young Azzo d'Este who was known as Azzolino and who had been betrothed to Marchesella degli Adelardi, had to face the disappointment of his fiancée's untimely death in 1186, intestate. This beclouded the Este claim to the political role of the Adelardi, and the Torelli were quick to seize upon the opportunity to exploit their dilemma. Prolonged civil strife—the fate of many other Italian towns—revolved around these two contenders, for whom family and clan loyalties probably bulked as large as the distant and nebulous powers of Pope and Emperor. Azzolino was elected *podestà* of Ferrara (generally a one-year appointment) in 1196, at the age of twenty-six. In the following years, his territories in the Ferrarese were augmented by several substantial ecclesiastical fiefs, but members of the Torelli family continued to serve as *podestà* and to hold other magistracies. In 1206, while Azzolino was serving as *podestà* in Verona, Salinguerra Torelli took over Ferrara, drove out the Guelfs, and installed himself as *podestà*. But Azzolino's counterattack was successful, and by 1208, it was he who was established as *podestà*. It had done no harm to the Este cause that in the interval Ferrara had come under a papal interdict, as a result of Salinguerra Torelli's confiscation of lands belonging to the Benedictine monks of Pomposa. Still, Azzolino and his forces were unable to stabilize the situation. The document produced by Muratori to claim that Azzolino was elected *podestà* for life upon his return in 1208, and accepted by generations of scholars as the foundation of the later *signoria,* has been proven (by William Montorsi) to be a forgery.[11] In fact, as the antiquarian Antonio Frizzi noted, the Guelfs were routed from Ferrara again in the following year, and the Torelli installed as *podestà* a German named Hugo von Worms.[12] Frequent periods of struggle and chaos followed. In no sense can it be maintained that the Estensi exercised effective control over the situation in Ferrara before the fifth decade of the thirteenth century.

Azzolino's death in 1212 left this problematical state of affairs in the hands of his eldest son, Aldobrandino, who at the time may have been in his early twenties. Because of the constant demands for military support made upon him by Innocent III, he was unable to act aggressively in dealing with his Ferrarese opponents, who were establishing increasingly close ties with Ghibellines outside the city.

[11] *Ant.Est.,* I, 387. But see now W. Montorsi, ed., *Statuta Ferrariae anno MCCLXXXVII* (Ferrara, 1955), pp. xxiii-xxiv.

[12] A. Frizzi, *Memorie per la storia di Ferrara* (Ferrara, 1791) I, 192; IV, 59; *Ant.Est.,* I, 389; cf. Montorsi, *Statuta Ferrariae,* p. xix. For a narrative of this period, see Chiappini, 27-45.

Upon Aldobrandino's early death in 1215, his brother Azzo VII, known as Azzo Novello, became the protagonist of the family's fortunes at the age of ten, and the Torelli dominated the political life of Ferrara. At every turn, the hopes of the Estensi seemed to be thwarted, locally by the mighty Salinguerra, elsewhere by the fierce and potent hostility of the notorious Ezzelino da Romano.[13] In 1222 Azzo and his men were driven out of Ferrara; he then returned briefly at the head of one hundred horsemen, and was driven out again. Two years later, Azzo and Salinguerra made another attempt to achieve a *modus vivendi* within the city, and Azzo returned. Such efforts (this was one of a series) reflected the difficulty both parties encountered in governing a city deeply divided by ideological and family loyalties in a time of general social instability. But those efforts never produced lasting results. Neither did the occasional benevolent intervention of various friars seeking to reconcile factional disputes by an appeal to the higher glory of God. Such efforts were made during the 1220's by Fra Giovanni da Schio, whose attempt to bring about a truce generated more popular than noble support.

It was not until 1240 that Azzo Novello d'Este had the military and diplomatic backing necessary to wrest Ferrara from the control of Salinguerra Torelli. His effort was one phase of a new Guelf war, backed by Pope Gregory IX and supported by the principal Guelf towns. With tactical support and adequate supplies, Azzo besieged Ferrara from March through June, and Salinguerra, now an octogenarian, surrendered and was deported to Venice, where he died four years later.[14]

---

[13] For the particular dangers posed to Estensi rule over Ferrara in this period see the volume *Studi Ezzeliniani* (Rome, 1963), esp. the works by C. G. Mor, " 'Dominus Ecerinus,' Aspetti di una forma presignorile," and P. Toschi, "Ezzelino da Romano nella leggenda."

[14] For a description of the gradual consolidation of Estense control, see A. Lazzari, "Origini della signoria Estense a Ferrara," *AF,* n.s. x (1954),

Azzo's defeat of Salinguerra was the first major step toward Estense hegemony in Ferrara. Naturally there were pockets of resistance within the citizenry, and the imperial faction continued to receive support from Ezzelino. The papacy, however, continued to respond cautiously to Azzo's professions of loyalty by granting tax exemptions on Este land-holdings (1247) and other legal privileges without, however, conferring vicarial rights on Azzo. The twenty-four years of Azzo's dominance in Ferrara were incidental to his major activity, which was fighting the Ghibellines all over Emilia and the March of Treviso, of which he was called "its very shield and guardian." [15] Regrettably, this able warrior was unable to extend the same degree of protection over his only son, Rinaldo, who, while held as a Ghibelline prisoner in Puglia, was murdered by poison in 1251. He in turn left a son, illegitimate but healthy, named Obizzo. Azzo decided to groom this child as his successor.

The triumphant campaigns initiated by Pope Alexander IV against the Ghibellines greatly strengthened Azzo's position by the year 1260. Ezzelino and his major supporters were dead, their forces routed, and the Marquess of Este collected a good portion of the spoils. His territories now included not only the traditional patrimony in the Paduan *contado* (Este, Monfelice, Calaone, Montagnana) but also the fertile and strategic Polesine di Rovigo, Anano, Adria, and the entire Ferrarese. An attempted *coup d'état* in 1261

1-68, esp. 26-44. This is a useful narrative, based on Riccobaldo's chronicle, the *Chronica Parva,* the work of Muratori, and some more recent scholarship.

[15] The phrase is Rolandino's, in *Cronaca in factis et circa facta marchie travixane,* ed., A. Bonardi, *RIS,* VIII: 1 (1906), 23; quoted by J. K. Hyde, *Padua in the Age of Dante* (Manchester, 1966), 69, who also gives an excellent account of the factional battles between partisans of the Estensi and Ezzelino in Padua (see ch. VII, "The Commune and the *Pars Marchionis"*).

was repressed with ease, and its protagonists beheaded, the only ripple on the smooth surface of Azzo's last years.

Transfers of power from one generation to the next were seldom smooth in thirteenth-century Italian city-states, and were predictably even less so when skipping a generation, particularly when the heir apparent was both illegitimate and a minor. Thus, the young Obizzo's orderly succession to Azzo in the year 1264 comes as something of a surprise, and would require explanation even if it were not for the special significance of the manner in which the change came about. For not only did Obizzo acquire the lands, revenues, powers, and obligations of his grandfather, but also, in a move without precedent, he was elected *signore* of Ferrara for life by plebiscite, and the office was made hereditary. The popular acceptance of the statute by which the Estensi were recognized as perpetual lords of Ferrara in 1264 must be regarded as the most significant single political act in the history of the city, before or since.[16]

Contemporary sources give evidence that Azzo VII had succeeded, where some of his predecessors had failed, in ingratiating himself with the people of Ferrara, both by personal qualities and by bringing about some measure of public order. Riccobaldo, who had nothing to gain by distortion in this case, regarded him as "Vir liberalis, innocens, tyrannidis inscius . . .," and the *Chronica Parva* notes that even his political rivals mourned his death, for "Hic vir saevus non fuit, sed benignus et pius."[17] After the

[16] For Obizzo's election as the first *dominus* of Ferrara, see esp. the study by L. Simeoni, "L'Elezione di Obizzo d'Este a signore di Ferrara," *ASI*, xciii: 1 (1935), 165-88; and the same author's earlier work "Ricerche sulle origini della signoria estense a Modena," *AM*, s. v, xii (1919). Also W. Montorsi, "Considerazioni attorno al sorgere della Signoria Estense," *AM*, s. viii, x (1958), 31-44, and A. Lazzari's article cited above (n. 14).

[17] See Riccobaldo, *Historia Imperatorum*, in *RIS*, ix, col. 135; *Chronica Parva*, *RIS*, viii, col. 487. It has been cogently argued, by A. F. Masserà,

funeral, the entire *popolo* of Ferrara, both citizens and foreigners, gathered in the main square, where Obizzo, now the second marquess of that name, was acclaimed *signore* of Ferrara, and his heir after him. Of course this was not, as some apologists have claimed, a spontaneous event, but rather a calculated political act. It was carefully arranged by one of Azzo's close advisers, Aldighieri della Fontana, who organized the Guelf nobility in support of the move and placed armed loyalists around the square, while the bearing of arms was prohibited for others. It was, as Simeoni noticed, exactly the same sort of representative institution as the Medicean *parlamentum*.[18]

Obizzo himself deserves little credit for the particular form of his succession, though in later years he took strong moves to further the tendencies already manifest here. Powerful forces were using him for their own ends as well as his own. For some years now, Ferrara had been a Guelf

"L'Autenticità della Cronaca parva ferrariensis," *Archivio Muratoriano,* I, n. 10, that the *Chronica Parva* is also the work of Riccobaldo.

[18] "L'Elezione di Obizzo d'Este a signore di Ferrara," 178-79 (hereafter "L'Elezione"). Simeoni takes issue with the opinion of E. Salzer, *Über die Anfänge der Signorie in Oberitalien* (Berlin, 1900), 42, no. 59, who argues that the *parlamentum* reveals that the Estensi took over with the support of a popular party, and rested on a democratic base. Simeoni believes that the only element of popular representation here was merely legal formality and that even this was made into a mere fiction: "come si faceva ancora a Firenze nel secolo XV nel parlamento per ellegere delle balie." He furthers this argument by adducing Obizzo's suppression of the guilds which occurred in 1287. It is to be noted that that event took place over two decades later, and probably only as a response to serious provocations. Simeoni provides no evidence to contest Salzer's very plausible argument that Obizzo's election was hailed by the people as a continuation of the successful rule of Azzo VII. But it must be said that *popolo* still remains a vague term in the Ferrarese context, where little serious research has been done to analyze post-communal social organization and political alignments. Pending further research (for which adequate sources may not be available) it remains an open question whether this nicely choreographed event expressed the "popular will."

citadel, the Ghibelline nobility had long been exiled, and those who supported the Estensi had a strong vested interest in continuing the *status quo*. Other Guelf cities, and above all the papacy, had much the same interest. The Guelf leaders of some of these cities—Mantua, Modena, Padua, Bologna—attended Azzo's funeral and remained in Ferrara for the "election," a fact strongly suggestive of magnate collusion.

The appeal of the maneuver rested in part on the weakness of Obizzo's personal situation. Riccobaldo reports that one of the arguments put forward for the move was that since no legitimate heir had been left by Azzo, it was necessary to create a man out of straw, "unum dominatorem constitueremus ex paleis." [19] The duplicity of the argument is striking. On the one hand, it suggests that a straw man is inherently weak, hence must be strengthened by conferring legally the privileges of despotism. On the other it implies that since the new signore is made "ex paleis," he will be manipulable by the real powers despite his new status.

How revealing this event is, and how typical it seems of the behavior of later generations of Estensi rulers! They must have learned a great deal from it. The façade of popular representation was scrupulously preserved (and "façade" in this context can be understood in the sense that certain sociologists currently use "face"). [20] A proper document was drawn up, duly witnessed, and signed by an archbishop, courts, other feudal lords, notaries, judges "et aliis multis." But can one really say, as one is tempted to,

[19] For this phrase, see Simeoni, "L'Elezione," 178; Montorsi, *Statuta Ferrariae,* lxxx, n. 5; also Chiappini, p. 54.

[20] See especially the following works of Erving Goffman; *The Presentation of Self in Everyday Life* (New York, 1959); "On Face Work," ch. I of *Interaction Ritual* (New York, 1967), 5-46; *Behavior in Public Places* (New York, 1963), esp. ch. 6, "Face Engagements," 83-111.

that Obizzo's "election" was *merely* the product of an atmosphere of repression and coercion? That has been suggested, but I cannot agree entirely.[21] I think that in general the people of Ferrara, and not only of Ferrara, weary of incessant strife, saw in the *dominus* a unique chance for stability in this period, and were therefore quite ready to accept one. Things had gone well enough for a long time under Azzo, and in a situation where the alternative to an orderly transfer of power might be another endless civil war among noble families (which would inevitably involve almost everybody else), they were prepared to follow the path of least resistance. And in any case, Obizzo was a mere boy. If the new lord's men trampled too heavily on the institutions and traditions of the commune, he could always be unseated. What appears in Ferrara in 1264, and subsequently in many other cities in northern Italy, is a kind of unspoken consensus to trade off a relatively narrowly-based, unstable republicanism (the commune) for a relatively broadly-based and comparatively secure despotism (the signory). In other terms, one effect of establishing a signory was to undercut the viability of party politics by transforming the conception of the chief of state from that of *capo* of the dominant party to *capo* of a dynasty, which would continue regardless of its changing political orientations.[22]

[21] This seems to be the basic view of Simeoni, sustained throughout "L'Elezione." The principal parts of the document, which appears in *Ant.Est.,* II, 25-6, have been translated by D. Waley, *The Italian City Republics* (New York, 1969), 235-36. Professor Waley seems to share Simeoni's view of the rise of despotism as a force imposed on an unwilling *popolo.* Though Waley's position is more clearly limited, better defined, and based upon the sources, he still seems in some ways to reveal a republican bias. A recent view closer to my own may be found in the stimulating article by L. Martines, "Political Conflict in the Italian City-States," *Government and Opposition* III: 1 (1967-8), 69-91, which does not include a discussion of Ferrara.

[22] It is partly for this reason that personal and family allegiances tend

It should be clear, then, that various groups saw something (and not necessarily the same thing) to be gained from the installation of a signory which would dominate the continuing communal bureaucracy. But very few could have realized, or even suspected, the costs of this transition. Since some of these costs became apparent early, it is appropriate to discuss them here.

When considering the political and social agencies acting on and within the matrix of the Italian city-state system, one is obliged to take into account, where possible, not only individuals and groups within a particular town, but also the roles and concerns of outside powers. The distinction, it should be noted, does not always involve a real difference, since "external" groups were often comprised, or closely represented the interests, of exiles or other groups with evident "internal" links or constituencies. Correspondingly, internal factions often played the perceptibly dangerous game of culling decisive support from outside powers, who then claimed new internal prerogatives, influence, and control. Naturally enough, as more recent experience plainly demonstrates, protective alliances such as these tend to turn elapsed time into a positive sanction, and to elicit *post facto* legal and historiographical rationalizations for their continuing effects.

Although our inquiry focuses primarily on Ferrara seen as a more or less self-contained society, and leaves the intriguing but at this point clearly unwritable history of its Renaissance administration and diplomatic history to future scholars who may be in a better position to pursue it (except

---

to supplant party allegiances in the popular tumults of the despotisms. Thus the terms Guelf and Ghibelline, for example, either tend to go into disuse altogether, or to be transformed into labels of purely local significance, and thus the emblems or symbols of a particular individual or family often become the rallying cry of an urban faction. Ferrara provides many examples, some of which will appear presently.

for the brief survey in Appendix I), this aspect of the subject cannot be ignored, least of all in connection with the consequences of installing the new *signoria*. For the Estensi, in gaining and maintaining control over Ferrara, played precisely that dangerous game cited above. Like most of its abler practitioners throughout history, they won handsomely, but they cannot also be said not to have lost as well. Moreover, they lost in two essential ways, one external, one internal, and both already clearly evident during the *signoria* of Obizzo II.

Ferrara, tempting prize that it had become in the course of the demographic, economic, and urban revival of the high Middle Ages, was far enough from most of the major Italian powers to maintain its liberty. The papacy, with its ancient claims to the city, was unable to keep much closer and weaker towns firmly in hand, and was content to have an ally in the Este lords (particularly if in later times when the relationship was legalized, they bothered to pay their annual rent).[23] The Florentines, separated by the high ridges of the Apennines, had plenty of troubles of their own and were happy when northern powers left them in peace, so that they could fight their own civil wars and build their own Tuscan *imperium*.[24] With its neighbor Bologna, twenty

[23] On the complicated question concerning the Estensi as papal or imperial vicars (which deserves further study) see especially the articles by G. de Vergottini, "Note per la storia del vicariato apostolico durante il secolo XIII," in *Studi in onore di Carlo Calisse* (Milan, 1940), III, 341-65; "Ricerche sulle origini del vicariato apostolico," in *Studi in onore di E. Besta* (Milan, 1939), II, 231-50; and "Di un vicariato imperiale degli Estensi a Ferrara sotto Ludovico IV," *Rivista di Storia del Diritto Italiano,* XI (1938), 289-316. More generally there is useful discussion of this subject in F. Ercole, *Del commune al principato* (Florence, 1928), esp. 344-52.

[24] The process is interestingly described in the recent studies by M. B. Becker, *Florence in Transition,* vols. I, II (Baltimore, 1967-68). Becker provides arguments to substantiate the view that empire-building is in no way incompatible with the systematic propagation of republican political ideologies domestically. Much of his argument is based on an explicit

miles to the south, Ferrara lived in an uneasy, but relatively permanent, truce. The two cities tended to harbor one another's exiles and unemployed artists, and their common obligations to Rome and fears of Milan and Venice tended to keep them from open warfare, though no love has ever been lost between them. Milan in the thirteenth century was yet to develop as a major Italian power. Though populous, it was plagued by internal divisions. The Visconti, still in the process of asserting dominion over the city, were in no position to undertake eastern adventures.

That left only Venice to play a significant role in the political history of Ferrara, and of course the opportunity was not missed. Of all the larger city-states, Venice was by far the closest to Ferrara. By land, the towns were separated by a journey of some sixty-odd miles over flat (though not entirely safe or easy) terrain. But Ferrara could be easily reached by boat as well. Its rich harvests and salt deposits, as well as its strategic position on that great inland waterway the Po, made Ferrara a special concern to the Venetians long before their mainland territorial involvements were expanded at the end of the fourteenth century to counter the growing power of the Visconti state. Apart from the straightforward economic and strategic considerations already mentioned, Venice may have also perceived the growing territorial state of the Estensi as a long-range potential threat to the Republic. If one makes such an assumption (for which I know of no documentary evidence whatsoever), Venetian policy towards the Estensi appears not only rational, but characteristically clever. For, first of

---

comparison with classical Athens, which indeed provides an excellent example of precisely that phenomenon, and in a city-state society. His discussion of "Florentine *paideia*," that is, of changing techniques for maintaining the republican value-system, advances our understanding of the survival mechanisms underlying Florence's prolonged resistance to despotism.

all, they supported the Estensi against the Torelli and Ezzelino, and helped them to gain control of Ferrara.[25] The most immediate effect of this policy was to move the center of Estense power and concern southward, from the area in the March of Treviso where the family had traditionally concentrated its political energies, to a more distant region from which for some time they would neither desire nor be able to continue to influence the political affairs of the immediate Venetian *contado* as they had previously done. Second, the Venetians, having supported the Estensi, could press them for some sort of reciprocal kindness, using the scarcely-veiled threat that the support used to help them secure dominion over Ferrara could equally well be used to unseat the new lords. Having by this means assured Estense collaboration, however reluctant, the Venetians would have extended their sway, somewhat indirectly but altogether painlessly, over an important and developing territory possessing considerable material resources which would be of immediate and lasting utility. Venice's critical support of Azzo, on his return to Ferrara in 1240, and subsequently of Obizzo II, was also in part based on the family's Guelfism, for while the papacy could by no stretch of the imagination pose a threat to the autonomy of the Serenissima, it was still conceivable in the thirteenth century that a powerful emperor could descend from the north to threaten the city on the lagoon. It may not even be completely nonsensical to suggest that the Venetians, whose city was founded as a refuge from invaders from the north, reacted with particular and perhaps sometimes unconscious alarm to this possibility.

[25] Ferrarese-Venetian relations in the late Middle Ages have been studied by A. S. Minotto, *Documenta ad Ferrariam Rhodiginum Policinum ac Marchiones Estenses spectantia* (Venice, 1873); by V. Lazzarini, "Possessi e feudi veneziani nel ferrarese," in *Miscellanea in onore di R. Cessi* (Rome, 1958), I, 213-32; and, above all, by B. Ghetti, *I patti tra Venezia e Ferrara dal 1191 al 1313* (Rome, 1907).

In any case, the Venetians, having acted consistently as power brokers to the Estensi, demanded their pound of flesh. In a series of treaties, Ferrara was obliged to grant an ever-widening range of commercial and other privileges to Venice and its citizens, including even the construction of castles in the Polesine di Rovigo, and, most important of all, the right of the Venetians to maintain a permanent magistrate in Ferrara, who would bear the title *Vice-dominus*. The latter would be one of the highest ranking officials in the city, with the sole purpose of seeing that the rights and privileges of Venice were scrupulously observed.[26] Bernardino Ghetti, in a study that has received too little attention, analyzed the treaties between Venice and Ferrara which legalized these arrangements, and revealed the pattern of concessions that emerge in the documents from the late twelfth century onward. From his work it would seem that the perennial popular hostility toward Venice in Ferrara follows directly from its legalized monopolies, commercial privileges, and legal and fiscal immunities.[27] It is worth suggesting that the major part of Ferrara's diplomatic, military, and external political problems in the fourteenth and fifteenth centuries may be traceable to this source.

The flexibility that the Estensi displayed in dealing with the Venetians is a foil to the rigidity and authoritarianism that characterize their treatment of potential opposition from within Ferrara.[28] Historians have often written, with

[26] For the crucial treaties between Ferrara and Venice which became part of Ferrarese public law, see W. Montorsi, ed., *Statuta Ferrariae,* esp. 229-39, where they are reproduced.

[27] For evidence of popular hostility toward Venice, one need go no farther than to consult the poems published by A. Segré, "Carmi latini inediti del secolo XIV intorno alla guerra di Ferrara di 1309," *Nuovo Archivio Veneto,* Ser. 3, vol. xv (1908), 322-59, from BEM Alpha, M, 5, 20 (Lat. 678).

[28] This distinction raises no problems. It simply reflects the realities of the limits of Estense power. With respect to their domestic constituency,

apparent precision but real vagueness, of Italian urban politics in this period in terms of a "class struggle." Ferrara has not been spared some of the confusing effects of this type of analysis. Thus, the Estensi have been regarded as the leaders of the aristocracy against the *popolo,* the Torelli as an essentially popular party resisting the thrust toward oligarchical tyranny. Such an interpretation appeals to our desire to place the signories of the Renaissance in a different moral realm from the republics, and therefore it has seldom been given the kind of critical scrutiny it requires. For Ferrara, at least, the model of "class struggle" seems not merely inadequate but misleading to the student of the thirteenth century, though this is more a hypothesis than a firm conclusion.[29]

I have already referred to the polarizing effects of papal and imperial factionalism in Ferrara. The Guelf and Ghibelline parties served as magnets attracting rival feudal clans, who had in common primarily the fact that their social origins and positions were more or less identical. Behind these families stood a wide range of supporters, drawn from no particular social group (except of course the clergy in the case of the Guelfs), and reflecting family

they had enormous leverage, and could if necessary call on almost unlimited force. With regard to the Venetians, the Estensi had the status of colonial client governors, and therefore had to respond with the proper tact and diffidence.

[29] I have written elsewhere about recent attempts to characterize Ferrarese political life in terms of the class struggle. See "Toward a Reinterpretation," 271-76. For a very useful critique and synthesis of the diverse interpretations of the transition from communal to signorial regimes, many of which have involved models of social change based on class struggle, or attacks on such models, see the article by G. Chittolini, "La crisi delle libertà comunali e le origini dello stato territoriale," *RSI,* LXXXII: 1 (1970), 99-120. In general, while agreeing with Martines, "Conflict in Italian City-States," 74, that the model works for many towns, I see little evidence of its validity for Ferrara. However, the main fact to bear in mind is that we do not yet have the data on which to base an interpretation.

loyalties, feudal or other tenurial obligations, geographical locations, or promises of rewards. There is nothing to suggest the existence of a popular party in Ferrara, or an awareness that popular interests as such were threatened by Estensi rule. On the contrary, in fact, it appears that Azzo won more esteem from the *popolo*—defined by Martines as "commoners of substance viewed as a political order"—than the Salinguerra despots who preceded him. During the first two decades of Obizzo's rule, the young marquess took no major steps which could be regarded as an attack on the *popolo*. But this situation changed dramatically when, in 1287, he abolished the guilds. This action, undoubtedly taken to consolidate his power, had a determining effect on the subsequent economic development of Ferrara. It was the second of the major costs involved in establishing the *signoria*.

To trace the legislative history of Obizzo's rule would be to witness a masterful exercise in the legal dismemberment of the remains of effective communal government, and an adroit gathering together of every string of power in the hands of a single individual. Not that communal institutions were simply legislated out of existence. Far from it. In general, they were scrupulously preserved, and most survived for centuries. At every stage, though, their representative character was undercut. The shell remained, but the living organism within had been removed. The statutes of 1287 leave no doubt as to Obizzo's methodical course. By 1271, for example, the promulgative language of new laws changes from that of personal edict ("statuit et ordinavit dominus Obiço") to the royal imperative ("Statuimus").[30] This relatively symbolic change had its counterpart in the removal of traditional powers from communal magistrates. As Simeoni observed, the *podestà* was reduced

[30] Cf. "L'Elezione," 179 (n.31); and also E. Salzer, *Über die Anfänge*, 25-86.

from a virtually autonomous figure—half chief justice, half chief-of-police—to a mere functionary of the *signore*. His original obligation to enforce the laws came to be transformed into a personal obligation to carry out orders, regardless of their legality.[31] By 1292, Obizzo had been given the right to designate his successor. Popular election was retained, to be sure, but the lord's candidate would be the only man running.

In no other area was the repression of communal institutions more significant than was the effect on Ferrara's economy resulting from the attack on the guilds. The guildsmen, who here as elsewhere included some relatively prosperous local merchants, bankers, and industrialists as well as many relatively modest entrepreneurs in the minor crafts, had clearly been willing to accept the man of straw in 1264. Subsequently the role of the guilds in vital political and economic decisions naturally diminished. Obizzo's close collaboration with Venice (with its exploitative interests) certainly gave grounds for discontent, particularly in the more internationally-minded, thus richer and more influential, guilds, or those engaged in transportation of goods. It is apparent, for example, that the boatmen's guild became particularly restive and troublesome in the 1280's, and at least possible that a broad and threatening current of discontent brought Obizzo to the point of taking pre-emptive action.[32]

In 1286, a new statute brought the guilds under the control of the lord's lesser council. By this first step, Obizzo gained the power to withhold ratifications of the statutes of individual guilds, to fine guilds for failing to submit to scrutiny, to limit the legal powers and destroy the autonomy

---

[31] E. Salzer, *Über die Anfänge,* esp. 25-86.

[32] See Montorsi's perceptive discussion of the relationship between the abolition of the guilds and the institution of a thoroughgoing autocracy, in *Statuta Ferrariae,* lxxxvii-xci.

of these groups. A year later, he dissolved them altogether, with a lengthy statute that imposed heavy fines for meeting or organizing in secret, and that stated:

> We command and wish it inviolably to be observed that every guild or college of the crafts of whatever sort, whether producing goods or engaging in trade . . . be, by the authority of the present statute, null and void. . . . And that henceforth no one may dare or presume to have any convocation, congregation, or meeting of them, whether by way of reforming or keeping observances, or for newly establishing said colleges, schools, statutes, and ordinances, publically or privately.[33]

Though the guilds were permitted to reorganize some years later, under the patronage and with the approval of the *signore,* this law had dealt a crushing blow to Ferrarese enterprise. Vital goods continued to be produced, essential services were rendered, but industrial and commercial growth stopped. A wealthy and politically ambitious class of burghers, such as existed in Florence, never arose to challenge the Estensi. Indeed, of the forty-seven volumes of guild statutes preserved in the Biblioteca Ariostea in Ferrara, not one represents the major guilds, in which popular wealth and political power tended to concentrate in other cities.[34]

---

[33] *Ibid.,* 390, Liber Sextus, stat. 60: De colegiis, scollis, matriculis et statutis tollendis; ll. 7-25.

[34] These statutes comprise an uncatalogued *fondo* which has been partially analyzed by P. Sitta, "Le Università delle Arti a Ferrara," *AF,* VIII (1896), 5-204. They include statutes of the *merzari* (2 vols.), *fabbri* (3 vols.), *bastaroli* (2 vols.), *strazzaroli, muratori, vasellari, fruttaroli* (2 vols.), *pelecanari, sartori* (3 vols.), *fabbri e orifici* (2 vols.), *brentatori e mastellari* (3 vols.), *drappieri, fornai, marangeoni* (2 vols.), *pelliciari* (2 vols.), *tornitori, carradori* (2 vols.), *speziali, sprocani* (2 vols.), *pastori o fornai, orefici, barbieri e parucchieri, sogari, preconi, callegari* (7 vols.). There is also an eighteenth-century copy of some printed statutes of the

Great wealth was to remain in the hands of the landowning nobility, or to those who were raised to the status of *gentil'-uomo* from the lower ranks by the *signori* for services rendered. In subsequent generations, the Estensi created a kind of *noblesse de robe,* even while they were controlling, domesticating, and turning to their own purposes the ancient feudal families.

What Obizzo had initiated was in effect a re-feudalization of what had been a nascent republican city-state. But the *popolo* had collaborated, and continued to collaborate, at the skillful subversion of its institutions. Were they making a virtue of necessity? Perhaps. Certainly later generations of Ferrarese humanist pamphleteers and panegyrists did, and it would be hard to deny that they possessed some solid evidence upon which to build their case for the qualities of Estense rule.

Arte della Seta, dated 1613, but nothing to suggest that this guild was founded early. For modern Italian equivalents of medieval guild-names, see A. Tagliaferri, *L' Economia Veronese secondo gli Estimi dal 1409 al 1635* (Milan, 1966), 207-16 (reference kindly supplied by Dr. Richard Rapp).

II   Ferrara in the Fourteenth Century

The consolidating and centralizing tendencies of Obizzo's rule extended beyond Ferrara. His territorial ambitions matched his dynastic hopes, and through the application of political skill and military strength, he assembled the basic elements of the extensive Este state of subsequent centuries.

Lendinara and its surroundings came under his control, in part by purchase, in 1285, and the Emperor Rudolf I confirmed the addition in the same year. In 1288, an embassy from Modena, which for years had been rent by a virtual civil war among its magnates, invited Obizzo to accept the lordship of that city. He was not slow to accept. After a triumphal entry into Modena in the following year, he proceeded to undertake a program of pacification, by recalling exiled factions and arranging the marriage of his second son, Aldobrandino, to Tobia Rangone, the daughter of the most powerful Modenese family. Not long thereafter Reggio, the next large town beyond Modena on the ancient Via Emilia, also elected Obizzo as *signore*.[1] The incorporation of Modena and Reggio into a growing territorial state occurred as a consequence of processes apparently similar to those that had brought about Obizzo's election in Ferrara. The magnates, debilitated by internal strife, not only were unable to maintain but actually served to break down public order. This raised the threat of popular uprisings, especially among the wealthier and politically more conscious guilds-

---

[1] On the territorial expansion of Ferrara under Obizzo II, see esp. *Ant.Est.*, II, 24-39; A. Lazzari, "Il marchese Obizzo II d'Este, signore di Ferrara," 53-63. Dante's aversion toward Obizzo is well known, and has provoked ample comment, for example A. Lazzari, "Il marchese Obizzo II d'Este signore di Ferrara nel poema di Dante e nella storia," *Giornale Dantesco*, XXXIX (n.s. IX, 1938), 127-50, and especially M. Catalano, "Dante e Ferrara," in *Studi Danteschi* (Bologna, 1921).

men. Thus threatened by the possibility of a popular insurrection from within and by Ghibelline forces from outside the city, the Guelf nobles decided to take their chances with the man who had brought a measure of stability to Ferrara, and who had known how to suppress the guilds there. I take it to be a fact of extreme importance that Modena and Reggio came in not under pressure, but by offering themselves, immediately after Obizzo had demonstrated his willingness and his ability to take an anti-popular stand in Ferrara. Having been elected in Modena, also by popular acclaim, he proceeded to eliminate the popular magistracies, from the office of *Capitano del Popolo* down. I believe that this strikingly paradoxical combination of popular election and anti-popular action can only be understood if one assumes not only pressure and intimidation by the noble Guelf clans, but also a growing sense of frustration and disenchantment, widely distributed throughout the citizenry, with politics by warring constituency.[2] The willingness to purchase security, even at a high cost in terms of personal or group privileges, seems to be an element in human nature that was just as clear to *signori* as it was to Renaissance students of signorial behavior, such as Machiavelli.[3]

[2] No one has fully succeeded in explaining why republics failed and were superseded by despotisms, which received popular acceptance despite often tyrannical behavior. The main attempts to come to terms with this problem are the works of E. Salzer, *Über die Anfänge*; F. Ercole, *Dal commune al principato* (Florence, 1929); and more recently E. Sestan, "Le origini delle signorie cittadine: una problema esaurito?", *Bolletino del'istituto storico italiano*, LXXIII (1961), 41-69, as well as the recent assessments by D. Waley, *The Italian City-Republics*, 221-39; D. M. Bueno da Mesquita, "The Place of Despotism in Italian Politics," in *Europe in the High Middle Ages*, ed. J. R. Hale, J. R. L. Highfield, B. Smalley (London and Evanston, 1965), 301-31. N. Rubinstein, "Florence and the Despots: Some Aspects of Florentine Diplomacy in the Fourteenth Century," *TRHS*, S. v, Vol. 2 (1952), 21-45, also considers contemporary views for and against the institution of despotism in the fourteenth century.

[3] The *signori* of course appealled to these fears and social goals in

It suited both the dynastic and the territorial aims of Obizzo to arrange for an orderly succession of power in the event of his death. This would have been desirable because of the legal ambiguities surrounding the succession to a *signore* who had been elected only for his own lifetime without hereditary provisions, but the likelihood of rival claimants from within the family made it imperative. In Ferrara, the latter problem remained to complicate transfers of power long after the former had been settled by the necessary statutory manipulations. That this must have been a concern to Obizzo can be seen in the fact that in 1292 the *consiglio maggiore* of Ferrara adopted an interpretation of Obizzo's original law of election enabling him to designate his successor. Oddly enough, as Simeoni pointed out, Obizzo does not appear to have done so.[4] This raises doubts about the tradition, which has never been proven, that the *marchese* was strangled by his two elder sons, Azzo and Aldobrandino.

When Obizzo died, in 1293, the Lombard law of primogeniture immediately took effect, and Azzo became his successor, the eighth Marquess of Este to bear that name. On February 21 of that year, the *consiglio maggiore* of Ferrara, recognizing Obizzo's death as imminent, had also elected his eldest son to succeed him, "pro bono et pacifico statu civitatis Ferrarie." The document explicitly (and perhaps, suspiciously) states that this action was taken without coercion, and calls for acceptance of the ruling by Aldobrandino and Francesco, the youngest of the three brothers: "And let those magnificent men the lords Aldobrandinus and Franciscus, the sons of the aforementioned lord Obizzo and the brothers of the potent and magnificent lord Azzo,

their own political propaganda, as N. Rubinstein has demonstrated in "Florence and the Despots," and as he intends to develop further in a forthcoming study. Machiavelli deals with this subject in several places, see esp. *Discorsi*, i. 16. 3-10; i. 10, 7; iii. 12. 3-4; *Il Principe*, ch. 17.

[4] "L'Elezione," 181-83; also *Ant.Est.*, ii, 40-43.

consent and will that the said lord Azzo their brother is, and is elected, and will be perpetual and general *dominus* of the state of Ferrara." [5] This apparently gratuitous action may have helped to forestall any general rising within the city by ratifying in public law a decision based on ancient laws of inheritance, but it in no way restrained Azzo's brothers from attempting to share in his rich legacy. Perhaps because he feared them, Azzo chose to exclude them from any form of authority, even lordships in outlying regions, and thereby created an insurgent party within his own family. His aggrieved brothers sought support in rival cities outside Este territories, and the first years of the *Trecento* reveal the kinds of challenges to princely authority in Ferrara that characterize much of the century there, and in the other *signorie*.[6] After the remarkable political successes of Obizzo, the reigns of Azzo and his successors up to the time of Niccolò II, well after mid-century, can only be described as a time of troubles.

The Estensi were always subject to strong pressures from

[5] The document is reproduced by Simeoni, "L'Elezione," 186-88. Simeoni states, relative to the problem of succession, that "Gli Estensi saranno fra i primi a credere superflua la elezione popolare e a ritenere sufficienti le investiture papali e imperiali per Ferrara e Modena." This view seems untenable in light of the fact—acknowledged by Simeoni—that the *popolo* had been convened in *parlamento* to ratify the decision. That there was no real alternative does not represent a new departure in the techniques of Estensi despotism, since precisely the same thing had happened in 1264, when Obizzo came to power. The point is that popular election was not destroyed by the Estensi, but rather was carefully kept alive because of its evident political value. The basis of their popular support, and indeed that of all despots in the city states, was the conviction that they would deliver a superior brand of justice, and the maintenance of such consultative mechanisms was an important instrument in sustaining that conviction.

[6] For the history of this epoch in the rise of the despotisms, see esp. Salzer, *Über die Anfänge;* L. Simeoni, *Le Signorie* (Milan, 1950) 2 vols., esp. vol. I, 245-50; and C. Cipolla, *Storia delle Signorie Italiane, 1313-1530* (Vol. I of the *Storia Politica d'Italia,* ed. P. Villari) (Milan, 1881), 1-83.

different sources and throughout the first half of the *Trecento* the major challenges to Este control over Ferrara came from the outside. Venice, as we know, guarded her commercial privileges there very jealously, and kept a watchful eye on Ferrara's military power, defence capabilities, and diplomatic alliances. Though within the Venetian sphere of influence, the Estensi wished to maintain a historic relationship with the papacy, to which they owed much of whatever legal justification they could muster for their control of Ferrara and its *contado,* especially to the south and east. Papal policy had a clear interest in maintaining Ferrara as a reasonably strong power, as long as she was dependably Guelf, so that she could serve as a buffer-state against a potentially expansionist Venice that might threaten the papal cities of the Romagna. At the same time, the rapid expansion of the Este state posed a threat, for the same kinds of considerations that had brought Modena, Reggio, and a number of lesser towns under Estean control might also apply in Imola, Forlì, Cesena, Ravenna, and Rimini. A firm line had to be drawn against such a potential misuse of the papal alliance. Thus, under Boniface VIII and again under Benedict XI, Este claims to Argenta, a potential staging-point for further southern incursions, were forcibly resisted. Even with the popes in their "Babylonian Captivity," the emergence of a powerful secular lord in their territories was of major concern.

To complicate matters further, dissident members of the family were not above conspiring with the enemy for their eventual personal gain. A good example is that of Francesco d'Este, who concluded, after Azzo's second marriage in 1305 to Beatrice, daughter of Charles II, Angevin King of Naples and Sicily, that a direct heir might be born to succeed his brother and that his chances for the succession were therefore reduced. Accordingly, he left Ferrara and, with the help of local Ghibelline forces, seized the fortified town of

Lendinara as a first step in challenging Azzo.[7] He failed, but the attempt is typical of the kinds of problems that Azzo and his successors encountered, and these struggles help to explain (just as they serve to reflect) some of the authoritarian tendencies of their rule.[8]

Such local disturbances were minor compared to the dangers posed by Venice or Rome. When these powers,

[7] A competent brief narrative of the events summarized in the two preceding paragraphs appears in L. Chiappini, *Gli Estensi*, ch. III, 53-63.

[8] The unflinching use of coercion, as well as the judicious combination of rewards and punishments, was an essential element in the mechanisms of control used by virtually all Italian urban despots. See D. M. Bueno da Mesquita, "The Place of Despotism in Italian Politics," who has argued that this in itself sometimes causes the positions of such rulers to be undermined (330-31): "Political loyalty was a crucial problem for the absolute rulers of Italy, beset as they were by the juridical ambiguities of their title, subject to the hazards of dynastic change, faced by the survivals of the communal tradition, and armed with the dangerous power of taking for their needs what their subjects had not consented to give. The good order which they promised in return would have seemed a more acceptable commodity if they could have come within measurable distance of attaining it, of suppressing the liberty of men to help themselves at the expense of their neighbours. As it was, their subjects were quicker to see the shortcomings of government than the benefits it conferred, and quicker still to resent the burdens it imposed; it was difficult to convince them that they had much to lose by listening to the often specious promises of others. . . . The old weapons of favour and disgrace, used in the search for political loyalty, in the long run narrowed the basis of support for the prince. Awareness of the narrowing basis of support bred fear of treason stimulated from outside the dominion. And fear of treason bred the tyrannical exercise of power." These insights seem particularly relevant to the smaller despotisms. In Ferrara, *per contra*, there was a broad enough base of feudal terrain and reclaimable territory to reward a large group of loyalists, so that the Estensi were not caught up in Bueno da Mesquita's interesting paradox. Other general aspects of the benefits and limitations of this sort of regime are analyzed by P. J. Jones, "Communes and Despots: The City-State in Late Medieval Italy," *TRHS*, s. v, xv, (1965) 71-96, esp. 94-99 (hereafter "Communes and Despots"); and in L. Martines, "Political Conflict in the Italian City-States."

rather than the feckless Ghibellines of Lendinara, were drawn into the melée of internal Estense dynastic politics, there was invariably a major crisis. A useful and consequential example was the Venetian-papal war over Ferrara that followed the death of Azzo VIII in 1308. Azzo, in an unwonted display of generosity, pardoned his rebellious brothers on his deathbed, but he had previously arranged that he would be succeeded by his grandson Folco, the legitimate son of his only son, the bastard Fresco, who would act as regent during Folco's minority. We do not know Folco's exact age at the time. Francesco and Aldobrandino, who had never hesitated to challenge their own brother, were not about to tolerate the rule of their grand-nephew, and they attempted to seize the city and the northern countryside. They failed because Fresco, with the help of troops from Bologna, forced an entry to Ferrara. But the diplomatic alignments behind these events is most surprising. Pope Clement V, now at Avignon, was backing Azzo's two brothers, from whom he hoped to gain closer collaboration. It was the Venetians who were supporting Fresco, who appears to have lacked popularity in Ferrara, and thus required outside help. Such alliances, then, were often formed for expediency, and tend to reflect neither real ideological commitments, nor lasting diplomatic alignments.[9]

Having taken Ferrara, Fresco now had to defend it against a papal army led by Francesco d'Este and Lamberto da Polenta, the lord of Ravenna. The history of this campaign has been described by G. Soranzo.[10] After some initial Venetian successes, a strong papal counterattack, following upon the customary interdict of the Venetians, succeeded

---

[9] See Chiappini, *Gli Estensi,* 59-61.

[10] *La Guerra fra Venezia e la Santa Sede per il dominio di Ferrara, 1308-1313* (Città di Castello, 1905), a thorough study that includes many of the relevant documents.

in breaking their hold on numerous fortified places in the Ferrarese. Francesco, at the head of the papal army, was for the moment in 1310 master of Ferrara, in the capacity of papal regent. To solidify papal control, a plebiscite was held in which approximately 3,500 people swore their loyalty to the Holy Father. The notarized oaths, taken from each of the city's twelve *contrade,* are still preserved in the Vatican Archive, and have been studied by B. Fontana and, more recently, by A. Ostoja.[11] The extent to which the results of the plebiscite really reflect popular attitudes is certainly undetermined.[12]

In any case the plebiscite, while interesting as a political tactic and a demographic source, seems to have had a merely transitory impact on Ferrarese political attitudes. In particular, it failed to provide a guarantee of permanence in the existing situation. Francesco could not be relied upon to act merely as a papal agent in the city where his father had been a virtually absolute ruler. Who could say when the pro-Venetian branch of the Este *signoria* might be re-established, and the staunch papal supporters subjected to savage reprisals? Who knew when Francesco himself might choose to betray the papal alliance, for the sake of a *rapprochement* with the Venetians, and his insurgent relatives? Guided, I believe, by such considerations, a plot against the Estensi

[11] B. Fontana, "Documenti vaticani di un plebiscito in Ferrara, sul principio del secolo XIV," *AF,* i (1886), 1-157, publishes the voting lists by *contrada,* and provides a useful analysis. But it should be used in conjunction with A. Ostoja, "La più antica rilevazione della popolazione a Ferrara: il plebiscito dell'anno 1310," *AF,* n.s. (1957), which analyzes the data from a very different perspective.

[12] Indeed the term plebiscite here is somewhat inappropriate. It would be closer to the mark to speak of a mandatory expression of allegiance, than an organized expression of popular will. In a sense, this process, by which statements of fealty were transcribed by notaries, would seem to be nothing more than an urban analogue of the tradition of feudal oaths, or a written analogue of the urban tradition of the *parlamento.*

was engineered in 1312. Francesco, having left the city for a day of hunting, returned to find the gates shut and an order for his arrest issued. Choosing to defend himself, he was overwhelmed and killed by the Catalan troops of Dalmasio dei Banoli, who with the rank of Captain General was chief of papal forces in Ferrara. In the aftermath of this event, the Estensi were banished from the city, and tight police controls instituted by the papal forces. Having never officially recognized Este rule, the Church had now restored its own sovereignty.

The papal garrison in Ferrara then was entrusted to Robert, the Angevin King of Naples, who instituted a repressive regime that inspired strong popular and noble hostility. This took the form of an insurrection in which the Catalan troops were besieged and finally eradicated, in August of 1317. After the Neapolitan governor, the Estensi possessed renewed appeal, and were recalled. Within ten days, Rinaldo, Niccolò, and Obizzo, the sons of Aldobrandino, and Azzo together with Bertoldo, the sons of Francesco, were elected *signori* of Ferrara. July 22, the day of this event, was proclaimed a holiday, and was for centuries thereafter celebrated as a day of independence. Ferrara, raised from a new, unwanted, and alien, to an older, desired, and local despotism, had restored what it understood to be its independence—not individual civil liberties or republican civic prerogatives, but the rule of an elected *signore* free from foreign control. The most important consequence of the anti-papal revolution of 1317 was precisely this: that the Estensi, far from being seen as usurpers, came to be regarded as the city's saviors, who had returned to regain its liberty, defined as its territorial and political sovereignty with respect to external powers.[13]

[13] Simeoni, *Le Signorie,* i, 248, makes the interesting point that to Ferrara *libertà* meant *signoria.* The Estensi came to be regarded as the defenders of the city's independence, as well as the guarantors of its

After 1317, the Estensi ruled uninterruptedly in Ferrara, but their problems continued to be legion. Uppermost was the task of restoring a *modus vivendi* with the papacy, which had predictably responded to the revolution with its most frightening weapons—excommunication and interdict. In the early 1320's, antagonized by this strategy and appalled by the growing chaos in the papal states, the Estensi even formed Ghibelline alliances and established relations with Louis of Bavaria.[14] It was not until 1329 that a new working relationship with the papacy was restored.[15] Rinaldo II, Obizzo III, and Niccolò I, the sons of Aldobrandino, were then recognized as papal vicars in Ferrara for a period of ten years, and required to pay an annual tax of 10,000 gold florins. Henceforth, even though the tariff was later reduced to 4,000 annually, and was paid only occasionally, the Estensi ruled as papal vicars in Ferrara. The papacy had cut its losses, and the Estensi had been rehabilitated and given new and enhanced legal status. Now they were to be the real rulers, as long as they recognized papal sovereignty, with its relatively small claims on their loyalty and wealth.[16]

---

internal stability and system of justice, especially after 1317, when the town rebelled against the Catalan mercenaries, and the Estensi were welcomed back to restore the city's freedom and maintain its independence from outside control.

[14] This complex problem has been studied by Vergottini in the articles previously cited (see above, Ch. I, n. 23). Vergottini argues that the emergence of the papal vicariate was a direct response to the prior use of the analogous institution by the Holy Roman Emperor, and that the first clear-cut instance of this process occurs with respect to the Estensi in the course of the 1320s.

[15] For the papal vicariate in general see, in addition to the articles by Vergottini, the interesting comments and useful reference provided by P. Partner, *The Papal State Under Martin V* (London, 1958), 186-92, esp. 190.

[16] Partner, *The Papal State Under Martin V,* agrees that the apostolic vicars were virtually independent, a view also maintained by P. J. Jones, "The Vicariate of the Malatesta of Rimini," *EHR,* LXVII (1952), 321-51.

In the following decade, Ferrara was caught up in the constant warfare of the Lombard states and differed little from other constantly warring principalities of the period. In 1336, Obizzo III regained Modena for the last time, after a rebellion similar to the one that had brought him back to Ferrara nearly two decades before. Rinaldo had died the year before, and Niccolò I followed in 1344. Thus Obizzo III, having proven himself in innumerable battles and by longevity, emerged as sole ruler of Ferrara. Obizzo attempted to repair some of his fractured alliances by marriage, others by a neutralism from which he was only reluctantly and occasionally drawn away, and by territorial acquisitions through purchase.[17] It should not be forgotten that the last years of his rule coincided with the outbreak of the Black Death, which of course must have contributed dramatically to the generally cautious and pacific policy he had already been pursuing since 1344. He died in 1352, leaving eleven children, all of whom were borne by the mistress whom he had married on her deathbed in 1347, Lippa degli Ariosti, the daughter of a Bolognese noble. His funeral was notably pompous.[18]

Partner's general statement applies exactly to Ferrara (p. 187): ". . . the gap between the theory and the practice of the apostolic vicariate was very wide. By these grants the Popes endorsed the title of rulers who were declaredly tyrants—*domini, signori*—and, inevitably, what these rulers did within their own domains could not in fact be called in question by any papal official." Partner's use of the word tyrant here is objectionable. Further support for this view comes from the recent study by I. Robertson, "The *Signoria* of Girolamo Riario in Imola," *Historical Studies,* xv (October, 1971), 88-115. This scholar has perceived the same kinds of implicit consensual relations between subjects and ruler that I propose as an essential element of signorial politics in Ferrara. For example (p. 115), Robertson writes of Riario that "He could no longer satisfy those criteria of 'good government' by which his Imolese subjects undoubtedly evaluated the worth of his *signoria* to them, and they were slowly being prepared to embrace the first viable alternative to offer itself."

[17] Chiappini, *Gli Estensi,* 64-76.

[18] *Ant.Est.,* ii, 117: "Poscia adì 20 dello stesso Mese passò all' altra vita,

During Obizzo's reign there occurred institutional changes that prefigure and in some respects perhaps initiate long-range developments in the modes of Estense control of Ferrara. In less dramatic, though possibly more enduring ways than his thirteenth-century namesake, Obizzo III may be regarded as an earlier contributor to the style of the *Quattrocento* despotism. It was during his reign, for example, that there appeared the first money coined in the name of an Este prince. This suggests a major advance in Obizzo's control of Ferrarese economic institutions, as well as an awareness of the moral and political advantages of having one's own coinage. As the engaging antiquarian studies of Vincenzo Bellini discovered, this early minting was quite unlike Ferrarese coinage in its developed Renaissance form, both in appearance and in value. But the essential transformation of Ferrarese coinage had begun, and the next major step followed fairly soon. In 1381, the old coins called "Ferraresi," "Bolognini," and "Aquilini" were discontinued, and the Ferrarese "Lira Marchesana" appeared.[19] The *marchesi* themselves were now the guarantors of Ferrara's monetary integrity.

Obizzo's appropriation of the monetary system, even in its initial piecemeal form, may be indicative of a decision to centralize controls and rationalize techniques in other areas as well. There is some evidence for this view in the language of court documents, which point to the earliest beginnings of an established bureaucracy in this period. Previously, there had of course been a court, in the sense of a group of advisers surrounding the prince. Some of these bore the title *iudex,* and may in addition to strictly judicial functions have aided in the formulation of statutes, edicts,

---

lasciando un gran desiderio di sè ne' suoi Popoli, e fu sepellito il suo Corpo a i Frati Minori con magnifiche esequie."

[19] V. Bellini, *Dalle Monete di Ferrara* (Ferrara, 1761), 97. (This work supersedes the same author's *Dell'antica lira ferrarese* [Ferrara, 1754].)

and proclamations. In addition, there was an ancient communal bureaucracy fairly typical of Lombard town governments of the *Duecento* which, in the time of Obizzo II, had already been subsumed by statute under the control of the *dominus*. This had come to include the office of the *podestà*, with his administrative, judicial, and police functions. According to the theory cautiously developed and presented by William Montorsi, it was also in the time of Obizzo I that the institution of the *savi* or *sapientes* made its first appearance.[20] This communal magistracy, consisting of twelve members and a *iudex, or giudice,* was for many centuries the town council of Ferrara, exercising broad judicial, administrative, and supervisory powers over other magistracies, the guilds, and administration of the civil law. With respect to the commune, the Estensi may be said to have simply taken over a reasonably functional set of bureaucratic institutions and services by improvising, and then codifying, means of controlling their membership and authority. But the early princes had no developed administrative machinery of their own for coordinating and supervising all of these bodies in town and country, in Ferrara and in the other cities and towns of their state. Like other growing, centralizing states of the later middle ages, the state of which Obizzo III was *dominus* required a growing, centralizing administration.

Though Obizzo II and his immediate successors obviously had plenty of lawyers, notaries, and scribes to attend to the growing task of generating and disposing of paperwork of all kinds and degrees, it is only at the time of Obizzo III that evidence appears of the existence of an organized chancellery within the court. A document from 1346 refers to the "cancelaria domini marchionis," and another, from

[20] W. Montorsi, *Statuta Ferrariae,* lxxxii-lxxxvii. For the institution of the *giudice dei savi,* and the *dodici savi,* see also A. Maresti, *Cronologia e istoria de' capi e giudici de' Savi della città di Ferrara* (Ferrara, 1683).

1358, indicates the office of Chancellor, "Canzellarius domini marchionis."[21] From these simple beginnings, as we shall see, a large, reticulated bureaucracy gradually grew. But in the second quarter of the fourteenth century, when the first major steps appear to have been taken, the new institutions were simple enough. The newly-formed *cancelleria* was comprised of the men who had previously borne the title of "notarius domini marchionis." Their competence and authority derived from their title as notaries, but their function derived from their assignment to the chancellery, the office with an essentially political and diplomatic mission. During the fourteenth century, the chancellery generally required a staff of between four and eight men. Alongside this group, there developed another specialized set of notaries delegated to the administrative and particularly the financial management of the court. Their office, as elsewhere, came to be called the *camera,* or exchequer. The officials charged with running the *camera,* and indeed all princely financial affairs, were given the title "factor generalis," or "fattore generale." The first known use of this title in the surviving documents dates from 1358. In this early phase of the organization of the administration of the court, these offices were small, and the division of labor may not have been as precise as it later became. But by 1380, the general trend is unmistakable, for court notaries now habitually identify themselves as being "in statione factorie,"

[21] Much work remains to be done on the administrative history of Ferrara, but the two recent articles by Filippo Valenti have made a good beginning. See "Note Storiche sulla cancelleria degli Estensi a Ferrara dalle origini alla metà del secolo XVI," *Bolletino dell' Archivio Paleografico Italiano,* n. s. 2-3 (1956-57), pt. 2, 357-65, (hereafter "Cancelleria"); esp. p. 357, where the archival references for the above statement appear. Also important is Valenti's study "I consigli di governo presso gli Estensi dalle origini alla devoluzione di Ferrara," in *Studi in onore di R. Filangieri* (Naples, 1959), ii, 19-40 (hereafter "Consigli di governo"). See also Appendix I, below.

or "in cancelleria nova." [22] These organisms had become physically, as well as functionally, distinct.

Obizzo's successor had neither the intelligence, experience, nor leisure to rival the political and administrative achievements—modest though they may appear—of his father. Aldobrandino III inherited the lordship of Ferrara in 1352. Seventeen years old, he was Obizzo's first-born son. Though his title was perfectly clear, and his popular acclamation conventional, he had to fight to keep his inheritance from his older cousins, Francesco II the son of Bertoldo, and Rinaldo, the son of Niccolò I, both of whom claimed a right to rule as legitimate children of the original vicariate, whereas Aldobrandino had been recently legitimized. After prolonged hostilities, Francesco was defeated in 1358, and stripped of all his conquests, including Modena. He was permitted to retire to the family seat at Este, where he lived out his life, and where generations of his descendants continued to live quietly in prosperous obscurity.[23] I have not been able to determine what happened to Rinaldo.

Upon Aldobrandino's death in 1361, his brother Niccolò II (1338-88) succeeded him. He had little to fear from Aldobrandino's three sons, who were little boys, and he moved quickly to reinforce his position among neighboring states. Though known as *Il Zoppo*, "the Lame," Niccolò II was a strong political activist who was not afraid of risks or crises.[24] His own marriage to Verde della Scala, of

[22] Valenti, "Cancelleria," 360.

[23] For Francesco, the son of Bertoldo, see *Ant.Est.*, ii, 104, 109, 118, 135, 148, 151; also E. G. Gardner, *Dukes and Poets in Ferrara* (London, 1904), 20, n. 1.

[24] For Niccolò II, see *Ant.Est.*, ii, 136-52 *passim*. H. Baron, *The Crisis of the Early Italian Renaissance* (Princeton, 1955), 112-14, gives interesting evidence of opinions of Niccolò offered by the humanist Giovanni Conversino da Ravenna, an outright admirer of the efficiency and progressiveness of despotisms (p. 113): "To Niccolò d'Este [reads Baron's paraphrase]

Verona, and the arranged marriages of other members of his family to other princely houses, most importantly the Malatesta of Rimini, immediately strengthened the flaccid alliances he had inherited from Aldobrandino. Moreover, he held the growing misgivings shared among the princes of northeastern Italy about the power, ambition, and expansionist policies of the Visconti lords of Milan, and worked to limit these. Among his efforts in accordance with this policy, he tried to pursuade Urban V to return from Avignon to Italy. The program of reassertion of papal powers, regional pacification, and legislative controls imposed on the papal states by the militant Cardinal Albornoz had, in Niccolò's view, laid the groundwork for Urban's return, which would provide a needed counterweight to Milanese ambitions in the Romagna and Emilia. Moreover, by pursuing this cautiously anti-Viscontean, Guelf line, Niccolò gained support not only from the traditionally Guelf nobles, but also from the strongly religious populace. The policy paid off handsomely, if temporarily, as a result of the Florentine War of the Eight Saints (1375-78), in which Niccolò was rewarded for his military support by the addition of several new papal territories.[25] Niccolò continued to maintain correct relations with the Venetians, recognizing the cornerstone of all successful Ferrarese diplomacy.

Niccolò's long reign also produced refinements in the institutional and administrative structure of the court. We have already noticed the increasing specialization of both

---

Ferrara owed its transformation from a mire-bound and evil-smelling place into one of the cleanest, healthiest, most populous, and sightliest of cities. Niccolò paved the streets and laid sidewalks, replaced tile structures with stone houses, raised forts and towers, and fortified the suburbs."

[25] Chiappini, *Gli Estensi,* 69-70. The territories received by the Estensi in return for services rendered in the war included the town of Lugo and the Archbishoprics of Ravenna and Faenza, which they acquired through purchase. Both of the latter were soon lost.

functions and offices that characterized the notaries, who may be regarded as the civil service of this period. What gives further evidence of an increasingly complex and differentiated structure of authority and responsibility within the court is the addition, in this period, of officers bearing the title of "counsellor." The first reference to a "consiliarius" dates from 1372, and the title denotes a new rank of administrators, interposed between the *signore* and the functionaries of chancellery and *camera* who executed his orders.[26] The *consiliarii* may be regarded as a kind of personal general staff. It would be misleading, though, to think of this structure as rigidly formalized and maintained. The *fattore generale* was not necessarily inferior in power or influence to a *consiliarius*. The same individual may have served as both, simultaneously or sequentially. If the evolving Ferrarese state is to be imagined in the metaphorical language of Burckhardt's "state as a work of art," we should not think in terms of sculpture or architecture, but in terms of more flexible or improvisory forms. For these changes, while considered, were introduced piecemeal, in response to specific requirements and circumstances as these developed. The process as I see it is one of improvisation, not of planning or composition. There is, perhaps, the ingenuity and inventiveness of *homo creator,* and perhaps his self-conscious artifice, but never the formality or finality of what we commonly think of as works of art.[27]

[26] Valenti, "Consigli di governo," 23-24.

[27] Cf. J. Burckhardt, *The Civilization of the Renaissance in Italy,* pt. 1 ("The State as a Work of Art"), especially section dealing with the Estensi. It is no longer credible that the manipulative and artificial skill of the *signori* exceeded that of the improvisers of techniques and institutions in Renaissance republics. For evidence of the latter, see the work of N. Rubinstein, *The Government of Florence Under the Medici* (London, 1966), esp. pp. 88-135. The same general point would seem to hold for the communes, and the structural innovations that occurred in that context may be sampled in the survey by D. Waley, *The Italian City-Republics.*

In the 1380's, another new and important position was created, that of the *referendarius*. This official was to serve as head of the chancellery, but the office was generally filled by a close personal advisor of the *signore*. Over the years, the *referendarius* became more than a functionary, however important, of the court. He became in some instances a virtual prime minister. Both in its specific charge, and in the opportunities for developing more personal powers, this office is clearly analogous to the position of chancellor in Florence. It is also totally different from the position of *referendarius* at Milan, where the term denotes a collector of duties.[28]

The appointment of *consiliarii* suggests the possibility that some sort of conciliar system may have come into existence within the court during the late fourteenth century. Filippo Valenti has shown, however, on the basis of careful research that though the existence of some such formal body can be proven for this period, it must have been of little consequence. He argues that such collegial bodies, which were widely used by other princes either for concrete aid in governing, for recognizing and conciliating powerful constituencies, or for reinforcing their political positions, were never used for such purposes by the Estensi. For these purposes, they were able to manipulate the magistracy of the *savi,* various judgeships, and a wide range of communal and aulic offices. Valenti showed that all of the committees known as councils in Ferrara were given essentially juristic functions, and did not participate in specifically political kinds of decision-making, at least until the late fifteenth century. Valenti regards this as evidence of an uncommonly absolutist tendency in Estense government, and this view has much to commend it.[29] The fourteenth-century *consilium*

---

[28] Valenti, "Cancelleria," 360-61.

[29] Valenti, "Consigli di governo," 20-29. The author observes that (pp. 19-20): ". . . i consigli non vengono mai menzionati nemmeno negli

domini marchionis, to which the first notarial reference occurs in 1372, is hardly ever mentioned in surviving records, and played no role in the promulgation of official documents. If such a body really existed during the time of Niccolò II, it was purely consultative in nature.

It has been noted that in 1381 Niccolò introduced the Ferrarese pound, the "Lira Marchesana," in a thoroughgoing reform of the state's coinage. The Ferrarese *lira* of Niccolò II, unlike the florin or the Venetian ducat, was a silver coin, the first examples of which show, on the obverse, the Este eagle, and around the border bear the inscription NICHOL.MAR.; on the reverse are the city's emblem and the words DE FERARI. But also unlike the great exchange currencies of the commercial centers, the *lira* was minted in small quantities and hardly used. Ferrara's numismatist called it "imaginary, and ideal." [30] What was exchanged was the Ferrarese *soldo,* or shilling, one-twentieth of a *lira.* *Soldi,* sometimes called *marchesini,* were also silver coins, originally containing twenty-three grains of the metal. The *soldo* appears to have devaluated slowly during the fifteenth century, in relation to its original purchasing power in Ferrara and to the great international coinages, and it was also gradually debased.

In the period of Niccolò II, the Este rulers continued to expand and develop their territories, moved farther in the direction of a monetary economy, and further elaborated their courtly administration, but they also endured some very serious difficulties. There were numerous and repeated

---

atti marchionali poi ducali come concorrenti alla formazione della volontà del Signore, e la loro figura, tolte le attribuzioni giurisdizionali . . . fu tutt' al più quella di organi puramente consultativi. Altro aspetto, questo, della tendenza all' accentramento personalistico del potere sempre presente, insieme con un caratteristico paternalismo, nelle tradizioni di governo della Casa d'Este."

[30] Bellini, *Delle monete di Ferrara,* 98.

floods and years of famine, and in 1382, an outbreak of the plague that killed 10,000 people, or about one-third to one-half the population of the city. In the aftermath of the plague, in particular, there was a period of social unrest that almost became a threat to the *signoria* itself. In 1385, a mob rampaged through the streets, demanding the death of Tomaso da Tortona, the judge of the *savi,* as a traitor. They were protesting against high taxes and forced labor. Their protest was not directed against the *signore,* much less the dynasty, but at a functionary, albeit an important one. The uprising reflects Niccolò's efforts to rebuild after the plague, on a reduced population base, and perhaps to carry out some costly hydraulic projects relating to the chronic flood problem. But it probably reflects more precisely his attempt to carry on the business and pleasure of the court as usual, despite the stricken population. The episode teaches another lesson. It is that the Estensi, though they did not share their power, knew how to take advantage, and always tended to benefit, from maintaining a chain of command. In this case, as in similar instances during the reign of Ercole I a century later, a scapegoat was always available. Popular unrest was sated by the sacrifice of a subordinate, the princely exactions moderated for a time, and life went on as before. In this instance, Niccolò II felt he had had a narrow escape, and he learned his lesson well. Having had his chancellery sacked, his staff terrorized, and his principal communal magistrate savagely mutilated, dismembered, and finally in part burned and in part paraded about the city and left as carrion, he set about to increase the security of the regime. Quietly, reprisals were carried out. The garrison was heavily strengthened. Finally, the architect Bartolino da Novara was retained to construct an impregnable castle within the city, to be connected by an elevated passageway to the Estense palace. Less than five months after the insurrection, Niccolò had secured a loan from the Gonzagas in Mantua, and the work was under way. The *castello,* dedicated to St. Michael, was the first great monument of Renaissance architecture in Ferrara, but its spirit is entirely medieval, at least in its outward aspect. It still dominates the city today, an eloquent monument to the unexpected. But when it was built, it must have exercised a more than physical dominance. It functioned, as other aspects of Estense rule also functioned, as a psychological deterrent against rebellion, a mighty fortress in more ways than one.[31]

Niccolò II died in 1388. He had been ambitious, lucky, ruthless, and clever. His brother Alberto—by contrast scholarly, pious, and benevolent—succeeded him, and ruled for only five years (Fig. 1). The most notable event of this period was the founding of the University of Ferrara, chartered by a papal bull of March 4, 1391. Alberto had arranged this during a pilgrimage to Rome, at which time he had also gotten the apostolic *camera* to consider past debts as void, gained new commercial privileges of various kinds, and seen to the legitimation of his bastard, Niccolò, aged eight, whose mother he had recently married.[32] When this child was acclaimed as *dominus* two years later, he inherited a state which had met not only the kinds of po-

---

[31] For the construction and design of the castle, see L. N. Cittadella, *Il Castello di Ferrara* (Ferrara, 1875). Its construction finds interesting echoes in the correspondence of Coluccio Salutati. See F. Novati, ed., *Epistolario di C. Salutati,* 4 vols. (Rome, 1891-1911), vol. II, pp. 176-80. In this letter to Alberto, Salutati pleads for leniency toward a courtier who, he thinks, may have been wrongly implicated in the uprising. The letter reveals strongly anti-popular attitudes, for the Florentine chancellor refers to the perpetrators of the rebellion as "quasi rabidi canes." Indeed this defender of republican liberty consistently flattered and cultivated the Estensi, and did not condemn them in the terms reserved for tyrants. In fact (Novati, II, pp. 359-62) he even wanted to get his cousin Francesco a position at the Ferrarese court.

[32] See Chiappini, *Gli Estensi,* 73-6; *Ant.Est.,* II, 152-59.

litical and social tests we have discussed, and improvised
the administrative and institutional changes we have traced,
but also one in which significant forms of cultural awareness and growth may also be discerned. No discussion of
Trecento Ferrara can ignore them.

Prior to the fifteenth century, Ferrarese civilization—including the visual and literary arts, and the more academic
and intellectual professions—was with a few notable exceptions qualitatively insignificant and quantitatively trivial.[33]
Ferrara, like such other principalities as Urbino, Mantua,
and even (though to a lesser degree) Milan, was a late
bloomer among the cultural centers of the late Middle Ages.
All of these principalities suffered greatly in the thirteenth
and fourteenth centuries from the chronic convulsions and
disorders of Northern Italian politics. But there were specific local problems as well, especially in the smaller states.
During the early reigns of the *signori* there was necessarily
a high budgetary priority placed on military expenses, a
special burden in states like Ferrara, where the activities
of the mercantile and industrial groups had been limited
or suppressed. Thus, that segment of the population which
in merchant oligarchies generated surplus wealth and found
new ways to enjoy it and invest it was smaller, more iso-
lated, and financially weaker in a town like Ferrara. Therefore, until the ruling family became both secure and
wealthy enough to provide positive stimuli for cultural life,
little could happen outside the patronage of the Church.
    In Ferrara, there were additional problems. Though the

---

[33] The best discussion of Ferrarese culture and courtly life in the
Trecento is still that of G. Carducci, "Della coltura Estense nei secoli
XIII e XIV fino alla signoria di Niccolò III," in *Edizione Nazionale delle
Opere di G. C.,* XIII (Bologna, 1954), 1-54 (first published in 1895); but
see also F. Novati, "Donato degli Albanzani alla corte Estense," *ASI,* s.
v, VI (1890), 365-85.

city had grown through the thirteenth century, it entered the *Trecento* as one of the less attractive towns of an urbanized peninsula. There was, to be sure, a fine cathedral, and a few other good features, but visitors found the place dank and insalubrious, the water unsanitary, the air oppressive, the streets muddy and incommodious, the houses flimsy and unappealling. Contemporaries did not hesitate to express their distaste for the place, and its baneful effect on the people. The inhabitants of the region were known for their loquacity, and Dante believed that from this indiscriminately garrulous little world no poet could emerge.[34]

In the beginning of the fourteenth century, Ferrara was retrograde even in comparison with its nearby neighbors. Both Modena and Bologna became important centers of learning, especially jurisprudence, in the middle of the twelfth century, and Reggio was not far behind. There is evidence that professors of law, medicine, and liberal arts were present in Ferrara during the reign of Obizzo II, but if they were, they can only have made a small and temporary impression. A statute from 1264 exempts them from military service, but there is no other evidence of their presence, and the clause may amount to little more than customary legal phraseology.[35]

The early *marchesi* may not have been very cultivated men, but they enjoyed some kinds of art, and saw the value of certain kinds of learning. During the thirteenth and early fourteenth centuries, troubadors from Provence were eagerly welcomed at the court, and their verses sufficiently

---

[34] *De volgari eloquentiae,* II, 15, where Dante talks about a certain garrulity peculiar to the Lombards; cf. Carducci, *op.cit.,* 19.

[35] Montorsi, *Statuta Ferrariae,* 73 (Liber Secundus, 82): ". . . statuimus quod omnes docentes in scientia legum et medicine et in artibus grammatice et dialetice, ire ad exercitum aut aliquam facere cavalcatam non cogantur; eo addito ut ad aliqua alia munera personalia subeunda non compellantur; et de hoc potestas precise teneatur. Quod statutum vendicet sibi locum in doctoribus continue docentibus."

appreciated to have been preserved in an important manuscript of the Biblioteca Estense.[36] The presence of these men, and the growing use of the *volgare* as a poetic language, may have inspired such local talents as Antonio da Ferrara, and his brother Niccolò, to try their hands at verse. Theirs are the first, unpretentious efforts at a local literature, willing, but not too able. Antonio, an acquaintance of Petrarch's (who found him somewhat scatterbrained), and a peripatetic physician, apparently spent little time in his native city.[37] A few of Niccolò's letters survive, but they are of small interest.

Just as Ferrara produced no notable known artists in the fourteenth century, so too was there no distinguished innovator in other creative or scholarly fields. Such modest claims as can be made for the city in that century are all attributable to the work of foreigners. Petrarch visited the court of Niccolò II and corresponded with his brother Ugo.[38] Other Tuscans were recruited to elevate the tone, and perhaps help professionalize the work of the court and the chancellery in particular. Foremost among these was Donato degli

---

[36] See the article and inventory published by Pio Rajna, "Ricordi di codici francesi posseduti degli Estensi nel secolo XV," *Romania,* II, (1873), 49-58.

[37] For the works of Antonio de' Beccari, see esp. A. Bottoni, *Saggio di rime inedite di m. Antonio da Ferrara* (Ferrara, 1878), and also Carducci, *La coltura estense,* esp. 28-33. He makes extensive use of the work of A. Zenatti, *Tre ballate inedite di Maestro Antonio da Ferrara* (Florence, 1886). A splendid recent edition of his *Rime* has been published by L. Bellucci (Bologna, 1967); see the review of this work by N. Iliescu in *Speculum,* XLVI: 4 (October, 1971), 721-23.

[38] For Petrarch's experiences in Ferrara, and his attitudes toward the Estensi, see his *Seniles,* Bk. XI, no. XII, to Pope Urban V (11 May 1370) which discusses his illness there; Bk. XI, no. XIII, to Ugo d'Este, brother of Niccolò II, which attempts to dissuade him from dangerous chivalric jousts; and Bk. XIII, no. I, to Niccolò II (5 August 1370, from Arquà) consoling him upon Ugo's death. Carducci gives erroneous references to these letters.

Albanzani, known as the dedicatee of Petrarch's *Of his own ignorance and that of many others,* and represented in Boccaccio's *Eclogues.*[39] Albanzani was an accomplished humanist, the first to reside in Ferrara. He probably settled there in 1377, already famous and well along in years. For four years he served as chancellor (almost certainly the post that later came to be called *referendarius*). In the later 1380's, he became tutor to the young Niccolò III and gave the young Marquess an appreciation for letters that eventually appeared in forms crucial to Ferrara's cultural development. Albanzani was the first of what was to become a familiar type around the Este court: a man of letters who combined both practical administrative skill with solid scholarly interests and achievements. At Niccolò II's request, he translated Boccaccio's *De claris mulieribus* into Tuscan, and followed that up by translating another work in the same genre, Petrarch's *De viris illustribus.* It should not be surprising that toward the end of his life he accepted a professorship in the new *Studium* of Ferrara. He died in 1411.

Though the presence of Donato degli Albanzani, who became a citizen of Ferrara, marks a growing interest in humanistic learning in the later part of Niccolò II's reign, it was under Alberto I that the first attempt occurred to place learning in Ferrara on a firm foundation. The charter of the *Studium* clearly reveals that Alberto nourished high hopes for it as a major center of learning, for it was established not only to give instruction in areas of immediate and obvious utility, such as law and medicine, but also in theology and arts. Documentation for the university is very

[39] Albanzani is also well known as the translator of Boccaccio's *De claris mulieribus* into the *volgare*. For his career in Ferrara, see the article by F. Novati, "Donato degli Albanzani alla corte estense," cited in n. 33 above. His correspondence with Coluccio Salutati has been published and extensively annotated by the same author.

sparse before 1450, but it appears that at least law, arts, and theology got started early, and that all of these fields eventually declined from their modest beginnings under the young Niccolò III, to the point where the institution was practically nonexistent by 1430. Only under Leonello's patronage did it begin to achieve real intellectual distinction and reputation.

However, the initial years of the *Studium* were of more than passing interest for the cultural history of Ferrara. They reveal that learning had come to be regarded as useful by the Estensi, whether for its practical value, its reflections of princely glory, or its inherent interest. More important, it brought to the city men of real competence in various fields, and for a while enabled them to teach and live there in relative dignity, a state of affairs taken for granted elsewhere, but previously quite unknown in *Trecento* Ferrara. Initially, professors were paid out of the communal treasury, though Alberto himself recruited the first appointees for the faculty, which commenced operations in the fall of 1391. Bartolommeo da Saliceto, from Bologna, and Egidiolo Cavitelli, from Cremona, were two of Alberto's first law professors, and they were soon joined by others. Classes met in monasteries and churches. But Alberto did not live to see the first diplomas conferred by the archbishop of Ferrara. The development of the university, and indeed of all of the relatively modest beginnings of Ferrarese culture that occurred in the reigns of Niccolò II and Alberto I, was greatly intensified in the fifteenth century, under significantly changed conditions.[40] But it clearly was in the

---

[40] For the foundation and early history of the university, see F. Borsetti, *Historia almi ferrariae gymnasii* (Ferrara, 1735) 2 vols; O. Venturini, "Dei gradi accademici conferiti dallo Studio Ferrarese nel primo secolo di sua istituzione," *AF*, IV (1892), 63-107; G. Secco Suardo, "Lo studio di Ferrara a tutto il secolo XV, *AF*, VI (1894), 25-294; G. Pardi, "Lo studio di Ferrara nei secoli XV e XVI," *AF*, XIV (1903), a monograph of

late *Trecento,* after the dynasty had emerged strengthened from the abortive revolt of 1385, that the institutionalization of culture and learning came to be seen as a desirable goal of Estense policy. In the following centuries, they came even to rival in importance the political, diplomatic and territorial goals of the dynasty.

274 pp.; the same author's *Titoli dottorali conferiti dello studio di Ferrara nei secoli XV e XVI* (Lucca, 1900); and also *Ant.Est.,* ii, 158. A recent survey is A. Visconti, *Storia dell' Università di Ferrara* (Bologna, 1950).

III   The Age of Niccolò III d'Este

"Sceptical as to the existence of unicorns and salamanders, the age of Machiavelli and Henry VIII found food for its credulity in the worship of that rare monster, the God-fearing Prince." [1] R. H. Tawney's trenchant observation offers an insight into the mentality whereby republics and principalities could be evaluated by contemporary observers *sub specie aeternitatis,* and the latter found in principle more Godlike, more reliable, and more just. What was true enough in the age of Machiavelli and Henry VIII was equally valid a century earlier for most of Italy.

[1] The quotation comes from *Religion and the Rise of Capitalism* (New York, 1926), 91; quoted by K. Popper, *The Poverty of Historicism,* 3rd ed. (London, 1961), 24. See also P. J. Jones, "Communes and Despots," 94-96. Jones makes the point that for political observers in pre-modern Europe the alternatives for government were not democracy on the one hand and monarchy on the other, but rather the choice between relative degrees of oligarchical or despotic control cloaked in various forms of popular representation. He argues cogently that to all Renaissance observers, including Bartolus, Machiavelli, and Vettori, Italian governments—regardless of their form—were tyrannies, whether of party, class, or of a single despot. To this point he quotes Dr. Johnson on alternative models of government: "Sir, that is all visionary. I would not give half a guinea to live under one form of government rather than another," suggesting that this attitude may have been fairly widespread in the Italian *Quattrocento.* Since modern political theory uses much the same vocabulary as that of pre-modern times, including such terms as republic, tyranny, despotism and the like, it is not easy to understand the inherent limitations on political speculation that existed before the French Revolution. But Jones' point has recently received added support from the intriguing study of Fred Weinstein and Gerald Platt, *The Wish to be Free: Society, Psyche, and Value Change* (Berkeley, 1969), in which the authors argue that social conflict in traditional societies was invariably directed toward the fulfillment of demands for the implementation of traditional values, and not toward the repudiation or overthrow of these values. See esp. ch. I "The Sociology of Value Change," pp. 20-44.

Nowhere was it more true than in Ferrara, where the brief reign of Alberto d'Este had given way in 1393 to a regency in behalf of his legitimized natural son, Niccolò. By 1441, when Niccolò died at the age of fifty-eight, there were few people alive in Ferrara who could remember the city without him, and even fewer who could have known his predecessors. In an age of short lives and even shorter reigns, Niccolò endured. That he not only survived but came to be worshiped with that ambivalent admixture of love and dread that Machiavelli understood so well reflects the fact that he not only was, but was perceived to be, one of those rare monsters, a God-fearing prince. His deeds generated useful myths, and he came to be regarded in the same terms as Cosimo de' Medici in Florence a few decades later, as *pater patriae*. There is no escaping the fact that this laudatory term was in the Renaissance reserved for figures of authority, even if they were not in the strict sense autocrats—men who knew how to keep the *popolo* in its place, men who knew how to draw on the desire to believe in a political father-figure, analogous to and cognizant of his universal counterpart, and willing to use these talents to produce a measure of public security and order.[2] Just as

[2] Niccolò III and Cosimo held an honorific title that was applied to many other contemporary rulers, as well as numerous earlier and later heads of state from Augustus to Atatürk, and even beyond. For historical uses of the phrase "pater patriae" see now A. M. Brown, "Cosimo de' Medici, Pater Patriae," *JWCI*, xxiv (1961), 186-221; S. Bertelli, "Petrus Soderinus Patriae Parens," *BHR*, xxxi (1969), 93-114; *idem*, "Pier Soderini: 'Vexillifer Perpetuus Reipublicae Florentinae,' 1502-1512," *Studies in Honor of Hans Baron* (Florence, 1971), esp. 351. The notion of patriarchal authority, and its role in traditional societies, has been explored by many writers, but see now esp. Weinstein and Platt, particularly 43, 69, 136-53, 160. Thus writers such as H. Marcuse have interpreted modern revolutionary behavior as revolts of sons against fathers, designed to change the pattern of patriarchal domination, the hallmark of traditional governmental structures. But Marcuse's conclusions are cogently challenged by Weinstein and Platt, esp. 300-301.

religion and politics are inextricably entwined in the personal and political lives of Cosimo de' Medici, or Henry
VIII, so too does this intermingling characterize the reign
of Niccolò III.

Perhaps for this reason, Niccolò has traditionally appeared
in the literature as a transitional figure, the man who
exemplifies both medieval and Renaissance characteristics,
the former waning through his long rule as the latter
emerge more strongly.[3] But I am reluctant to accept that
as an adequate, or even interesting, interpretation of this
key figure. For one thing, I use the terms "medieval" and
"Renaissance" as consistently as possible to refer to periods
of time, the one ending, the other beginning, around 1300.
The terms themselves are loaded with misleading implications of all sorts, but if they are quite consciously limited
to such chronological referents, the damage can be minimized. They are in such common usage that one can hardly
speak the language of early modern history without them,
but I think they can be used without the full range of
Burckhardtian assumptions and evaluations. Moreover, even
if I were convinced that the terms "medieval" and "Renaissance" could still be used as meaningful analytical (as distinct from chronological) categories, I could not agree that
Niccolò is in any convincing way a "transitional figure"
in that sense. The entire continuum of Este princes throughout the fourteenth and fifteenth, and even to a large extent
the sixteenth, centuries reflects certain more or less common
values and styles. Though these princes differed significantly in their interests and tastes, with far-reaching effects,
their political careers and personal life-styles represent

---

[3] For scholarly judgments of Niccolò III, see A. Lazzari, "Il Signor di
Ferrara al tempo del concilio del 1438-9, Niccolò d'Este," *AF,* n.s. x (1954),
69-96 (previously in *Rinascità* i [1938], 672-702, cited here because of its
greater availability). Also A. Manni, "Terzi ed Estensi, 1402-1421," *AF,*
xxv (1925).

variations on an autocratic theme, the *leitmotif* of which remains relatively constant over several centuries. What have traditionally been regarded as "medieval" and "Renaissance" elements are found in the reigns of Niccolò II and Alberto I, just as they are in those of Niccolò I, Ercole I, or even Ercole II. This is not to assert that there are no fundamental changes or long-term developments over hundreds of years. To claim that would be absurd. But it is to say that the simplistic model that historians have used to characterize such changes and developments does not begin to offer the explanations it purports to provide, and that it can therefore be safely abandoned. Whether "medieval" or "Renaissance," Ferrara's society was unusually stable, structurally almost static.[4] In this it bears comparison with Venice, its metropolis.

Niccolò came to be regarded as the father of his country, *pater patriae,* because to him was credited the achievement of providing for Ferrara something it had never had before: relative security and relative stability. Cosimo de' Medici won his sobriquet for the same reasons, of course, and on much more difficult terrain. Unlike Cosimo, who had to build a new autocracy within the unpromising framework of a proudly self-conscious republic controlled by an entrenched oligarchy, Niccolò had only to consolidate and build upon the foundations well established by eleven predecessors from his own family.[5]

[4] Florence, on the other hand, provides an almost diametrically opposite example of a society which, despite notable elements of continuity (particularly in its structures of authority), is none the less mobile in extremely dramatic ways. For the profound psychological and sociological implications of these structural characteristics, see esp. M. B. Becker, *Florence in Transition,* vol. II (*The Rise of the Territorial State*), esp. 201-50.

[5] The difference is significant. Niccolò was the twelfth marquess of Este and the latest in a very long series of rulers of Ferrara from his own family. That is not to say that he could have maintained his position without noble and perhaps even popular support. Indeed, the willingness

But it was no foregone conclusion that he would succeed in that task, when he first inherited the titles of his father in 1393. At that time Azzo, the son of Francesco d'Este, attempted to seize power for the collateral line descending from Obizzo II's son Francesco. Both Niccolò's youth and his original illegitimacy stood against him. But in his favor were the facts that the much-esteemed Alberto had designated him, that he immediately received full legal confirmations of his inheritance, and, most important perhaps, that he had full Venetian support.[6] The situation posed one problem for which Ferrarese institutional precedents offered no ready solution. It was clear that Niccolò would not be able to govern personally for many years, and there was no reliable senior member of the family to act as regent. At the same time, after over a century of despotism, Ferrara had no tradition of conciliar bodies with executive powers. It was in this context that after Alberto's death, his close advisors formed a body that might have become permanent, but in the event served only an *ad hoc* function. This was the council of regency, which in effect ruled Ferrara until Niccolò attained his majority.[7]

The regency was established at the same time that Niccolò

to be dominated was—as has been suggested—a crucial condition to the success of the Estensi and many other despots. What was lacking in Florence was a general consensus, especially among the merchant oligarchy, as to how their rule should be embodied; or, more simply, who should rule. Thus the Medicean oligarchy not only had to supersede that of the Albizzi, which had generally controlled Florence since 1384, but also had to perform the delicate political task of at the same time appearing to rule by virtually unanimous popular consent, and without significant office-holding. N. Rubinstein has shown how they did it in *The Government of Florence under the Medici, 1434-1494*.

[6] *Ant.Est.*, ii, 159-66.

[7] For the regency council, see especially F. Valenti, "Consigli di Governo," 20-2. The document of its incorporation is in *ASM, ASE*, Cancelleria, Leggi e Decreti, Sec. ii, vol. ii, f. 1.

was confirmed as *dominus generalis,* and the permanent members of the council were to include the noblemen Filippo and Gabrino de' Roberti and Tomaso degli Obizzi, and the *referendarius* Bartolommeo della Mella, who was not a nobleman. These were considered Niccolò's representatives on the council. In addition, there were to be six additional citizens, elected every two months, representing the state and people of Ferrara. This group originally included a physician and two notaries. Evidently, then, the council attempted to represent the various constituencies of Ferrarese political life in such a way as to maintain popular and noble support for the threatened regime. It is interesting to notice that the structure of this council conferred real power on the permanent members only. This method must have proven unsatisfactory, because it seems to have been abandoned after a year or so, whereupon the entire membership became permanent and seems to have been drawn from and generally limited to the great noble families loyal to the Estensi. This suggests that after an initial period of uneasiness, even such token representation of the *popolo* as the council had created was no longer a political necessity. Notarial protocols suggest that the council became and remained a powerful institution until the late 1390's, when it suddenly disappeared almost completely from mention, as the young *Marchese* consolidated his personal dominion. During its term, though, the council of the regency acted with extreme loyalty and vigor to defend Niccolò's interests. It prosecuted the war against Azzo, investigated and severely punished attempts at treason, and attempted to deal conservatively with financial problems.[8]

[8] But Valenti shows (23) that the council became coterminous with the principal functionaries and advisers of Niccolò d'Este as he became more active in government, and included such intimate familiars as Uguccione Contrarii, the Archbishop of Ravenna, Alberto del Sale, the *referendarius*

In 1397 Niccolò, then thirteen, married Gigliola, the daughter of Francesco Novello da Carrara, the lord of Padua. After the glow of the joyous festivities had subsided, Francesco attempted to seize Ferrara, and for a short time he succeeded. Della Mella, the *referendarius*, was jailed, the council dissolved, and Paduan troops stationed throughout the city. A virtual protectorate had been established over Niccolò's state, and the young man was a mere puppet. But by 1402, he had gotten rid of the Paduans, by threatening the Venetians with a Milanese alliance, and for the first time had established personal control over Ferrara. In 1402, with the Paduans at bay and Giangaleazzo Visconti of Milan dead, Ferrara had survived a long series of crises. Niccolò's rule was never seriously challenged thereafter.[9]

In the tumultuous politics of Northern Italy from 1402 to 1415, Niccolò played a relatively cautious role. He seems to have realized the advantages of a basically defensive strategy for a second-class power surrounded by greater states. Thus he avoided over-reaching, but resolutely fought all attempts to whittle away the edges of the Este territories. He understood the importance of containing the Milanese, an essential ingredient in his continuing good relations with Venice. At the same time, he tried not to antagonize the Visconti either by outright bellicosity or by conspiring with their enemies. The decline of Milanese power after the death of Giangaleazzo made this cautious policy possible. Its revival, some years later, after Niccolò had built a powerful state of his own, gave him new opportunities to play off

---

Bartolommeo dela Mella, the *giudice* of the *savi* and other office-holders, including the *magister camerarius,* the vicar-general of the court, the main cameral officials (*factores generales*), and so forth. He also regards it as a forerunner of the later *Consiglio Segreto* (cf. Appendix I, below).

[9] For the Carrara-Estense problem see esp. A. Frizzi, *Memorie per la storia di Ferrara,* III, 407-14; *Ant.Est.,* II, 162-64; Chiappini, *Gli Estensi,* 86-88, gives extended descriptions of all these events.

the Venetians and the Milanese against one another, and to raise the price to both for his continuing non-intervention.

Despite the occasional opportunities for gain that this strategy presented, Niccolò recognized a longer-term, deeper interest in establishing stable and peaceful relations between the two jealous powers that surrounded him. In fact he came to be regarded as a potential peacemaker, a genuinely neutral power whose best interests would be immediately served by a reconciliation of differences between surrounding hostile powers. Thus, in a letter dated January 27, 1424, he wrote to his cameral officials: "There should come to Ferrara on February 3 next the ambassadors of the Duke of Milan and those of the Florentines to treat for peace, [a matter] which we have in hand. And we are sure that they will not want to stay in the same inn." [10] The letter gives instructions on how the ambassadors are to be lodged separately, and order the *fattori* to make certain the accommodations are adequate, "che habiano bono et bello alogiamentj." Niccolò offered similar facilities in other years, such as 1426, 1428, and 1433, and 1441 as well. In these years, Ferrara came to be known as a peaceful city, and Niccolò as a ruler of extraordinary political acumen. Guarino da Verona believed that Niccolò had a literally prophetic in-

[10] *ASM, ASE,* Cancelleria, Registri dei Mandati 1424, f. 13 v°: "El debe venire a dì iii de febraro proximo futuro a ferrara li ambasaduri del duca de milano et quelli de fiorentini per tractare la pace la quale nuy havemo in le mane. Et semo certi che egli non vorano stare in una medesima hosteria. Et per questo volemo che vui mandiati per Antonio Galgano, hosto alangelo, et per laltro da ciglo, et ordinati con loro che egli mettano Impunto quelle due o tre camere che a vuy et a loro para bixogno o piu se piu credeno ne debia essere di bixogno, acioche quando vegnerano dicti ambasadurj trovino in tute due quelle hosterie alcunza le cose che stagano bene e che habiano bono et belo alogiamentj." Quoted by L. A. Gandini, "Saggio degli Usi e delle Costumanze della Corte di Ferrara al Tempo di Niccolò III (1393-1442)," *AR,* S. iii, ix (1891), 163-64 (hereafter Gandini").

sight into political and military matters.[11] Though that is surely a case of politically motivated humanist rhetoric in a princely context, it is clear enough that Niccolò well understood the nature and limits of Este power. Content to recover and strengthen his hold on the ancient centers of the original territories, he was also well aware that his state was surrounded by Mantua, Padua, Verona, and Bologna, with Venice and Milan not far beyond. He knew that he lacked the manpower base for fighting of states like Urbino, where there was a surplus of men not needed for farming and public works. He realized that Ferrara owed its continuing independence to its dominion-like or semi-colonial status in relation to Venice. He recognized that his popularity within his states depended in large part on his ability to preserve their *libertà,* in the sense of freedom from foreign control.[12] He thus chose to be primarily (though not exclusively) an observer, rather than an actor, in the political dramas of his time.

It is possible, though I have found no documentary evidence to confirm the notion, that Niccolò's pacifistic inclinations are linked to his strong and very public religiosity.

[11] Guarino's judgments of Niccolò may be sampled in his funeral oration, published by R. Sabbadini in his *Epistolario di Guarino Veronese,* comprising vols. 8, 11, and 14 of the series *Miscellanea di Storia* of the Deputazione Veneta di Storia Patria. The edition recently has been reprinted by the Bottega d'Erasmo (Turin, 1969). These are cited as vols. i, ii, and iii. See vol. ii, pp. 413-20. Guarini says (p. 415): "Per eam non modo praesentia intelligebat, verum etiam perinde ac ab excelsa specula ventura prospiciebat et ut vates divinus agnoscebat, bellorum non tantum ortus, sed etiam exitus praedicebat, ut non futura praemonuisse, sed praeterita narrese videretur." The passage is slightly misquoted by Lazzari, "Il Signor di Ferrara," 695.

[12] For this use of the word *libertà,* and others current in the period, see above all N. Rubinstein, "Florence and the Despots;" *TRHS,* s. v, ii (1952), 21-45. I have found no early Ferrarese uses of the term; they may appear in time.

His life in fact reveals a combination of formal piety and personal transgression that is remarkable even by the standards of the time. On the one hand, Niccolò's public religious life made him the very model of the Christian prince. In 1413, for example, he made a pilgrimage to Jerusalem, where he visited the holy sites. The entire trip, which lasted three months, was duly chronicled by the courtier Luchino dal Campo, who gives a vivid description of the ebullient and chivalrous company and its escapades.[13] For their fidelity in accompanying him, several of Niccolò's advisors were knighted at the Church of the Holy Sepulchre, and literally won their spurs. In later years, Niccolò undertook pilgrimages to many other places, and seems always to have enjoyed himself hugely in the process. He never made the great journey to Santiago de Compostela, but his son Ercole later set out to repair the oversight.[14] Such pilgrimages were to an extent conventional, ritualistic acts; they offered a sense

---

[13] All of the Ferrarese chronicles for this period cover Niccolò's trip to Jerusalem, but by far the best source is Luchino da Campo's eye-witness account, which has been published by G. Ghinassi, in *Collezione di opere inedite e rare dei primi tre secoli della lingua* (Turin, 1861); but see also the other account published by L. Simeoni as an appendix to the chronicle of Giovanni da Ferrara, *Fr. Johannis Ferrariensis Ex Annalium Libris Marchionum Estensium Excerpta, RIS,* xx, pt. 2 (Bologna, 1936), 51-52.

[14] It is possible that Niccolò's trip to the shrine of St. Anthony in Vienne may have had as its original destination Santiago de Compostela, but this is not certain. Simeoni has published the account called "Viaggio de S. Antonio de Viena in Franza" taken from the *Cronaca* of Paolo da Legnano, *ASM*, f. 108 v°, which gives a strong indication of how much of a pleasure trip a religious pilgrimage of Niccolò's could be. The point is confirmed by Ugo Caleffini's *Cronaca in Rime,* which was published by A. Cappelli, "Notizie di Ugo Caleffini . . . con la sua cronaca in rime di Casa d'Este," *AMP,* S. I, Vol. II (Modena, 1867), 267-312. Ercole had every intention of going to Spain in 1486, but upon his arrival in Milan he was dissuaded from the undertaking by papal officials, who convinced him to visit the Pope in Rome instead.

of a divine mission combined with the pleasure of a grand tour. In Niccolò's case, it suggests that the domestic situation was well in hand, and that his régime could survive his absence.

Though Niccolò ranged abroad to express his religious devotion, he did not fail to do as much at home. In February of 1414, he entertained Pope John XXIII (Baldassare Costa) for a week, before leaving on a pilgrimage to Spain that ended in Piedmont. Five years later, Martin V visited the city.[15] Most important, of course, was Niccolò's hospitality to the Council of Ferrara-Florence in 1438. The choice of Ferrara as the site of this historic assemblage was less a papal recognition of Niccolò's religiosity than of his success in maintaining a peaceful and neutral state. At the time, though, it seemed to reflect both.[16]

At the same time that Niccolò paid dutiful attention to routine religious observances, as well as to extraordinary events of the type cited above, he also managed to live the life of a princely libertine. His lovers were legion, and his hordes of children proverbial:

> Di quà, di là, sul Pò;
> Tutti figli di Niccolò.

With due allowance for exaggeration, there would appear

[15] See *Diario ferrarese dall'anno 1409 sino al 1502 di autori incerti,* ed. G. Pardi, *RIS,* xxiv, pt. vii (Bologna, 1928), 15 (hereafter "DF"): "MCCCCXVIIII, a dì VIII de Febraro, Papa' Martino vene a Ferrara et era Colonexe. E desmontò in Corte con grande honore et a dì XII del dicto mese dete la benedictione al populo de Ferrara."

[16] E. Cecconi, *Studi storici sul Concilio di Firenze* (Florence, 1869), i, Doc. clviii. The pontifical bull speaks of Ferrara in these terms: "locum quidem gratum Graecis, rebus gerendis utilem, idoneum et accomodatum omnibus regibus et mundi principibus et praelatis, tutum et liberum." The use of the word "liberum" here is especially interesting, in the context of our previous comments on *libertà.* Quoted by Lazzari, "Il signor di Ferrara," 673. See also Giovanni da Ferrara, 27.

to be some substance to the legend.[17] But Niccolò did not owe his amatory successes solely to his political stature. Contemporaries saw him as a charming, attractive man. Aeneas Sylvius described him as "fat, jocund, given over to pleasure," but also praised his good judgment.[18] The chronicler Ugo Caleffini, who in his somewhat fanciful rhymed chronicle puts the number of Niccolò's loves at 800, noted the Marquess' appeal even to the foreign ladies he met on his pilgrimages.[19] His escapades—which were not limited to noblewomen—may have been a distraction from Niccolò's complicated family situation, but they certainly did not make the latter any easier.[20] His first wife, Gigliola da Carrara, died in 1416. Described by Caleffini as "ugly, unpleasant, and bad," she was also childless, and probably quite neglected, for during this period Niccolò was enjoying the favors of a host of courtesans and women of the town, and producing numerous offspring. His favored mistress was Stella dei Tolomei, also called dell' Assassino, a Sienese noblewoman whose family had emigrated to Ferrara. She was the mother of Ugo, Leonello, and Borso. All three of these sons were treated as legitimate children by Niccolò, and Stella herself was accorded the respect

[17] No one knows exactly how many children Niccolò had, but a conservative estimate based on a cautious extrapolation from the number of known children would put the figure somewhere in the thirties.

[18] Aeneas Sylvius Piccolomini, *De viris illustribus* (Stuttgart, 1843), 15: "Fuit vir pinguis, laetus, voluptati deditus." Quoted by Lazzari, "Il Signor di Ferrara," 699, and Gardner, *Dukes and Poets,* 29.

[19] See the *Cronaca in Rime,* 286.

> Quando questo signore zunse in la Franza
> le donne vedendo pur el signor zentile
> più se innamorava de lui cha de li mariti
> e da quelli baroni gli era fatt' grandi inviti.

[20] Aeneas Sylvius Piccolominii, *Historia Rerum Federici Tertii Imperatoris* (Strassburg, 1685), 95, comments on Niccolò's eclectic tastes as does Caleffini, *Cronaca in Rime.*

owed to a royal favorite. She was popular, too, for her beauty and kindness. She was accorded full honors at her funeral in 1419, but the distinction of being Niccolò's second wife had been given the previous year to another, Parisina de' Malatesta.[21]

Parisina was young, energetic, happy in the customary activities and pleasures of the court. Cameral records reveal her as a conscientious administrator of her accounts and those in which she was interested, as an able housekeeper, and a devoted mother to her twin girls and her son, Alberto. Gradually, however, the routine of life at court must have become tedious. A young woman married to a much older man who was also a dedicated philanderer, she was surrounded on the one hand by her husband's loyal professional attendants and on the other by his bastard children. Of the people around the court, only Ugo, Niccolò's first-born son, was of her own age and rank. Neither the bored young wife nor her handsome, lively stepson was unaware of Niccolò's philandering, and their own growing friendship culminated in a passionate love affair.

Ordinarily, in Ferrarese law, rape, incest, sodomy, and adultery were the serious sexual offenses. It is, however, most improbable that the adultery provisions were ever enforced as stringently as those relating to crimes that more directly threatened public security and order. In this respect, Niccolò indulged a certain princely license which probably extended to some extent to other citizens, until he learned what was going on in his own household. Despite care and discretion, Parisina was betrayed by one of her confidants. In May, 1425, Niccolò secretly witnessed one of Ugo's trysts with Parisina. His rage was implacable, and the full

---

[21] For the incident of Ugo and Parisina, *Ant.Est.*, II, 190; but more recently A. Lazzari, *Ugo e Parisina* (Florence, 1949), which is to be preferred to his earlier study, *Ugo e Parisina nella realtà storica* (Florence, 1915).

sanction of the laws was brought to bear on his two most beloved people, despite pleas for clemency from his favorite advisers. The *Diario Ferrarese* drily reports:

> 1425, in the month of May, a Monday, at the 24th hour, the head of Ugo, son of the illustrious marquess Nicolò da Este, was cut off, and that of madonna Parisina, who was stepmother of the aforementioned Ugo; and this because he had consorted carnally with her. And with them was decapitated one Aldovrandino di Rangoni da Modena, a familiar of the said *signore,* for having been the cause of this evil. And they were put to death in Castel Vecchio, in the Torre Marchesana; and that night they were brought in a cart to San Francesco, and there they were buried.[22]

It is interesting to see that even in the midst of his terrible rage and thirst for vengeance, Niccolò remained willing to follow the prescribed legal forms. After the executions, copies of the official sentence were dispatched to Ferrara's allies, to explain and justify an act the ferocity of which might be hard to accept under any circumstances, and which appeared practically unintelligible in the light of Niccolò's own sexual proclivities.

[22] *DF,* 17: "MCCCCXXV, del mese de Marcio, uno luni, a hore XXIIII, fu taiata la testa a Ugo, figliolo de lo illustre marchexe Nicolò da Este, et a madona Parexina, che era madregna de dicto Ugo; et questo perchè lui hevea uxado carnalmente con lei. Et insieme fu decapitado uno Aldovrandino di Rangoni da Modena, famio del dicto signore, per essere stato casone di questo male. Et furno morti in Castel Vechio, in la Tore Marchexana; et la nocte furno portati suxo una careta a Sancto Francesco et ivi furno sepulti." See also Palla Strozzi, *Diario, ASI,* s. iv, vix (1884), 8, quoted by Sabbadini, *Epistolario di Guarino Veronese,* iii, 184-85, n. 1. The scandal obviously aroused great interest throughout Italy. See, e.g., Aurispa's questions about it in his letter to Niccolò d'Ancona, sent from Bologna in August, 1425, in R. Sabbadini, *Carteggio di Giovanni Aurispa,* vol. lxx of *Fonti per la Storia d'Italia* (Rome, 1931), 31 (hereafter *Carteggio di Aurispa*).

Niccolò produced more children in the following six
years, but it was not until 1431 that he married again, for
the third and last time. His new wife was Ricciarda da
Saluzzo, who gave birth in the same year to Ercole, and
then to Sigismondo in 1433. In addition to providing Niccolò
with legitimate sons, the prospect of a new marriage had
prompted him somewhat earlier to arrange for the formal
legitimation of Leonello, a move that can only be understood in the context of the problem of succession. In fact,
there is evidence that Niccolò took considerable pains to
satisfy the ambitions and aspirations of his sons after the
affair of Ugo and Parisina. They got new positions and
commands, new titles or privileges, and even new recognition of their personal interests. The hiring of Guarino da
Verona in 1429 may signify less a new concern on Niccolò's
part to patronize men of learning than to satisfy the particular desires of his heir apparent.[23]

Niccolò's biographers agree that his foreign policy during
the last two decades of his reign was increasingly devoted
to keeping Ferrara out of war, and that he succeeded in
this goal largely because of continuing diplomatic efforts
directed toward balancing off the competing claims of
Venice, Milan and the papacy. To each of these jurisdictions, Niccolò could explain his obligations and historic
relationship with the others, and thus win a measure of
forbearance. Moreover, as long as the Estensi maintained
their traditional relationship with Venice, there could be
little danger of conquest by any other power. Secure in their
private wealth, surrounded by smaller principalities, suspi-

---

[23] Aurispa for one seems to have thought of Niccolò III as a man with
few sympathies for and little interest in scholars. See *Carteggio di Aurispa,*
57-8, where, writing to Ambrogio Traversari, he says: "Ea quae ad quietem
animi mei pertinere dicebam, ex industria in hac cedula scribo, ut intelligas
rem occultissime agi maxime oportere, praesertim ne ad huius principis
aures perveniret."

cious of change, the Estensi took a defensive stance in the political tumults of the 1420's and 1430's. In this, during that time, they were successful. An impressive indication of Niccolò's increasing autonomy and independence may be seen in his gradually strengthened hand toward the papacy. His annual *census vicariatus* was reduced by a greater percentage than any of the other reductions accorded to papal vicars in a period of declining and uncertain receipts. Boniface IX reduced Ferrara's *census* from 10,000 to 8,000 florins, John XXIII lowered the annual toll to 6,000, and then to 5,000, of which, under Martin V, 1,000 was to be refunded to the Este as a pension. Moreover, the Este appear to have paid their 4,000 florins quite irregularly: on at least one occasion the papal legate settled for a partial payment of 3000 to settle all arrears (1426). No state as powerful and remote as Ferrara could be held fully accountable for its debts to Rome. But the popes valued the Este as military as well as financial tributaries. The papal vicar has been characterized as a quasi-feudal officer, and Niccolò, for one, was occasionally asked for military assistance.[24]

In his domestic policies, Niccolò revealed himself as an Este prince cut from the traditional cloth of Niccolò II and Alberto I. Known for his accessibility and joviality, as well as his religiosity and libertinism, his personality appears to encompass qualities we are accustomed to consider contradictory. In a typical medal, he looks very much as Pius II described him—thick, stocky, with a passionate severity that could give way to coarse humor (Fig. 2). And that, apparently, is what he was like. His great popularity also attests to the fact that he was not a man of either fancy or intellectual tastes. At the same time, he appreciated the uses of learning, and began on a modest scale the consistent patronage of humanists, lawyers, and physicians for which

[24] P. Partner, *The Papal State under Martin V,* 190.

his successors became famous.[25] His clemency and respect for law were celebrated. Indeed, the Ferrarese statutes, though freshly revised in 1394, were once again thoroughly reviewed and systematized under Niccolò in 1420. The famous judicial murder of Ugo and Parisina, which darkened Niccolò's reputation among Romantic poets,[26] was a unique and totally uncharacteristic event, if Guarino's funeral oration is to be trusted. Giovanni da Ferrara's *Annals* dwell on Niccolò's ingratiating personality, his delight in people of all degrees, his popular appeal.[27]

A good part of Niccolò's efforts appear to have been devoted to the extensive projects of construction that were undertaken in Ferrara throughout his reign. This includes not only structures built for his own use, such as the *castello* and the new palaces of Belriguardo and Belfiore (which was begun by his father), but also extensive public works, such as roads, levees, and other hydraulic projects. Examples of this concern are reflected in the *Diario Ferrarese*. On July 13, 1415, work began on the bell tower of the cathedral. In May of 1417, masons began to pave the *piazza del commune*. On October 25, 1419, the Po broke through its banks at Malonga, flooding a large region north of Ferrara: "And it was decreed, under penalty of the gallows, that every man go to repair the Argene Tra-

[25] See A. Venturi, "I Primordi del rinascimento artistico a Ferrara," *RSI,* i (1884), 591-629; G. Gruyer, *L'Art Ferrarais à l'époque des princes d'Este* (Paris, 1897), 2 vols., i, 16-34, *et al.;* D. P. Lockwood, *Ugo Benzi, Medieval Philosopher and Physician, 1376-1439* (Chicago, 1951).

[26] The main damage was done by Byron in "Parisina," which has been called "perhaps the most exquisitely versified poem that ever the author produced." See *Works of Lord Byron,* vol. x (Boston, 1900), pp. 145-76, for interesting historical notes, and the text. In the poem, Niccolò is called Azo, for metrical reasons.

[27] Giovanni da Ferrara, *Excerpta,* 28, ll. 18-24: "Praetereo eius inenarrabilem humanitatis dulcedinem, urbanitatem, sales, iocos, quos cum civibus, cum rusticis indicibili familiaritate exercebat. Tanta benivolentia, tanto amore suos complectebatur cives, et omni studio incumberet, tum suis tum alienis fortunis, eos ceteris omnibus locupletiores fieri."

versagno, so that the waters would not pass that point; and [even] priests and friars went there. And on the eighth of November that dike broke, and flooded many villages in the Ferrarese." [28] The local chronicles record an impressive series of floods, earthquakes, fires, and crippling storms through the century. From these sources it is obvious that for Ferrara at least, pestilence, famine, and natural destruction posed much greater, more frequent, and more sustained threats to the common weal than war, which could be more effectively deterred through human effort, and was in any event less dangerous. [29]

If Niccolò could point to certain solid achievements in

[28] DF, 15-16.

[29] In the Ferrarese, perhaps especially, war was something of a rarity throughout the Quattrocento (except for 1482-84), whereas pestilence and famine were as common as elsewhere in the peninsula. There was no five-year period when some sort of famine failed to occur, and during these periodic failures in the grain supply, hundreds of people died of starvation. In addition to that there were recurrent outbreaks of plague which also took a great toll. In contrast, historians of war in Quattrocento Italy have found that it did not offer such high risks of mortality as one might expect. See, for example, J. R. Hale, "War and Public Opinion in Renaissance Italy," in Italian Renaissance Studies, ed. E. F. Jacob (London, 1960), 105: "The Quattrocento, then, had been a time when wars were restricted in scope, when casualties had been moderate and the impact of war on civilians had been slight. . . ." Apart from the fact that casualty rates were relatively low, compared to both later periods of warfare and mortality from other disasters, great advances had occurred in the technology of protecting populations from the ravages of warfare, which had become in any case increasingly the work of professionals. The continuous efforts of the Estensi princes throughout the Quattrocento to improve the walls of Ferrara bear witness to the seriousness with which they took their responsibilities to the popolo in this respect, as well as to their desire to perpetuate and strengthen their own control in the city. For other examples of this technical revolution in defense (in large part inspired by prior changes in the technology of destruction) see J. R. Hale, "The Early Development of the Bastion in Italy: An Italian Chronology, c. 1450-1534," Europe in the Late Middle Ages, ed. J. R. Hale, J. R. L. Highfield, B. Smalley (London and Evanston, 1965), 466-94.

the administration and care of his territories, this was in no small part because of the exceptional energy and abilities of his most trusted subordinates. Niccolò, a shrewd judge of men, knew how to reward excellence and punish dereliction. His associates show an exceptional pattern of personal loyalty and length of service. Bartolommeo della Mella is a case in point. A Florentine who served as *referendarius* during Niccolò's minority, he continued to hold that office until 1425, and served as a "virtual prime minister," as Filippo Valenti has written.[30] A day of mourning was declared for his funeral. An even closer and more powerful counsellor of the *Marchese* was Uguccione Contrari, a Ferrarese nobleman who was his constant companion, his most trusted general, diplomat, and military adviser, and his closest friend. Uguccione had been in command at Ferrara during Niccolò's pilgrimage to Jerusalem. He and Niccolò together held the bridle of the Pope's mule when John XXIII came to Ferrara in 1412. But for his countless services he received much more tangible rewards, as well. In addition to honorific titles, he benefited from feudal grants that made him a man of extreme wealth.[31] Other close servants of the *Marchese* were similarly rewarded, but a man could fall more quickly than he rose. Such was the case of Giacomo Giglioli, one of Niccolò's secretaries, and a noble Ferrarese. He was condemned to be hanged for treason, but instead hanged himself in prison. His goods and properties were confiscated and his main house was sold to another courtier, Giovanni Gualengo, for 6,000 *lire mar-*

[30] F. Valenti, "Cancelleria," 361; *DF,* 17.

[31] For Uguccione Contrari, see esp. *DF,* 9, 11-13, 31. The Contrarii had been a powerful family in Ferrara for centuries, but Uguccione was the first to attain a position second only to that of the *marchese.* He died in May, 1448, but many of his descendants served subsequent Este princes. He figures in Decembrio's *De Politia Litteraria* as an adviser and friend of Leonello's. See also Sabbadini, *Epistolario di Guarino,* iii, 359-60.

chesane. It is a typical instance of Estense retribution for real or suspected injury.[32] In the aftermath of this affair, the Giglioli survive, but regain no significant political influence for nearly half a century. And the emergence of Giovanni Gualengo marks the rise of a family that was to distinguish itself under Leonello and Borso. Niccolò knew how to yield the carrot and to wield the stick. These lessons were not lost on his successors.[33]

Niccolò does not appear to have been a bookish man, but he was not ignorant of letters nor of the uses of learning. The first lord of Ferrara to have been tutored by a humanist, Donato degli Albanzani, Niccolò had been exposed to the work of Petrarch and Boccaccio, and probably to a large number of Roman authors. During the course of his reign, the beginnings of a library began to accumulate at court, and the books were borrowed from time to time by members of Niccolò's circle.[34] The earliest records—those before 1440 —suggest a predominantly religious tone of the book collections within the Marquess's circle. Thus Parisina ordered

[32] *DF,* 20: ". . . fu preso messer Jacomo Ziliolo, secretario de lo illustrissimo marchexe Nicolò da Este, e in quello giorno proprio fu preso messer Ziliolo, suo figlio, il quale era capitaneo di Regio, e fu menato a Ferrara e fu messo in Castello . . . per tradimento che voleano fare al dicto marchexe. Et fuli atrovato, tra denari et roba, la valuta de doxento miara de ducati, computando de denari che havea a Fiorenza e Arimine . . . e fu venduta la sua casa a Zoanne Gualengo lire sei sei mila marchexine. El dicto Iacomo fu atrovato impichado per la golla in la dicta torre, e sì s'apichò per la gola per desperatione e fu sepulto al teraio." See also A. Cappelli, "La Biblioteca Estense nella prima metà del secolo XV," *GSLI,* xiv (1886), 1-30, esp. pp. 7-11, where the author lists the law books confiscated among Giglioli's possessions.

[33] See below, pp. 180-84.

[34] The inventory of Niccolò's library has been published by Cappelli, 12-30. Documented instances of borrowing survive, and have been published by several scholars, particularly G. Bertoni, *La Biblioteca Estense al Tempo di Ercole I d' Este, 1471-1505* (Turin, 1903), esp. App. iii, 255-64.

payment of three gold ducats to her chaplain Maginardo, to reimburse him for a psalter he had gotten for her. On another occasion, her *factores generales* informed Parisina that they had paid twelve pounds to one Bartolomeo *cartolario* for an Office of the Blessed Virgin Mary, bound in black velvet.[35] But Parisina's tastes, as her biography would lead us to expect, were not exclusively religious. From the same Bartolomeo she ordered, in 1423, "uno libro in francexe che se chiama Tristano." There, as Carducci observed, she read the archetypical tale of fatal adultery and *lèse majesté,* to which her subsequent career provided a parallel.[36]

Of Niccolò's personal literary tastes, we know practically nothing. It is clear enough, though, that while he often turned up to listen to a sermon offered by some itinerant friar, he preferred to engage humanists when it came to the education of his children. Thus the Sicilian Hellenist Giovanni Aurispa, who had taught at Bologna and Florence, was invited to the court to serve as tutor to Meliaduse d'Este, Niccolò's twenty-one-year-old natural son, who later became a gifted ecclesiastic.[37] Two years later, Niccolò was able to attract Guarino da Verona, the greatest scholar and teacher of the Ferrarese *Quattrocento,* to serve as tutor to Leonello, then twenty-two.[38] In 1431, Giovanni Toscanella arrived, to become tutor to Borso, who had just turned twenty.[39]

[35] *ASM, ASE,* Cancelleria, Registri dei Mandati, 1424, f. 53 v° (quoted by Gandini, "Usi e costumanze," 152). Gandini gives other examples as well.

[36] "Della coltura estense nei secoli XIII e XIV fino alla signoria di Nicolò III," 53.

[37] For Meliaduse d'Este see *DF,* 17, 24, 27, 37; Also Giovanni da Ferrara, *Excerpta,* 29, 31, 37.

[38] Apart from a trip to Egypt and the Holy Land, which he made in 1440, Meliaduse came to be known not only as the patron of Aurispa, whom he eventually helped (*Carteggio di Aurispa,* 34-35), but also acquired a certain renown as Bishop of Pomposa. He died in 1453.

[39] For Toscanella, see R. Sabbadini, *Epistolario di Guarino,* III, 375-76;

(I cite these ages because it strikes me as intensely interesting that such tutors were hired for grown men. Though more complex hypotheses could be framed, I believe that this reflects quite simply a particular order of priorities. Military education—the preparation of a *condottiere*—came first, frills later. "Ars et Mars" was how the ancient commonplace read, but Niccolò, like most of the despots, took it in reverse order.)

It was during this period of Niccolò's reign that he began to acquire a substantial collection of books, many of them illuminated. Probably under the influence of the prestigious humanists who now surrounded his sons, and through the use of their connections with scribes and bibliophiles all over Italy, he began to assemble the nucleus of the great Biblioteca Estense. The classics, mostly Latin or in Latin translation, and vernacular works in Italian and French were sought in diverse subjects.[40] During various moments during Niccolò's reign, there appear also to have been several half-hearted attempts to reactivate the University, but these were of little consequence. In the period from 1402, when Niccolò first tried to re-establish the *Studium* founded by Alberto, to 1442, when Leonello and Guarino inaugurated a new and sustained effort to reform and improve the institution, only about two hundred students had matriculated in all fields. Moreover, about half of these attended the *Studium* between 1402 and 1407, the first five years of that forty-year

---

idem, Vita di Guarino Veronese (Genoa, 1891), 33, 185, 218; *id., La scuola e gli studi di Guarino Veronese* (Catania, 1896), 87 (both reprinted as *Guariniana* [Turin, 1964]); also V. Rossi, *Il Quattrocento*, rev. ed. (Milan, 1954), 45-47.

[40] There are abundant examples of the Ferrarese search for texts. One need only consult the *Epistolario di Guarino* to find many, but see also the compilation of G. Bertoni, *Guarino da Verona fra letterati e cortigiani a Ferrara, 1429-1460* (Geneva, 1921), and the works of Sabbadini cited above.

period.[41] Such culture as there was had become purely aulic and unofficial by the time Guarino and his associates arrived.

The court itself was a world of immense contrasts, an analogue in miniature of Ferrarese life. In it, the extremes of learning and ignorance, virtue and vice could be found together, sometimes even in the same individual, the heights of wealth and the depths of squalid poverty could be found within the same room. Thus, in a period when Parisina was buying musical instruments, colorful birds, and other expensive knick-knacks, many of the servants were practically naked because funds had not been released for their new uniforms. Indeed, poverty was an endemic problem at court as elsewhere, though its study is complicated by lack of statistical information or quantitative data. It is not surprising that Parisina reacted to the phenomenon and sought to help at such close quarters.[42] But there is some evidence to suggest that the Estensi also concerned themselves with the problem on a larger scale. In 1422, Parisina ordered her tailor to make a new dress for a "povera donzela" who was about to marry. Niccolò is reported to have solicited the wealthy personally in order to raise money for poor relief, and was reputed to be open-handed toward

[41] The most accurate study of enrollment figures in the *studium* of Ferrara are those of C. Pinghini, "La popolazione studentesca dell' Università di Ferrara dalle origini ai nostri tempi," *Metron: Rivista internazionale di statistica* vii:1 (1927), 120-44.

[42] Gandini, "Usi e costumanze," 160. Gandini points to the extreme contrasts and gives this example from Parisina's Registro dei Mandati, 1424, f. 24 vº: "Messer Prosdocimo Conte si dete a Meliaduse como compagno, el quale come ce scripto e uno valente huomo et segli repete la lectione et quello fa bisogno. Et e stato sego uno bon tempo senza salario. Et per quello per nuj sentimo lo si puo dire nudo che non torna ad honore del signore che cossi nudo staga a la compagnia del figliolo, unde, compensando ogni cossa, volemo che vuj provediati che luj habia tanto panno che se fazo uno vestodo, uno paro de calce et uno capuzo." The same Parisina may also be found ordering seeds imported from Venice for her parrot (157).

needy people who came to his attention.[43] But at this time in Ferrarese history, there was no institutionalized, formal means for alleviating economic hardship, except in time of famine. Then, according to a time-honored practice, the prince would undersell the market price of wheat from his own stocks.

Despite what scholars have regarded as a substantial income based on land rents, taxes, and financial commutations of feudal dues, Niccolò himself was often unable to meet his obligations. His creditors often had to manifest great patience, and he himself was sometimes reduced to humiliatingly mercenary behavior.[44] Even in relatively easy times, he took care to control some of the expenses of the court. Thus, though he was willing to pay a series of tutors to his eldest son, Meliaduse, he tried to limit the young man's travel and maintenance expenses, by controlling the size of his entourage. His apparent negligence in the payment of the vicarial *census* appears fully compatible with the picture that emerges from Gandini's study of the cameral registers.

The long reign of Niccolò d'Este as *Marchese* of Ferrara is a period of beginnings. It was the beginning of the heyday of the Este dynasty, the first consistently stable regime of a series that was to endure in the city for the next two centuries, and that was in the end to give way only because of the lack of a direct heir to Alfonso II. It produced beginnings in a biological sense as well, for all

---

[43] Giovanni da Ferrara, *Excerpta,* 28.

[44] "Usi e costumanze," 160-61, which gives this example: After the death of Niccolò's tailor, Anechino, the latter's daughter also became very ill. Niccolò, thinking that she too might die, and that the horse he had given his tailor might then be sold by the estate to pay for her funeral expenses, sent in advance to ask that the horse be given back to him. There is also much evidence of tradesmen being kept waiting for their pay.

three subsequent rulers of Ferrara were not only born then, but also received their essential formative training in the world of Niccolò III, their father. We can discern other kinds of beginnings as well. This period reveals the emerging formulations of Ferrara's pacifically-oriented diplomacy, the beginnings of a sophisticated courtly culture, and the start of the remarkable building programs that transformed Ferrara in the *Quattrocento*. That the three men who ruled Ferrara from 1441 to 1505 were brothers helps to explain the continuity previously cited. And in perhaps more subtle ways, we see the despotism cultivating a new style, an operational tone rather different from that of its predecessors. Niccolò is the first truly princely figure in Ferrarese history. He cannot in any sense be regarded as just another Emilian petty tyrant. His vices and virtues, his excesses and repentences, his largesse and his parsimony, all of these appear on a grand scale. He is a recognizable figure, an individual man, full of unresolved contradictions, majestic in his unresolved complexity.

In fact, there is much about Niccolò III that reminds one, perhaps, of Henry VIII. To return to Tawney's phrase, he was, like Henry VIII, a "God-fearing Prince," but he acted on the assumption that God was prepared to allow him some rather exceptional privileges. Like the Tudor monarch, he remained very much the feudal lord, rewarding loyalty and punishing real or imagined defectors. Though the parallel could be extended further, he appears above all to have enjoyed, like Henry, a powerful sort of personal magnetism, which made people like him even if they could not quite approve of him.

This God-fearing prince died on an errand of the type he particularly enjoyed. In November, 1441, he went to Milan with Uguccione Contrarii, in the aftermath of a Venetian-Milanese truce he had helped to arrange. The ailing Duke of Milan, Filippo Maria Visconti, having great confidence in Niccolò's ability, had summoned him to serve as governor of the Milanese state. Within a month of his arrival, on December 26, Niccolò died of a sudden and unexplained illness, at the age of 58.[45] That he was poisoned has been suggested and may well be true, for in taking over Milan, he raised many anxieties. Francesco Sforza, the Duke's son-in-law, feared that his claim to the duchy might be lost. The Venetians as well as the Florentines could not ignore the possibility of an expansion of Este control over the entire northern part of the peninsula. There were motives enough, but nobody knows what happened. By December 30, Niccolò's body had been returned to Ferrara, where it lay in state in the Church of Santa Maria degli Angeli, the newly completed Franciscan church north of the city. On New Year's Day, at midnight, he was buried there, "nude, without any pomp, for so did he command in his will." [46]

[45] *Ant.Est.*, ii, 201; Frizzi, *Memorie per la storia di Ferrara*, iii, 489-90; Chiappini, *Gli Estensi*, 98; Lazzari, "Il signor di Ferrara," 698.

[46] *DF*, 26: "Et il lune sequente, che [fu] il primo giorno di Zenaro, . . . fu sepulto nudo senza alcuna pompa, perchè così comandè nel suo testamento."

IV   Leonello d'Este and the Formation of Ferrarese Culture

Just as Niccolò III came to be regarded by Ferrarese historians and antiquarians as the *pater patriae,* or, to put it more accurately, *pater civitatis,* so did his first heir and successor, Leonello, appear to be the progenitor of Ferrarese culture, *pater civilitatis.* It may be unfashionable to say so, but the traditional view in this case would seem to be perfectly correct. In fact, as we learn more about Leonello's impact on the growth of art, literature, and learning in Ferrara, we begin to discern his broader and subtler influence upon the evolving styles, tastes, and manners of *Quattrocento* despotisms. In carrying out, and trying to justify, this re-evaluation of Leonello's role in the formation of northern Italian cultural developments in the fifteenth century, the historian is handicapped by Leonello's own greatest handicap—the brevity of his life, and especially, of his reign. But before turning to the actual rule of this extraordinary man, it may be useful briefly to review his career up to the year 1441.[1]

Leonello's early years—he was born in 1407—were spent in Ferrara, where he received instruction from a succession of tutors in various disciplines, but mainly in warfare. Military skill was essential for any nobleman, but it was paramount in the training of scions of ruling families who had historic obligations of territorial defense, feudal service, and dynastic continuity. Since practical experience was considered necessary in this area, Leonello spent several years in the field in Umbria and Tuscany with the celebrated *condottiere* Braccio da Montone. Though some scholars

---

[1] The only biography of Leonello is that of G. Pardi, *Leonello d'Este* (Bologna, 1904); it should be supplemented by the various studies of Sabbadini and Bertoni cited earlier, and especially by reference to the *Epistolario di Guarino,* vols. II and III.

have assumed that this experience "had not made a soldier of him," probably owing to his later interests, I think it is evident that Leonello really knew the art of war.[2] To Niccolò, he would otherwise have been clearly unacceptable as an heir.

But when Leonello, trained in the military arts, returned to Ferrara in 1424, he found himself in the position of a supernumerary. Trained for the battles that Niccolò assiduously avoided, Leonello had to find other pastimes. The only fact we have is that he eventually found his way to humanistic studies. Unfortunately, almost nothing is known about the crucial five-year period from 1424 to 1429, during which this interest somehow developed. But develop it did. The view that Leonello's mind was a kind of *tabula rasa* shaped and informed by Guarino after his arrival in Ferrara in 1429 is greatly exaggerated. However, no correspondence prior to Guarino's decision to move to the city indicates that the young prince had become enchanted with the idea of capturing the secrets of the ancient world.[3] But after all,

[2] Aeneas Sylvius Piccolomini, *De viris illustribus,* 16; Giovanni da Ferrara, *Excerpta,* 31; *DF,* 197.

[3] See Sabbadini, *Vita di Guarino Veronese* (Genoa, 1891), 84-88. Carducci believed that Leonello had written to Guarino for the first time during his period of apprenticeship to the *condottiere* Braccio da Montone, and that Guarino had replied to this letter, but that the evidence had been lost. See *Delle poesie edite ed inedite di Lodovico Ariosto* (Bologna, 1875), 29. However this notion has been completely refuted by Sabbadini, *Epistolario di Guarino,* III, 262-63. It should be noted, though, that Guarino did have extensive correspondence with humanists of the Ferrarese circle before moving to the city in 1429, most of which involved discussion of manuscripts and the search for books of various kinds, together with complaints about their status. He had also been in contact with Giacomo Giglioli, at the time one of Niccolò's most trusted advisers, since 1422, and it was the same Giglioli who personally issued the official invitation to Guarino to make the permanent move to Ferrara. For the letter of invitation, se Sabbadini, *Epistolario di Guarino,* I, no. 468, and also another reference in no. 473.

he was young, noble, well-traveled, had time on his hands, and was bright enough to perceive that the *studia humanitatis,* as his contemporaries understood the meaning of this term, had engrossed and were continuing to engage many of the best minds of his own generation. And his own father, who was not a learned man but could appreciate a good secular mind when he found one, was anxious to have his sons well educated according to the newest theories. Niccolò must have known full well what kinds of activities and values were being fostered at such centers as the palace school in Mantua, for his decisions as a patron of humanists clearly indicate that he thought the model established by Vittorino da Feltre was worth emulating. His relationship to Leonello may have been a bit like that of Gargantua to Pantagruel, in Rabelais's famous letter, for Niccolò looked at humanism with the sympathetic and admiring, but perhaps also somewhat envious and relatively ignorant, eyes of a prince who had been superficially and doubtless quite traditionally educated, and who had had the serious responsibilities of government thrust upon him at an early age. As a practical man, the range and balance of humanist education appealed to him, and he was obviously willing to pay reasonably competitive stipends in return for the tutorial services of some respected figures in the movement.

Niccolò, unlike Gargantua, made no effort to benefit from these tutors himself, and until Guarino arrived, and conferred on courtly literary circles a new order of prestige, it was clearly not easy to be a mere humanist in Ferrara. Aurispa, having arrived in 1427, could hardly wait to leave (though he ended up staying over thirty years). In 1428 he wrote to Ambrogio Traversari in secret, "chiefly lest it should come to the ears of this prince," in hopes of arranging a teaching position at the *Studium* in Florence, if there were an opening.[4] But by 1431, things were going better.

---

[4] *Carteggio di Aurispa* (Rome, 1931), 57-58.

He writes to his Sicilian compatriot Bartolomeo Guasco, a teacher of rhetoric in Savoy, that Meliadusa d'Este had gotten him a diaconate and an annual stipend of 200 gold pieces per year.[5] With additional income from his extremely tight-fisted trading in manuscripts, Aurispa must have been doing very well. He was receiving more than Guarino had earned in Venice (150 ducats), though a good deal less than the great scholar's Ferrarese stipend (350 ducats), which easily supported a large household in good style.[6]

At the same time that Niccolò was willing to pay the price for all of this instruction and reflected glory, he also insisted on keeping it within the limits of the court, and refused to commit substantial sums to public instruction and the restoration of the *Studium*. Within the court itself he seems to have been quite generous. By 1436, the date of the first inventory, we can begin to speak of a real Este library, much of it acquired during the previous decade. The inventory, compiled by "Ser Jacomo" and "Raynaldo," lists 279 volumes, including works in a variety of fields.[7] There are many religious and pious works, patristic writings, and French romances, but there are also humanists and classical authors represented in diverse fields. Thus among the ancients one finds Frontinus on aqueducts, Caesar, Suetonius, Florus, Josephus, Isidore, Vegetius,

[5] *Carteggio di Aurispa,* 74-75, for the improvement of his fortunes; for evidence of his brisk manuscript business, see pp. 64-70, *et al.*

[6] Sabbadini, *Vita di Guarino Veronese,* 121-22; According to Sabbadini, Guarino was assigned a stipend of 150 ducats by the "Consiglio," by which he probably means the *dodici savi,* on March 29, 1436, when he undertook his duties as public lecturer. This provoked his dissatisfaction since as Leonello's private tutor he had received 350 ducats. A month later, his salary was adjusted to 400 *lire marchesane.* His duties involved two lectures on weekdays, one on holidays, and the prohibition of taking additional funds for his services.

[7] Published by A. Cappelli, "La Biblioteca Estense nella prima metà del secolo XV," 12-30.

Seneca, Aristotle, Valerius Maxiumus, Priscian, Ovid, Statius, Cicero, Juvenal, Lucan, Festus Rufus, Terence, Vergil, Lucian, Sallust, Martianus Capella, Apuleius, Horace, Eutropius, Quintus Curtius, Boethius.[8] Among the moderns the most frequently represented are Petrarch and Boccaccio, though works by Dante, Albertino Mussato, Riccobaldo, Cecco d'Ascoli, and Giovanni da Ravenna are also listed.[9] There are also a number of works for which no author is given, including calendars, chronicles, geographical and devotional texts, and of course the large collection of Arthurian and Carolingian fables and romances, all in French, which was studied in the nineteenth century by Pio Rajna.[10] The collection had four obvious areas of con-

[8] It is sometimes impossible to know precisely what works were represented because references in the inventory are sometimes vague or misleading. Here are some examples: "51. Libro uno chiamado Julio Frontino, in membrana, couerto di chore rosse. . . . 60. Libro uno chiamado el dialogo de San Gregorio, in membrana, couerto de chore roso. . . . 62. Libro uno chiamado Prisciano minore, in membrana, couerto di chore verde. . . ." On the other hand, many citations are quite precise.

[9] It is interesting to note that these books are not listed in any particular order. Vernacular literary works are intermingled with ancient historical and moral writings and patristic texts. The several works dealing specifically with the history of Ferrara are nos. 19, 36, 54. There seems to be a marked preference for the vernacular works of such authors as Petrarch and Boccaccio, and the latter is more heavily represented.

[10] "Ricordi di codici francesi posseduti degli Estensi nel secolo XV," *Romania*, II, (1873), 49-58. The self-conscious maintenance of chivalric traditions and styles at the court of Ferrara is an essential element in its cultural continuity and conservatism, one of the characteristics that distinguish it from the other Italian courts which had shared the voguish acceptance of French courtesy in the fourteenth century but later abandoned it. In Ferrara this was synthesized with the newly-emerging and autochthonous Italian humanist styles, to result in a kind of Italian gothic humanism toward the end of the century, a process that culminates in the works of Boiardo and especially Ariosto. Notice too the recurrent use of such names as Rinaldo, Marfisa, and Bradamante in the Este family, as evidence of this cultural penchant. Cf. the interesting study by A. Vallone, *Cortesia e Nobiltà nel Rinascimento* (Asti, 1955).

centration. There were religious works, from Augustine's *City of God* to the *Decretals* and writings of the schoolmen, especially Thomas. There was contemporary literature, in which Petrarch in particular was strongly represented, with Boccaccio not far behind. There were the classics, strongest in Aristotle, Cicero, Ovid, and Seneca, and in authors of real practical use, like Frontinus on aqueducts, the grammarians, Vegetius on fortifications, and so forth. And finally, the romances of chivalry, popular with the ladies, and probably, along with religious works, the oldest part of the collection.

The inventory may be presumed incomplete. Court records (*guardaroba*) mention fairly frequent borrowings from the library, either through cameral notations to that effect, or by secretarial copies of requests for the return of particular volumes. At any given time, a number of courtiers, secretaries, and ladies might have had particular works in their possession, and there is even evidence that books were lent to ordinary citizens on occasion. Similarly, other sources indicate the presence in Ferrara of authors not included in the 1436 list. Plautus is perhaps the most important example.[11] At this early stage the court was probably the principal book collector in Ferrara, but it was certainly not the only one. Guarino had a noted library of classical texts, which was dispersed after his death. Aurispa was a bookdealer, and he tried to hold on to some of his better codices.

---

[11] Eight of Plautus' comedies were known in the Middle Ages, but Nicolas of Cusa had discovered an important MS., including sixteen new ones. These of course aroused great interest in Ferrara, as throughout Italian humanist circles. See R. Sabbadini, *Le scoperte dei codici latini e greci nei secoli XIV e XV* (Florence, 1905), 11-12. The same author's *Storia e critica dei testi latini* (Catania, 1914), 327-36 details the difficulties encountered in obtaining copies of the new MSS. This is also illustrated in Aurispa's letter to Paolo da Sarzana (September 11, 1431), in which he says: "Comoedias Plauti nondum habuimus, expectamus eas tamen, quas quamprimum acceperimus eris tu quidem aut primus aut inter primos illarum particeps." See *Carteggio di Aurispa,* 77.

Other members of the court, particularly such cultivated men of letters as Tito Vespasiano Strozzi and Ludovico Casella, tried to build personal libraries. Men in specialized fields, such as law or medicine, often collected in their specialities.[12] Finally the religious orders needed the tools of their trade. There was work in the 1430's and 1440's for a goodly number of scribes and *cartolai*.

Leonello, of course, was in the thick of all of this in the last decade of Niccolò's life. Under the benign guidance of the gentle and learned Guarino, Leonello became what by the standards of the time was considered an intellectual, or at least, an *homme de lettres*. He wrote sonnets, gave Latin orations on ceremonial occasions, corresponded with scholars on learned subjects, engaged in colloquys with friends and colleagues, collected gems, cameos, and ancient medals. But above all, he learned to know, enjoy, and appreciate professional excellence in the arts and scholarship, and possessed both the generosity and the tolerance needed to encourage and stimulate others. His was the patronage not of the Maecenas, but of the passionate devoté, not of the disinterested philistine, but of the discriminating mind and eye, not of the seeker of sensations, but of the self-conscious searcher for aesthetic canons and scholarly criteria.

How do we know this? In the first place, that is in effect what almost every source tells us, or at least invites us to conclude. Gasparo Sardi was simply reciting the received wisdom when he wrote of Leonello in 1566:

> He was a peaceful prince, and most of all a lover of learning and of men of knowledge, rather than arms and soldiers. Even though in his youth he had learned

[12] Thus Giacomo Giglioli had an important legal library, the contents of which are listed in A. Cappelli's article "La Biblioteca Estense," 10-11; Aurispa's book collection was also well known, and so was Guarino's. The latter left his library to his son Baptista, but in the sixteenth century it was dispersed.

the art of war from Braccio da Montone, the greatest general in Italy. He composed light verse, recited a prose oration, which he had written, to the Emperor Sigismund, when the latter knighted him in Ferrara, and another to Eugenius IV. . . . He always surrounded himself with men learned in every doctrine, reasoning and disputing with him. . . . To these he made very great gifts, and also to those [scholars] who were not with him but whom he knew to be wise men. . . . In his palace he had a chapel gracefully painted, and decorated with beautiful marble and hangings, and he had men come from France who sang the divine offices well, which Ercole I later had done in the church he built in the new courtyard, called the chapel of the court.[13]

Much of this is taken almost *verbatim* from the *Annales* of Johannes Ferrariensis, the Franciscan chronicler who continued the *Chronicle* of Jacobus de Delayto into the Borsian period. It is the most reliable contemporary source for Leonello's reign, and its judgments are amply borne out by the anonymous diarist, and by such outside observers as Pius II.[14]

Superimposed on his enthusiasm for good letters, Leonello had the Christian piety of the Estensi, a fact that lost him no credit with the humanists since Guarino himself manifested a marked devotional streak. The Prince's adornment of the chapel mentioned by Sardi reveals one aspect of his religious concerns, but there are other more convincing manifestations. For example, the anonymous diarist characterizes him using the adulatory vocabulary reserved for a "Christian prince." Leonello was "a lover of justice, of most

[13] *Libro delle Historie Ferraresi del Signore Gasparo Sardi* (Ferrara, 1646), 151.

[14] Giovanni da Ferrara, *Excerpta,* 30-4; Aeneas Sylvius Piccolomini, *De viris illustribus,* 16.

righteous life, a lover of piety, devoted to the divine religion, a friend of the poor and of needy domestics, generous, a studious auditor of the Holy Scriptures, patient in adversities and moderate in prosperity. He governed his people in peace with great wisdom." [15] The sentiments are echoed by the Franciscan annalist: "Non fuerit vir pietate maior Leonello quisquam nec iusticia melior nec virtute clarior," and he gives details.[16] The field of poor-relief was one in which Leonello made significant contributions. Shortly after taking office, he repealed some of the regressive taxes which had been weighing heavily on the artisans. He also worked, together with the learned bishop Giovanni da Tossignano, to establish the Hospital of Santa Anna, a combination of poorhouse, asylum, and medical hospital for the people of Ferrara. It was meant to replace a number of small first-aid stations scattered about the city. Having grown continuously throughout the fifteenth century, and having received benefactions from individual as well as institutional donors over the years, it remains Ferrara's principal medical facility even today.[17]

The same concern for the institutionalization of public services may be partly responsible for Leonello's early decision to reopen the *Studium* on an enlarged scale, but it is more likely that his desire to attract learned men to Ferrara was the decisive factor. But in this area the commune itself perceived that it had an interest. A thriving university would mean foreign teachers and students seek-

[15] *DF*, 33: "Questui fue amatore de la iusticia, de honestissima vita, amatore de la pietade, de la divina religione devotissimo, amatore de li poveri et domestici bisignozi, liberale, de le Sacre Scripture studioso auditore, in le adversitade paciente et in le prospere moderato. Li populi suoi in pace con grande sapientia guvernò."

[16] Quoted by E. P. Garder, *Dukes and Poets in Ferrara* (London, 1904), 66 (hereafter *"Dukes and Poets"*).

[17] See *DF*, 30, n. 3. For other early evidence see B. Zambotti, *Diario ferrarese dall'anno 1476 sino al 1504*, ed. G. Pardi, *RIS*, 2nd ed. xxiv, pt. 7, 124, 346 (hereafter "Zambotti, *Diario*").

54055

ing lodging, clothing, and food, frequenting the taverns and marketplaces, spending money. It would mean new prestige for Ferrara, and perhaps new papal privileges. It would bring to the city new professional skills. Above all, it would provide a facility for the education of the middle-income guildsmen who could not afford the expense of sending their children elsewhere. In 1418, the magistracy of the *savi* had, with Niccolò's approval, resolved to reopen the *Studium* for the public benefit, but nothing had come of it.[18] On January 17, 1442, Leonello and the *savi* promulgated a similar resolution, but this time they appointed a commission of six *riformatori* to work with the lecturer in alleviating discontent by remedying certain unspecified abuses. At the same time, Leonello wrote letters to his friends throughout Italy, attempting to recruit both teachers and students for the reformed university. Leonello had been *marchese* for only three weeks when these steps were taken.[19]

Even in fifteen-century Ferrara, when classes met in the Franciscan and Dominican churches, a university involved substantial expenses. There was a certain amount of maintenance, doubtless some small administrative expense, and especially salaries. Most of the funds for the professors' stipends came from the communal treasury, but they were sometimes augmented by princely contributions. It seems that the maintenance of the *Studium* occasionally imposed a strain on communal revenues. In 1447, for example, the *savi* had to impose a surtax on all meat sold in the district of Ferrara, for its support.[20]

Owing to this palpably serious commitment to the de-

[18] *ACSF,* Determinazioni, C, 3, 18, f. 24, dated October 6, 1418.

[19] *ACSF,* Risoluzioni del Commune, Libro F, 4, 6, cc. 54 v⁰-55, for January 17, 1442.

[20] *ACSF,* Deliberazioni, Libro G, 5, 14, f. 25 v⁰ (May 4, 1447). The tax imposed was two *soldi* and one *denaro* per *peso* of meat. The *Registri dei Mandati* in *ASM* also contain many references to payments out of Leonello's *camera* for support of the *studium*.

velopment of the *Studium,* it enjoyed a remarkable growth during Leonello's reign. We have no firm information as to the size and compensation of the faculty during the period from 1441 to 1450, but it is evident that it grew substantially, as the need for increased revenues despite unquestionably augmented tuition receipts makes clear. The first *rotulo* listing faculty stipends dates from the 1450's, and indicates that professors in the arts faculty were paid generally less than law professors, except for especially distinguished men like Guarino. The medical faculty, too, rated high compensation.[21] The differentiation in salaries bore no relation to the magnitude of the instructional task, as enrollment figures show. It is, instead, a result of the fact that lucrative alternative careers were available to doctors and lawyers, so that the *Studium,* like the contemporary western university, had to compete for them in a much more expensive market. And I suppose that it was also a consequence, then as now, of more general, implicit priorities and values.

As to enrollments, Carlo Pinghini has shown that they increased tenfold in the 1440's, from an average of 34 students per year in the last decade of Niccolò's reign to an average of 338 per year under Leonello. Of this figure, an average of 310 were enrolled in the arts faculty, and only 28 in law. More than two-thirds of all these students were Italians from outside Ferrara. Of the rest, about 75 percent were foreigners. The balance, averaging only 19 students per year, were natives of Ferrara.[22] In the same period, the

[21] See esp. A. Solerti, "Documenti riguardanti lo studio di Ferrara nei secoli XV e XVI conservati nell archivio estense," *AF,* IV (1892), 1-65; G. Pardi, "Lo studio di Ferrara a tutto il secolo XV," *AF,* XIV (1903); and G. Secco Suardo, "Lo studio di Ferrara," *AF,* V (1893).

[22] See C. Pinghini, "La popolazione studentesca," 140-43. I have computed these average figures from the enrollment figures compiled by Pinghini.

average number of students receiving doctoral degrees increased fifteenfold, from one to fifteen per year. The records reveal no natives of Ferrara in this category, which is
puzzling.

These facts and figures, though fragmentary and perhaps
even faulty, serve to reveal a quantitative growth which
is in itself important. But they do not tell us very much
else. Was the *Studium* of Ferrara a Renaissance equivalent
of the modern degree-mill, or was it a serious institution of
higher learning, comparable to Pavia or Bologna in its
academic standards? Did the great professors, such as
Guarino and Theodore Gaza, really teach, or were their
positions merely sinecures that underwrote primary functions within the courtly circle? Was there a good number
of students of real intellectual distinction, or were the students dullards and mediocrities? Questions such as these
can at least be taken up for the second half of the century,
but for the age of Leonello there is precious little evidence
to resolve them.

What we do know, and this is not trivial, is that the
burgeoning little *Studium* made it possible for Leonello to
surround himself with a fairly stable circle of poets and
scholars, and to get to know many more.[23] In addition to

[23] The entire literary circle around Leonello has been studied extensively
by G. Bertoni, *Guarino da Verona fra letterati e cortigiani a Ferrara, 1429-
1460* (Geneva, 1921), esp. chs. II and III. Bertoni, essentially an able com-
piler, put together biographical notes and archival references on the
humanists of the court, together with other documents illuminating cultural life in the Leonellan circle. See also his *La Biblioteca Estense* (Torino,
1903), 25, n. 1, which lists the codices dedicated to Leonello by such
figures as Flavio Biondo, Tommaso Cambiatore, Francesco Ariosto, Basinio
Basini da Parma, Tito Vespasiano Strozzi, Giovanni Bianchini, and
Guarino. Pardi, *Leonello d'Este,* 173-77, lists other works, including
Guarino's translation of the *Nicocles* of Isocrates, and Plutarch's *Lives* of
Alexander and Scilla; Trapezuntius' *Invective* against Guarino; Aurispa's
translation of Lucian's *Amicitia;* Giovanni Marrasio's elegy, and orations

the many writings dedicated to Leonello by humanists, there is first-hand evidence of the activities of this cultivated circle in the important book *De Politia Litteraria,* written by the Milanese humanist and physician Angelo Camillo Decembrio, and dedicated by him to Pope Pius II. More than any other source, the first book of this treatise informs us of the cultural life of Ferrara under Leonello d'Este.

The *Politia* has attracted the attention of several scholars, but it really needs a modern abridged and annotated edition that would make it accessible to a wider audience. The published versions are rare as well as defective, but the Vatican manuscript, which is the presentation copy to Pius II, is both contemporary and accurate.[24] The work itself, as Michael Baxandall has observed, is "a very long and

by Basinio Parmensis, Bartolommeo Imperiali, Pier Candido Decembrio, Ciriaco d'Ancona, Apollonio Bianchi, Angelo Gambiglioni, and of course the *Philodoxos* and *Theognis* of L. B. Alberti. To this list may now be added the poems by Felino Sandeo found in a MS. in Lucca. See G. Arrighi, "Canzone per Leonello d'Este raccolte da Felino Sandei dello Studio di Ferrara, nel un codice lucchese del quattrocento," *Rinascimento,* n.s. II (1952), 203-10. These are very pleasant *volgare* love sonnets.

[24] The most reliable way of consulting this text is the MS. in the Biblioteca Apostolica Vaticana, Vat. Lat. 1794 (microfilm in University of Pennsylvania Library, Film no. 1434). Citations here refer to the Augsburg edition of 1540, a copy of which may be found in the Rare Book Collection of the Van Pelt Library, University of Pennsylvania. There is a slightly better version (Basel, 1562). Our references have been collated with the Vatican MS. The *Politia Litteraria* needs a full-scale study. See A. Della Guardia, *La 'Politia litteraria' di Angelo Decembrio e l'umanesimo a Ferrara nella prima metà del sec. XV* (Modena, 1910), and the relevant passages in G. Bertoni, *Guarino Veronese fra Letterati e cortigiani;* also the recent article by M. Baxandall, "A Dialogue on Art from the Court of Leonello d'Este," *JWCI,* xxvi (1963), 304-25, who publishes and helpfully annotates and discusses one chapter. For acute and just criticism of the works of Della Guardia, Bertoni, and Sabbadini, see E. Garin, "Motivi della cultura filosofica ferrarese nel rinascimento," in *La cultura filosofica del rinascimento italiano* (Florence, 1961), 402-31.

badly written book that repels attention in several ways." [25]
Baxandall does not exaggerate the obscurity of Decembrio's
syntax, the frequent omission of logical transitions, and the
sometimes confusing style of argumentation, not to mention
the subject matter, which shifts back and forth between
antiquarian pedantry and topics of almost universal interest.
Divided into seven books (of which apparently only three
comprised the first version, dating back to 1445 or there-
abouts), the *Politia* was clearly completed in its present
form not later than 1462. Therefore, though an appreciable
part of the manuscript is undoubtedly retrospective, Books
I, II, and V are contemporary, and appear to be based on
actual dialogues occurring at the court of Ferrara during the
middle period of Leonello's reign. In fact, Decembrio states
that he was present during these dialogues, and he is known
to have spent much of his time after 1432 in medical and
literary studies there.[26] Of these books, only the first is
entirely of general, as distinct from quite narrowly philological, interest.

The author is a rather able *metteur-en-scène,* and he provides delightful and plausible settings for the discussions.
Leonello is invariably patient, gentle, and friendly to his
associates, whom he addresses without condescension, and
who reply without flattery. The participants in the dialogue
are all gentlemen of the court—foremost among them is
Guarino, whose particular *forte* is the elaboration of pen-
dantic philological arguments. The others serve mainly as
interlocutors, though some of them occasionally make im-

[25] Baxandall, "A Dialogue on Art," 304.

[26] For the most comprehensive discussion of Decembrio's career, see
R. Sabbadini, "Tre autografi di Angelo Decembrio," *Scritti varii di erudizione e di critica in onore di Rodolfo Renier* (Turin, 1912), 11-19. It is
clear that Decembrio spent a good deal of the 1450s in Spain, but then
returned to Ferrara in the 1460s (cf. Bertoni, *Guarino Veronese,* 78, which
cites payment to Decembrio for certain minor diplomatic missions).

portant points. These include Feltrino Boiardo, Lord of Scandiano, an intimate of Niccolò III and grandfather of the poet; the courtiers Alberto Costabili, Giovanni Gualengo (whom we have already encountered), and the everpresent Uguccione Contrari, Niccolò and Tito Strozzi, Alberto Pio da Carpi the elder (still a young man), and the humanist Carlo Nuvolone.[27]

But the unquestioned master of ceremonies, the leader of every major discussion in the work, is Leonello himself. Angelo's verbal portrait is quite compatible with the paintings and medals by Pisanello, Oriolo, and others:[28] "There was great care and gentility in his manner of speaking. His face was calm but his eyes were aglow with vitality. Physically, he was very well coordinated and particularly striking was the grace with which he used his arms and hands." "Grace," in fact, might serve well as the key word to summarize the ensuing description:

> His style of dress—and one's dress can be a source of respect and good will among gentlemen—was noteworthy for its tastefulness. He was not concerned with opulence and ostentation, as some other princes are. But—now you will find this remarkable—he thought out his wardrobe in such a way as to choose the color of his garments according to the day of the month

[27] It is noteworthy that of this company, only Guarino himself was a professional humanist. The others were all noblemen of the court, including Niccolò and Tito Strozzi who, though Florentine *fuorusciti,* had the highest status in Ferrarese society. For an assessment of the effects of noble domination of Ferrarese cultural life at the court, see below, pp. 221-25.

[28] The best discussion of Leonello d'Este's physical appearance is that of Ernst Kantorowicz, "The Este Portrait by Roger van der Weyden," *JWCI,* iii (1939-40), 169-80 (reprinted in the same author's *Selected Studies* (Locust Valley, N.Y., 1965), 366-80, to which I refer here. Though much of Kantorowicz's article is devoted to Leonello's illegitimate son Francesco d'Este, who spent most of his life as a courtier in Burgundy, there is much useful information on Leonello and his circle, his portraits, and their iconography.

and the position of the stars and planets. What shall I say of his great commitment to the worship of God? Simply that he was like a saintly monk who daily offered prayers to the lord. And though he lived among men, he was not less than the very angels of heaven who, it sometimes seemed, took counsel from him.[29]

In a sense, the graceful Leonello, carefully selecting his clothes with an eye to astrology, seems a very tame and perhaps slightly dull figure, when compared to his flamboyant father. However, his restraint, his temperance, his balance, and his learning, those quiet virtues, were balanced by a certain intensity, which also appears in the portraits (Fig. 3), and which is reflected in his determined efforts to elevate the level of civilization of his state.

Basically, though it is misleading to be categorical when discussing the *Politia,* this is a book about language. Decembrio concedes that Cicero and Quintillian together have covered most of the essential rules of eloquence, and he does not intend to duplicate their effort. At the same time, he clearly wants the dialogues to serve as a kind of *vademecum* for people who would like to speak well (f.2): "And so we shall define Politia Litteraria not in legal

---

[29] A. Decembrio, *Politiae Literariae Angeli Decembrii Mediolanensis Oratoris Clarissimi, ad Summum Pontificem Pium II libri septem* (Augsburg, 1540), f. 1, v⁰. I wish to thank my former student, Dr. Raymond E. Wanner, who has translated the first book of the *Politia Litteraria,* for allowing me to quote his translation here. The passage reads in part: "Tanta ab eius ore dicendi mansuetudo, in fronte serenitas, in oculis enhilaratio, denique in omni corporis gesta modestia in proceritate membrorum aptitudo. . . . Nam in vesta non decorem & opulentiam solum, qua caeteri principes honestari solent, sed mirum dixeris pro ratione planetarum, & dierum ordine, colorum quoque coaptationem excogitant. Quid de perpetua eius in divinum cultum pietate dixerim, ut tanquam sacer Monachus quotidianas ad Dominum referret orationes, ac inter mortales vivens, non minore cum Diis ipsis, que hominibus concilio frui videretus."

categories, nor as the *Res Publica* of the Greeks . . . but rather according to our own usage as polite or urbane conversation. We should like, therefore, that you understand 'politia' or 'expolitia' . . . as an expression of the concept of elegance itself or as the cult of elegance." Thus, he plans to present some of the innumerable discussions that were carried on at the court on this subject, and related ones. Taken as a whole, the dialogues provide an astoundingly detailed and specific picture of courtly literature and artistic canons, assumptions, and tastes. Let us consider a few particularly interesting examples, taken from the most general section of the work, Book I.

A substantial portion of the first book is devoted to the care and adornment of a library, and the criteria according to which a book collection should be built. Angelo presents this as a subject over which the discussants often disagreed, particularly with respect to the quality of individual books and authors. Together with the surviving inventories, the attitudes revealed here are helpful in understanding the particularly erudite and far-ranging character of Ferrarese humanism. In this setting, physical care, appearance, and order are first of all important. One's books require both a suitable location and a suitable order. They are best kept in chests or boxes, in a room that is clean and not damp. If bookcases are used instead of boxes, the volumes should be chained, "as in monastic libraries." At the same time that privacy and security are maintained by these devices, there should also be adequate ventilation. Fragrant herbs and flowers in the room will help prevent musty odors. No pets of any kind should be admitted, and the site chosen should be free of noise. The decor must be sober, and conducive to contemplation:

> There can also be some good paintings on the walls, painting which represent the Caesars or the meaning

of the gods, or classical heroes. Thus it is good, from time to time, to look at that wonderful picture of Jerome writing in his hermitage, for this picture reminds us of the solitude, the silence, and the zest for study and writing that must characterize a library.[30]

Thus, the physical aspect of libraries receives great attention. Beauty follows cleanliness and order as the requirements of a well-established collection. After general agreement on these subjects, Feltrino Boiardo interrupts to divert the discussion to more substantive matters. He interjects the opinion that Livy, not Vergil, is the greatest of the Roman writers, for he deals with truth, rather than imagination "as is the custom with poets."

But Leonello refuses to take Feltrino's lure, and continues to analyze the physical properties of libraries. Now he has moved a step closer to the texts, for he turns to the way books themselves are made. They too must be beautiful—skillfully written and tastefully illustrated, and well bound: "Look at my *Aeneid* with that idiotic picture on it . . . adding decorations to an old horse does not make the horse more beautiful." [31] He then complains about careless and inaccurate scribes, and laments that even good scribes perpetuate the errors of the defective manuscripts from which they copy. Only then, after presenting the arguments for

[30] *Politia Litteraria*, f. 3 v°-iv: " 'Quae nisi eam volumus nihil instrepit, Honestas quaque picturas, caesuras ve quae vel deorum, vel heroum emoriam repraesentent. Ideoque saepenumero cernere est quibusdam iucundissimam imaginem esse Hieronymi describentis in heremo, per quam in bibliothecis solitudinem & silentum, & studendi scribendique sedulitatem oportunam advertimus.' "

[31] *Ibid.*, f. 4 r°: " 'Non tamen omnis in hoc politiae genus, nec ni imbicilis titentibus aut phaleris, litterarum ve picturis, & tabularum tegumentis nostra versatur intentio, ut Aeneae contigit, cum pictura inani pasceretur, sed vulgo ferunt equum qualencunque addita phalerarum ornamenta, veluti pulchiorem, non meliorme tamen efficere.' "

and against adorning books with "pearls and gold and silks and fine purples," does he turn to Boiardo's view of Vergil.

It is in these discussions concerning the merits of ancient authors that Leonello's good judgment and common sense appear. He takes a relativistic position, and gently reproaches Feltrino for not having thought the matter through. In elegance, Livy and Vergil are in many places equal. As regards grace, metre, and soft cadences, Vergil is clearly superior. Beyond that, says Leonello, it depends upon the reader's particular interests:

> For there are those whose interests are very definitely in history such as our Feltrino and you Alberto who only very rarely read poets. . . . Others, however, are attracted by a love for poetry as bees are to flowers. Still others apply themselves to the study of philosophy, and they are considered truly wise. And still others place before all other disciplines that moral and natural reality which they call metaphysics.[32]

This relativistic approach is somewhat remarkable in view of *Quattrocento* debates over precisely these kinds of subjects.[33] Leonello's intellectual sympathies here are clearly broad enough simply to accept the various disciplines without attempting to establish or enforce invidious distinctions between them. Let us just admit, he says, that men's literary tastes will reflect their own most urgent concerns.

To acknowledge that fact did not imply for Leonello that every author might not be evaluated both on his own terms, and by general criteria of utility. For, having established this tolerant framework, he turns "to the criteria by which we have selected from that vast array of authors what we believe are the more outstanding works—note that I did not say the most outstanding works—for inclusion in

[32] *Ibid.*, f. 4 v°.

[33] Cf. E. Garin, ed., *La Disputà delle arti nel quattrocento*, vol. ix of *Ed. Naz. dei Classici del Pensiero Italiano* (Florence, 1947).

our library." The first quality by which any author must be judged is whether he stimulates eloquence and industry in his readers. He must not induce foolish levity, like Plautus, or irrational depression, like Lactantius. Among poets, therefore, he chooses first Vergil and then Terence. To these he immediately adds "Cicero, the teacher of virtues, especially in his *De Officiis,* and Sallust, the enemy of vice. From them we learn eloquence, a sense of propriety, and a knowledge of matters military and civic." Prince Leonello's emphasis here on the acquisition of civic virtue through reading republican authors like Cicero and Sallust should not be overlooked, despite his evident literary preference for Vergil.

At this point Leonello really warms to his subject. After a long encomium of Vergil, he embarks on an analysis of Terence, in which he emphasizes the moral lessons that are to be drawn from the comedies, if one looks beyond the window-dressing of funny Greek names, and the common-place subject matter he often treats. In fact, to Leonello this is a positive attraction, for it makes Terence more accessible and relevant: "The works of Terence are useful to every class of men and to every type of situation." Though elegant, even deceptively elegant, in style, Terence is realistic, for he "wrote in accordance with the nature of things."

Harmony with nature is also one of Cicero's most important qualities, and he, like Terence, bases his values solidly on the truths of "moral philosophy." Both stimulate and teach virtue to a race inclined toward evil, though Terence is more practical and less elitist. But again the venerable Boiardo interrupts, and asks Leonello to get on with it, and list other authors who ought to be represented, "lest people might think that we are collecting this library for a poor man." [34] Leonello agrees, and goes on to discuss Ovid, Aesop, Horace, Seneca, Juvenal (who should not be read publicly,

[34] *Politia Litteraria,* f. 7. Of all Cicero's works, the *De Officiis* is taken by Leonello to be the most important.

"but rather . . . in the privacy of your library"), Plautus, Statius, Tibullus, Catullus, Martial, Propertius, and Claudian. Then he refers to some minor authors, whose works are "more suited, perhaps, for filling up a library, rather than for improving its quality," and he amusingly twits Guarino for having so many of them.[35]

It should be clear from the above list that Leonello personally preferred poetry and drama to other literary forms. But notwithstanding the superior literary skills of the poets, he could not pretend to regard them as the most effective teachers of eloquence. For this he turned back to Cicero and the other rhetoricians. Cicero is presented as a model for eloquence in general, but first of all for letter-writing in particular. Here, Leonello ridicules those who puff up Ciceronianism into a bombastic and unnatural affectation. An elegant, though simpler, epistolary style is that of Pliny, which Leonello highly recommends. Juvenal and Quintillian are also essential as teachers of eloquence.

Interestingly, Decembrio devoted an entire chapter of the first book to Leonello's discussion of histories as an aid to more eloquent speech. At first glance, this is an uncommon justification for the study of history, but it is closely connected with Leonello's emphasis on reality. For to Leonello, the cardinal virtue of the historians was that their eloquence had to be confined within the limits of truth. Livy in this context is not scorned, but Leonello with mild disdain attributes his pre-eminence to the amount of work he produced. Though often pleasing, Livy's style is subject to lapses of taste, and he also makes factual errors. Sallust is adjudged

---

[35] *Politia Litteraria,* f. 8 r⁰. Leonello goes on to say, " 'I shall omit their names lest my naming them be cause for some to become angry with me, and be cause for ridicule. All of these works, however, are part of the library of our friend from Verona, so that since it is sometimes necessary for him to lend books to his less intimate friends, we might receive something of value.' "

superior in these respects, though too little of his work survives. The same is true of Quintus Curtius, whom Leonello admires. He also likes Caesar, but more as a reporter of events than as an elegant author. Leonello also lists Florus and other summarizers, comparing them favorably with prolix historians whom he calls "asses," referring to Eusebius, Orosius, and similar compilers. On the other hand, he is willing to provide space for Josephus, Hegesippus, and a group of historians who concerned themselves eloquently with monarchs—Suetonius, Tacitus, Plutarch. But about these he has practically nothing to say.[36]

The first five chapters, then, are concerned exclusively with Latin letters. But Leonello now changes the subject to vernacular authors, and their claims to be taken seriously in the formation of the model library. He expresses reservations about translations from the ancient tongues into Italian, not because he thinks there is anything illegitimate about this effort, but because it reveals a lack of literary training on the part of the reading public:

> If works of this kind, and especially histories, are to be done because of the whims of certain Princes, we have no serious objections. But since classical works are being put into the vernacular, I do wonder about both the Prince and his people, for both seem to lack training in literature. To be content with a translation is like being content with earthenware and coarse cloth rather than pearls and things of great value.

Moreover, notes Leonello, translators often do a poor job, and misconstrue the difficult passages.[37]

---

[36] *Ibid.*, ff. 8-10.

[37] *Ibid.*, f. 10. Ferrarese humanists for the rest of the century manifest embarrassment about using the *volgare* in serious works, and often apologized for so doing. Their protestations reflect the need to satisfy the requirements of the courtly circle, and above all later princes like Borso and Ercole, who were quite indifferent to their own lack of Latinity.

But vernacular literature as a category consists primarily of original works, not translations, and here Leonello is not much more appreciative of contemporary efforts. Most vernacular writers are "illiterate idiots." [38] Even the better ones, those who write "correctly and grammatically" like Petrarch and Boccaccio, are unworthy of comparison with the ancients: "We cannot admit them to the more refined kind of library we are preparing." He lumps them in with the medieval encyclopedists, and archly pronounces his verdict: "To this category are to be relegated all who depart from the classical style of composition." [39]

Having dismissed the lot of modern writers, Leonello reopens the discussion of his beloved Cicero, this time under the aspect of moral philosophy. Here, Leonello is revealed as conversant with the teachings of Plato, Aristotle, Aristippus, Epicurus, and a number of Stoic and Peripatetic authors. All are worthy of inclusion, though none so much as Cicero. Indeed, for Leonello, the Greek authors present something of a problem. In the Ferrara of Aurispa and Theodore Gaza, the importance of Greek letters could not be minimized, but it is evident that Leonello himself did not succeed in acquiring the language, and could not have responded to Greek literature with the same intensity of feeling that he reveals for Latin letters. Thus, though he has high praise for Homer, because of his perseverance over blindness and his compendiousness as a Vergilian source, he misses the

---

[38] *Ibid.* Leonello also says, " 'Which of the classical authors ever composed a work in the vernacular?' " This argument is turned on its head by proponents of the vernacular in the French Renaissance. Writers like Du Bellay, Pasquier, and Le Roy argue that just as the ancients spoke and wrote in their vernacular, so must the moderns do. See my *Life and Works of Louis Le Roy* (Geneva, 1966), 77-78, 139 (no. XII). For a comparison with Florence, where the *volgare* played a different role, see H. Baron, *The Crisis of the Early Italian Renaissance* (Princeton, 1955), esp. ch. 15.

[39] *Politia Litteraria,* f. 10 v°: " 'In quo genere omnes adiucandi sunt, ut brevi sententia concludam, qui a veterum more dissentiunt.' "

poet's unerring touch, his own bardic eloquence. To Leonello, Homer was "as garrulous as Greeks were wont to be," and his work suffers by a lack of selectivity and focus. Vergil he finds superior, for his nobility, and for his concentration on elevated themes. Other Greek authors whom Leonello finds worthwhile are Apollonius, Pindar, Euripides, Sophocles, and Aesop, but he has no specific comments on any of them. Then he lists, among philosophers, Plato, Aristotle, Diogenes Laertius, and Xenophon. But for Leonello, the most eminent Greek literary undertakings are to be found in the field of history. Here he praises Herodotus and Thucydides, but again in vague terms. Though Leonello is clearly aware of the Hellenic revival, he seems to regard it as a curiosity, which has not affected his own values at all:

> It is scarcely believable how many of our people have almost turned into Greeks, and learned how to work with the Greek language and with Greek books. It is like being in Attica. Whatever we say is the best in Greek literature will, certainly, be examined very carefully. But so much for the Greeks.

Leonello's obvious limitations here were not lost on his contemporaries. To this impatient and unenlightening survey, Feltrino replied (jovially), "You will soon seem like a barbarian yourself, Leonello, if you continue to use Latin to tell us about the Greeks." [40]

Thus chastised, Leonello turns back to the safer terrain of Latin and vernacular authors, this time in the previously undiscussed area of sacred writing and ecclesiastical jurisprudence. Leonello observes that this field is not all that it used to be, but that it is still worth knowing something about. Theology is an old man's subject, "exception made, of course, for those who are in Holy Orders." If we want

[40] *Ibid.*, ff. 11 v°-13 r°.

to prepare ourselves for old age, we cannot ignore it. But Leonello is very selective in his choice of theologians, and his attitude toward religion reflects the fact that here too his critical faculties were brought to bear. For the library, Leonello would collect the better works of Ambrose and Augustine, Jerome (for his Ciceronian eloquence), Lactantius and Chrysostom (in the Traversari translation), and the Bible. After this miniscule list, so notable for its omission of every Catholic author after Augustine, Leonello pulls himself up abruptly, and accuses himself of digressing.

The first nine chapters of Book I establish a canon of distinguished authors and works, and offer reasons for the choices. Leonello's taste is precisely cognate with the Ciceronian and rhetorical humanism of the Florentine chancellors and their entourages.[41] There is not the slightest preference for authors of a non-republican stamp. The criteria are aesthetic and functionalistic, but this may be a distinction without a difference, for elegance of language (though not only of language) to Leonello, as to most humanists, was not only a source of pleasure and beauty in itself, and for its own sake, it was also an immediately practical and productive skill. In the *Politia* both aspects are recognized, and neither is placed above the other.

With this notably secular, classicizing canon now estab-

[41] See E. Garin, "I cancellieri umanisti della repubblica fiorentina da Coluccio Salutati a Bartolomeo Scala," *La cultura filosofica del rinascimento italiano*, 3-37, and the various studies of H. Baron, esp. *The Crisis of the Early Italian Renaissance* (Princeton, 1955), and *Humanistic and Political Literature in Florence and Venice at the Beginning of the Quattrocento* (Cambridge, Mass., 1955); H. Gray, "Renaissance Humanism: The Pursuit of Eloquence," *JHI*, xxiv (1963), 497-514; J. E. Seigel, *Rhetoric and Philosophy in Renaissance Humanism* (Princeton, 1968); W. Ruegg, "Die scholastische und die humanistische Bildung im Trecento," *Das Trecento* (Zurich, 1960), 141-81; idem, *Cicero und der Humanismus* (Zurich, 1946); and most recently, N. S. Struever, *The Language of History in the Renaissance* (Princeton, 1970), chs. I, II.

1. Alberto d'Este, Marquess of Ferrara (1388-1393). Statue by an unknown artist. Ferrara, façade of the Cathedral. To the right is an inscription of a bull of Pope Boniface IX, listing various privileges conceded to Alberto

2. Niccolò III d'Este, Marquess of Ferrara (1393-1441). Ferrarese, resembling the work of Amadio da Milano. National Gallery of Art, Washington, D.C. Samuel H. Kress Collection

3. Leonello d'Este, Marquess of Ferrara (1441-1450). Pisanello, Italian (c. 1395-1455). National Gallery of Art, Washington, D.C. Samuel H. Kress Collection

4. Borso d'Este, Marquess, then Duke, of Ferrara (1450-1471). Biblioteca Estense, Modena, MS. Alpha L, 5, 16 (Ital. 720), *Genealogia Estense*, f. 3r°

5. Borso d'Este in Triumph. Miniature painting from Biblioteca Estense, Modena, MS. Alpha, M, 7, 21 (Lat. 82), Gasparo Tribracho da Modena, *Divi ducis Borsii estensis triumphus*, f. 2r°

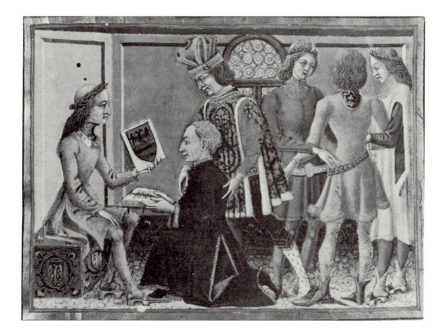

6. Giovanni Blanchini presenting his *Astrological Tables* to the Emperor Frederick III, in the presence of Borso d'Este and courtiers. Miniature painting in Biblioteca Comunale Ariostea, Ferrara, MS. Cl. I, n. 147, f. 1r°

7. Bartolommeo Pendaglia, Merchant of Ferrara. Sperandio, Italian, c. 1425-1504. National Gallery of Art, Washington, D.C. Samuel H. Kress Collection

8. Ludovico Carbone (c. 1436-1482). Sperandio, Italian (c. 1425-c. 1504). National Gallery of Art, Washington, D.C. Samuel H. Kress Collection

9. Ercole I d'Este, Duke of Ferrara, Modena, and Reggio (1471-1505). Baldassare d'Este, Italian (active 1461-c.1504). National Gallery of Art, Washington, D.C. Samuel H. Kress Collection

10. St. Martin dividing his cloak with the beggar. Miniature painting in
Biblioteca Comunale Ariostea, Ferrara, MS. Cl. I, 346, *Statutes of the
Confraternity of St. Martin*, 1494, frontispiece

Lerique mortales studio et glorie
Seculari maniter dediti Dux
IIL me exinde sui nominis Im
mortalem gloriam querere putaruut si claro
rum uirorum uitas scribere agorederentur:
Que res utiq non perennem quidem sed tempo
raneum concepte spei fructum afferebat: quia
& si per labentia tempora suam memoriam
propagarent et magnorum uirorum propositis
exemplis non parua emulatio legentibus exci
taretur Tamen labor iste suus hec ingliit La
cubrationesq nihil ad immortalem nominis
memoriam in eterna uita capescendam pertii

11. Ercole d'Este receiving a book from its author, an unknown monk.
Biblioteca Comunale Ariostea, Ferrara, MS. Cl. I, 306, *Vita B. Ioannis
a Tauxignano Episcopi Ferrariae*, f. 11r

12. Portrait of Ercole I d'Este. Dosso Dossi. Galleria Estense, Modena

Ad Illu̅ᵐ principem D̅n̅m. d. Herculem Duce̅
preclariss̅imu̅ Flo̅ide̅ ciuitatis fer̅arie̅n̅ Mutine̅
ac Regij. Marchio̅e̅m eſte̅n̅. Rodigijq̅, comite₃
& c̅j. Libellus per fratrem Andream pannoniu̅
ordinis chartuſie̅n̅ editus prefatio.

RINCI
PVM uere
Illuſtriſſime
preclare tue
co̅uenit excel
lentie illud
p̅p̅m̅ Macha
beorum xij.
Poſuit te do
mi̅ ducem
uniu̅ſarum

uirtutum. Scribendi nempe de rebus
magnis & multiplicib9 a te pelariſſi
me geſtis latiſſimu̅ m̅ campu̅ aperit
magnitudo uirtuti tuaru̅. Accedit₃
ad uteriore̅ ſtili materia̅ recoſe du
calis dignitas altiſſima diuina diſ
poſita prouidentia. Q̅ uſatq̅ue his

13. Ercole d'Este as a Christian Prince, enthroned with the motto
"Dominus Fortitudo Mea"—"God is my strength." Biblioteca Estense,
Modena, MS. Alpha Q, 9, 12 (Lat. 108), Andreas Pannonius, *Ad D.
Herculem Ducem Civitatis Ferrariensis Libri duo*, frontispiece

A LA ILLVSTRISS·ETEX
EL·M·M·LEONRA·DRA
GON·DVD·FERR·DL
MOD·DREGERE·EDRE
GNRE·ANT·CRNZAN·

14. Eleanora d'Aragona, Duchess of Ferrara (1472-1493). Miniature painting, attributed to Cosimo Tura, in the Pierpont Morgan Library, MS.
M 731, f. 2v°, Antonio da Cornazzano, *De modo regere et regnare*

15. Cosimo Tura, The Roverella Altarpiece (central panel). Reproduced by courtesy of the Trustees, The National Gallery, London

16. Covered stairs in the courtyard of the municipal building of Ferrara, formerly the Este Palace. Attributed to Pietro Benvenuti, 1481

17. Bird's-eye view of the Palace of Belriguardo, showing courtyards, gardens, and waterways. Detail of Archivio di Stato, Modena, Mappe in rotolo, 2: Topografia di tutti gli Stati Estensi di Marco Antonio Pasi, 1481

18. Niccolò da Correggio (1450-1508). Sperandio, Italian (c. 1425-c. 1504). National Gallery of Art, Washington, D.C. Samuel H. Kress Collection

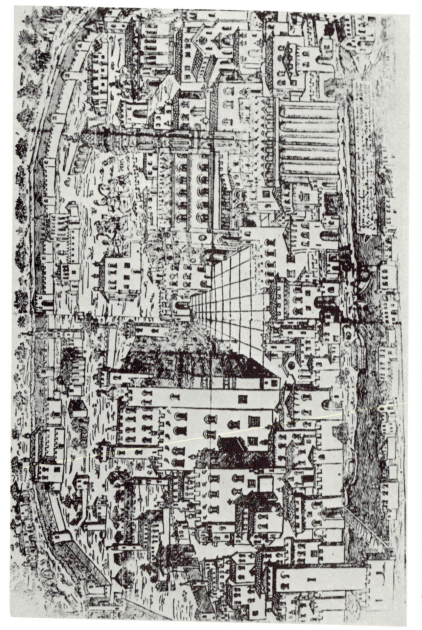

19. Planimetric view of Ferrara, 1499, showing the Herculean Addition. Anonymous woodcut. Biblioteca Estense, Modena

lished, Leonello goes on in the tenth and final chapter to purge it of forgeries, false attributions, and unworthy works by otherwise acceptable authors. The most interesting casualty of this process is the pseudo-Ciceronian *Rhetorica Ad Herennium*. That this was recognized as a pseudepigraphical work by the humanists in Ferrara in the 1440's will come as a surprise to historians of classical scholarship, who have traditionally credited the discovery to Raphael Regius, whose treatise *Utrum ars rhetorica ad Herennium Ciceroni falso inscribatur* was dedicated to Cardinal Giovanni de' Medici, the future Pope Leo X, in 1492, having been written in the previous year.[42]

Leonello offers a lengthy list of works falsely attributed to ancient writers, leading up to a general statement on the criteria by which such forgeries may be identified. He discusses interpolations, neologisms, anachronisms, stylistic variations, and deliberate forgeries. In the case of *Ad Herennium,* though, he tends toward more historical arguments. It must have been written after Cicero's lifetime, since an older work would not be attributed to him. Moreover, it is impossible that Herennius would have had the nerve "to approach a man of Cicero's stature and attempt to commission a second work on oratory. No one would have been so forward, and even if Herennius had committed such an impropriety, it is unthinkable that Cicero, with all of his other responsibilities and commitments, would have complied." Finally, the work is inferior to the *De Oratore,* and therefore could not be authentic:

"It is then clear that this work is far inferior, terribly obscure, and unbearably dull when compared to the

---

[42] For the bibliography of this problem, see esp. H. Caplan's introduction to the Ad Herennium in [M. T. Cicero] *Ad C. Herennium De ratione dicendi,* in Loeb Classical Library (London, 1954), pp. vii-xxxix, and the appended bibliography. Cf. F. A. Yates, *The Art of Memory* (London, 1966), 125.

depth of eloquence, utility, and scholarship that one finds in the original work [that Cicero wrote,] even though he was overburdened with other duties and responsibilities." . . . The others seemed to agree with the Prince, for what he said was true.[43]

Though Leonello's arguments were all wrong, he reached a sound conclusion.[44]

The other books of the *Politia Litteraria* deal with related themes, including many detailed points of classical philology.[45] Scattered throughout the work, like kernels of wheat in a great heap of chaff, are passages which reflect Leonello's guiding search for normative standards in all fields of culture. Michael Baxandall has called attention, for example, to Leonello's comments on the art of painting. The painter is a simple craftsman, in no way comparable to the poet.[46] He has no *ingenium,* no matter how developed his skill in representing nature. Leonello gives some grudging respect to those contemporary artists who imitate the ancients, and reveals the influence of Alberti's aesthetic of painting in

[43] *Politia Litteraria,* f. 16: " 'Quamobrem illud opus deterius, imperfectius, obscuris, incuriosius praemisisset, quod nunc utilius, copiosius, disertius, praesertim aliis officiis vel negotiis familiaribus tantopere occupatus aggrederetur. . . .' Videbantur cuncti quia vera diceret, sententiae principis assentiri."

[44] According to Leonello's argument in the *Politia Litteraria, Ad Herennium* was a later, derivative work done by a forger drawing on Cicero. Modern scholars have concluded that it was a pre-Ciceronian work of the schools, popular before the *De Oratore* was written. See *Oxford Classical Dictionary,* ed. M. Cary *et al.* (Oxford, 1949), 768.

[45] Thus Book Three deals with Latin parts of speech, Book Four considers the properties of the letters of the alphabet, Book Five and Six consider philological arguments regarding Latin poetry, and Book Seven analyzes the diphthong in Greek and Latin.

[46] "A Dialogue on Art from the Court of Leonello d'Este," 309: "Leonello repudiates the painter's claim to *ingenium* and the rejection becomes in turn part of the highly restrictive view of the range of painting and sculpture put forward at the end of his speech."

many passages. But he rejects decorative art as frivolous—except for the representation of nude figures in exact imitation of nature—and asserts many other expressive limitations of visual arts.[47] He reserves special scorn for northern taste, especially in tapestry, though he admires the craftsmanship involved. Leonello's cultural values are indeed so overwhelmingly literary that at the end of the chapter the poet Tito Strozzi himself interjects a plea for the visual arts, displaying the framed image of " 'a golden-haired maiden—no ancient Roman monument, but one of the modern glories of our Ferrara girls. . . . Nothing, it seems, is lacking in it but her voice.' And, as he said this, he opened a pyxis that held the image of a maiden, a sight sweet to all."

How accurate is Decembrio's presentation of the cultivated circle around the court of Leonello d'Este? It is hard to say. On the one hand, we know (for he says so himself) that Decembrio was writing in imitation of the *Atticae Noctes* of Aulus Gellius, and one scholar has on the strength of that viewed the work as an "idealizing account." [48] Yet

[47] Baxandall observes that Leonello's preference for the nude follows from the view that it offers greater naturalness, and less likelihood of conformity to fashion, with its threat of obsolescence. Baxandall rightly sees no Platonic influence here, though Garin, "Motivi della cultura filosofica ferrarese del Rinascimento," 416, writes somewhat vaguely of Platonism in the Leonellan court. Later, of course, Neo-Platonism exalts nudity, as shown by E. Panofsky, "The Neoplatonic Movement in Florence and North Italy," in *Studies in Iconology* (New York, 1939), 129-69.

[48] At the beginning of Ch. III of *Politia Litteraria* (f. 3, Decembrio writes: ". . . Aulus Gellius . . . will serve as our model. . . ." See H. Baron, "Aulus Gellius in the Renaissance: His Influence and a Manuscript from the School of Guarino," *Studies in Philology* XLVIII (1951), 107-25; reprinted in *idem, From Petrarch to Leonardo Bruni* (Chicago, 1968), 196-215. For the passage in question, see p. 215. If all humanist writing modeled on ancient works were dismissed as idealized, there would be few humanistic treatises that could legitimately be taken seriously, let alone at face value. The problem is to establish, wherever possible, ex-

there is a question of the extent to which literary antecedents affect the truthfulness of an author's work. From those elements that are susceptible to verification, Decembrio seems to be quite accurate. His references to specific physical objects, places, and works of art all check out well enough. His characterizations of individuals are confirmed by other sources. There may be a serious issue in Leonello's domination of the discussion, but even there I tend to give Decembrio the benefit of the doubt. After all, by the time he finished the book it was no longer dedicated to Leonello, who had long since passed beyond flattery, but to Pius II, who knew a lie when he heard one and had no special love for the Estensi. In any case, it really matters very little whether Leonello or somebody else said the things attributed by Decembrio to him. What is significant for present purposes is that these kinds of issues were what formed the substantive matter of Ferrarese courtly culture during the 1440's. Clearly, the Prince participated very fully in the formation and contribution of the circle in which ancient literature, history, and moral philosophy were passionately discussed, analyzed, and scrutinized for their relevance to contemporary art and life. One cannot imagine so much as a single page of Decembrio's account taking place in the company of Leonello's father.

In other aspects of his rule, Leonello revealed less portentous and less radical departures from the interests and policies of Niccolò III than in what might be called cultural affairs. Though unostentatious in his personal appearance and manner, he shared his father's love of elegant decoration, and pompous display. Leonello's first marriage—to Margherita Gonzaga in 1435—was lavish enough to require a special and substantial tax for the enormous festivities

ternally verifiable criteria for distinguishing between literary idealization on the one hand and plausible historical description on the other.

that were held at public expense.[49] But his second marriage, to Maria of Aragon, the illegitimate daughter of Alfonso the Magnanimous, in 1444, was even more elaborate. After a most impressive solemn entry into the city, the marriage ceremonies lasted through two weeks, with an incessant round of balls, jousts, and other spectacles and feasts.[50] To top it all off, a collection of wild animals was released in the garden at Belfiore, and as the newlyweds watched from a balcony, hunters killed them all. Leonello's love of pretty things led to a tremendous increase in household property during his reign, especially luxury goods of all kinds—brocades, tapestries, books, jewelry, and the like.[51]

Politically, Leonello maintained a strict continuity with his father's policies. The Venetian alliance remained intact, and continuous attempts to placate Venice were always in

[49] *ASCF*, Deliberazioni, D, 4, 9, ff. 13-14 (November 12 and 22, 1434) record a communal collection of 12,000 lire for Leonello's wedding and repairs to fortifications. Four years earlier, in anticipation of the wedding, the commune collected a special tax of 2,000 lire, and the *savi* were authorized to raise additional funds, "Per usura" if necessary (see *ASCF*, Deliberazioni, C, 4, 1, f. 17).

[50] *DF*, 27-8: "A le noze veneno li ambasiaturi veneziani [etc.] . . . et li ambasiaturi de Tuti li Signori de Italia d'presso. . . . Ne le qualle noze 12000 libre de cira se gli brusò, se gli mangiò 15000 mila de confectione de chucaro, 40000 para de polame, 2000 bestie bovine; fasani, columbi, pepioni senza numero; 20000 sechie de vino se bevette avantazato; mogia 200 fra formento et biave de cavali."

[51] The best studies of the decorative arts and the so-called minor arts in Ferrara are still those of the Marchese G. Campori, done in the nineteenth century. They include "Gli Orologieri degli Estensi," *AF*, n.s. II (1877), 1-23; "I Pittori degli Estensi del secolo XV," *AMP*, s. III, vol. III (1885-86), pt. 2, 525-603; "Gli architetti e gli ingegneri civili e militari del secolo XIII al XVI," *AMP*, s. III, vol. I (1883), 1-70; "Le carte di gioco dipinte per gli Estensi nel secolo XV," *AMP, vol.* VII, 1-15; "I miniatori degli Estensi," *AMP*, VI (1872), 245-74; *Notizie della maiolica e della porcellana di Ferrara nei secoli XV e XVI* (Pesaro, 1879); "L'Arrazeria Estense," *AM*, VI (1877), 415-59; *et al*. See also G. Gruyer, *L'Art ferrarais à l'époque des princes d'Este* (Paris, 1897), esp. vol. II.

progress. Thus Venetian neutrality, together with adroit diplomatic activities that have been studied and described by Giuseppe Pardi, kept Ferrara at peace throughout the reign.[52]

Domestically, the situation too was exceptionally stable. Borso proved an able and loyal second-in-command, while Niccolò's legitimate children by Ricciarda da Saluzzo— Ercole and Sigismondo—were in the traditional manner sent away for schooling. After his initial popular acclamation, Leonello had to confront a severe grain shortage in the winter of 1442, and managed the situation well enough. A small insurrection in the remote Garfagnana region was put down with typical Estense firmness, the only serious disturbance of the public order during Leonello's rule.[53] In fact, this decade was in all respects peaceful, even as measured by serious crime against persons and property, according to the evidence available in the Ferrarese *Libro dei Giustiziati.*[54]

The activities of the *signore* continued to be financed out of receipts from the extensive private holdings of the family, and the many and varied taxes paid into the marchesal and communal treasuries. Indeed, the Estensi were well known

[52] *Leonello d'Este,* esp. 67-81, 124-26.

[53] *Ant.Est.,* II, 204-205, says that Leonello handled the uprising "con buon modo et colla forza." *DF* does not mention the incident.

[54] The *Libro dei Giustiziati,* Biblioteca Comunale Ariostea di Ferrara, Fondo Manoscritti, Cl. I, MS. 404. It has been briefly discussed by Melchiorre Roberti, "Il 'Libro dei Giustizati' di Ferrara", *Atti del R. Istituto Veneto di Scienze, Lettere ed Arte,* LXVI, pt. 2, 837 ff. See also D. Zaccarini, "Delitti e pene negli stati Estensi nel secolo XVI," *AF,* XXVII (1928), 3-66. I have discussed this MS more extensively in "Crime and Punishment in Ferrara, 1441-1505," in L. Martines, ed., *Violence and Civil Disorder in Italian Cities: 1200-1500* (Berkeley and Los Angeles, 1972), 104-28, (hereafter "Crime and Punishment"). The *Libro* indicates an insignificant increase in capital crimes, as well as some shifts in the methods of capital punishment, during the last quarter of the century.

for their subtly developed skill at discovering and exploiting new sources of revenue. Income came from taxes on real property, but also from sales taxes, personal property taxes, commodity taxes, and others. There was a tax to be paid on livestock, and then another on butchered meat. Crops were taxed in the field, and then again when sold in the marketplace. Special levies could always be invoked for new projects of defense, public works, or non-recurring expenses of the court, such as weddings and other celebrations. In addition, funds were generated through the sale of licenses and permissions to hunt, fish, travel, bear arms and—in the case of the Jews—engage in banking. Weights and measures were taxed, as were wheat, bread, and flour, wine, fish, fruit, combustible materials, and building and other trade supplies. Non-residents of the Estense state were also caught in its tightly-woven fiscal net. For them, there were border taxes, import duties, travelers' tolls, hostelry taxes. Additional revenues came from the annual contributions paid by each commune within the territory to the signorial *camera,* from various "miscellaneous" sources such as fines, legally-acquired confiscated goods, and the alienation of marchesal lands.[55]

Against these rather imposing sources of credits must be placed the substantial operating expenses of court and state, even in peacetime. Public works—especially walls, dikes, and land reclamation projects—were costly and were often expedited by tax credits to particular districts or

[55] Pardi, *Leonello d'Este,* 124-40, discusses the nature of the receipts and expenditures during Leonello's regime. The *Registri dei Mandati* in *ASM* for Leonello's rule have been carefully studied by such scholars as Campori, Bertoni, and Venturi, in their pursuit of the history of artistic and literary patronage of the court. They remain to be carefully analyzed from the point of view of economic and social history. In the meantime, the only substantial work available on the economics of the court is that of P. Sitta, "Saggio sulle istituzioni finanziarie del ducato Estense," *AF,* III (1891), but this must be used with extreme caution.

workers. In addition there were the usual civic costs in relation to sanitation, charity, police, administration of justice, public instruction, and the various licensing, taxing, and administering bureaucracies. All of these, and the funds they utilized, deserve the attention of economic historians.

But above all, there were the expenses of the court. Leonello was the first of the Estensi to spend money lavishly on culture, in the broad sense. He started new palaces and continued work on the foundations begun by Alberto and Niccolò, sponsored costly festivals and public spectacles, hired expensive academic talent in several fields, patronized illuminators, goldsmiths, tapisseurs, painters, engineers, architects, and musicians.[56] Then there were the irreducible expenses of the court—clothing and food for all, offices to be run, diplomatic missions to be financed, hunting, hawking, the expenses of maintaining big houses and gardens, stockpiling grain, traveling, giving presents, maintaining fortifications, guards, and hundreds of horses. Finally, there came the pleasant special expenses—births, weddings, coronations, official visits; and those that were not so pleasant—funerals, unexplained inflation, floods, epidemics, earthquakes, wars, and the costs of trying to prevent or anticipate these. Once all of these expenses were paid, there remained the papal dues of 4,000 florins per year.

Given its negligible industrial base, its marginal role in Italian banking and finance, its strongly seasonal agricultural economy, and its high cash requirements, it is not surprising to find that Ferrara, like Mantua, became a city hospitable to Jews.[57] There are indications that there were Jews in Ferrara as early as 1088, though the first documentary evi-

[56] See above, n. 51.

[57] The best work on the Jews of Ferrara is A. Balletti, "Gli Ebrei e gli Estensi," *AM,* s. v, vol. vii (1913). But see also A. Pesaro, *Memorie storiche della communità israelitica di Ferrara* (Ferrara, 1878), and his *Appendice alle Memorie,* the whole work reprinted recently (Bologna, 1967). For the general background, A. Milano, *Storia degli Ebrei in Italia* (Turin, 1963),

dence of legal immunities granted to Jews in the Este territories dates from 1275. Under Alberto, Jewish banks were encouraged to provide service, especially during market days, and under Niccolò, an association of Jewish creditors was allowed to organize in 1413.[58] Despite occasional papal opposition, the *signori* persevered in protecting Jews in their territories, and by the middle of the fifteenth century, there were certainly small but stable Jewish communities in Ferrara, Modena, and Reggio. The Jews of course lived under carefully regulated conditions. They almost certainly had to pay for marchesal protection in a variety of ways, but by and large conditions were relatively benign under the Estensi. In 1446, the *giudice de'savi* issued an ordinance prohibiting Jewish bankers from opening their establishments, including doors and windows, on religious holidays, and from making any loans on those days, a fact that suggests that such abuses of the Christian Sabbath had been tolerated to the point where they had become problematical.[59] In 1452, land was granted for a Jewish cemetery in Ferrara.[60] And Jews, like all others, were tried in the regular civil and criminal

---

203-204, and C. Roth, *The Jews in the Renaissance* (Philadelphia, 1959). In addition to their traditional roles it should also be noted that there were Jews from time to time at the Este court in such occupations as *bombardiere,* and also dancing master. See Zambotti, *Diario,* 124; and the anonymous MS. in B.E.M. Alpha J. 9, 4 (Ital. 92), "Dell'Arte del Ballo" (title added later), for which see O. Kinkeldey, "A Jewish Dancing-Master of the Renaissance: Guglielmo Ebreo," in *A. S. Freydus Memorial Volume* (New York, 1929), 329-72. And for the similar position of Jews in Mantua, cf. G. Coniglio, *I Gonzaga* (Varese, 1964), 290-91.

[58] For similar arrangements elsewhere, see the recent article by A. Molho, "A Note on Jewish Moneylenders in Tuscany in the Late Trecento and Early Quattrocento," in *Renaissance Studies in Honor of Hans Baron,* ed. A. Molho and J. A. Tedeschi (Florence and Dekalb, Ill., 1971), 99-117. Molho seems to me to overestimate the on-hand cash requirements of Jewish bankers, whose credit network would appear rather to have rested on fiduciary arrangements of a more sophisticated kind.

[59] See *ACSF,* Deliberazioni del Maestrato, 1445, v, 14, f. 17 (April, 1446).

[60] *ACSF,* Deliberazioni del Comune, G, 5, 14, f. 63.

courts. With only occasional exceptions, they were not obliged to hear Lenten sermons or submit to similar forms of harrassment that were common elsewhere, and on occasion, the *signore* himself intervened to suppress anti-Semitic preachers.[61]

Had Leonello lived as long as his father, or his brother Borso, the political history of Ferrara would probably have been much the same, but its cultural history would have been vastly different. The *marchese's* death at 43 in 1450, resulting from a "terrible headache," deprived the circle of learned humanists at the court of the only genuinely interested protector of their scholarly, Latinate circle. But during the scant decade of his rule, Leonello put Ferrara on the literary map of Europe. It had by 1450 become a center of linguistic and philological studies rivaled only by a few other towns. Its university was thriving, its court was a refined gathering place of cultivated humanists and renowned artists. The prince's library had been embellished with important new works, dedicated and presented to him by scholars who knew they could expect a warm reception. Though the influence of these developments remained at work through succeeding decades, Ferrara was changed in subtle but crucial ways in the long reign which followed.

[61] See below, pp. 206-207. Balletti's position is that Jews in Ferrara had an exceptionally tranquil and flourishing life, characterized by much tolerance (p. 176). But he also observes that they paid the usual high price—both economically and in terms of personal freedom—for their protection by the *signori*. Their security was contingent on provision of the banking services provided for the dukes. Still, as Balletti shows (pp. 222-25), by the standards of the time, Jews were relatively well off in Ferrara. Under Ercole I, whose religious impulses occasionally led to coercive measures, they were sometimes forced to wear identifying badges or to attend Lenten sermons, but this policy was sporadic. See Zambotti, *Diario*, 12; Frizzi, *Memorie per la storia di Ferrara*, IV, 182; Pesaro, *Memorie storiche*, 17.

V   Borso d'Este and the
Transformation of Ferrarese Culture

Of all the Este *signori,* none loved praise more than Borso, the younger brother of Leonello. The trappings and the rhetoric of power delighted him, and he was never embarrassed to be called "glorious," "heavenly," or "divine." Indeed, having riches and power, he spent a good part of his political and diplomatic energy in the pursuit of new titles, and accepting the fulsome congratulations of his many admirers upon his rising status. His vanity was so shameless, so obvious a source of pleasure, that it almost becomes a cause of admiration (**Fig. 4**). One can spend quite a few happy afternoons browsing through the panegyrical—one is tempted to say devotional—treatises dedicated to Borso that survive in the Biblioteca Estense in Modena. There is, for example, the piece by the court physician Michele Savonarola, *De felici progressu Illustrissimi Borsi Estensis ad Marchionatum Ferrariae* . . . , a presentation copy which narrates Borso's career and his election to power upon the death of Leonello, and takes time to expatiate upon Borso's myriad virtues.[1] The classically obsequious treatise by Ludovicus Argenteus, *Oratio de Laudibus Illustrissimi Principis et Excellentissimi Domini D. Borsi,* also a presentation copy,

---

[1] B.E.M. Alpha W, 2, 15 (Lat. 215). Definitely a presentation copy, the MS., a quarto in 45 ff., narrates the careers of Leonello and Borso, and prescribes what is required of a good prince. Its interest lies mainly in the identity of its author, many of whose other works also survive in early mss. in the Estense and the Biblioteca Apostolica Vaticana. For this MS. see P. O. Kristeller, *Iter Italicum* (Leiden, 1963) I, 370 (hereafter *Iter*); D. Fava and M. Salmi, *I manoscritti miniati della Biblioteca Estense in Modena* (Florence, 1950), 163; D. Fava, *La Biblioteca Estense nel suo sviluppo storico* (Modena, 1925), 59. Michele Savonarola deserves a new monograph, though the work of A. Segarizzi, *La vita e le opere di Michele Savonarola* (Padua, 1900) is still useful.

is as effusive as its title suggests.[2] There is the idolatrous and, let it be admitted, somewhat tedious poem by Gasparo Tribraco da Modena, called *Divi ducis Borsii estensis triumphus per Tribrachus Mutinensem*.[3] A miniature painting illustrates this work (Fig. 5). It shows Borso on a triumphal chariot, shaded by a *baldacchino*. The chariot is drawn by two white horses, upon one of which a blindfolded Cupid is seated. In front of the horses are four women, who bear the symbols of office.

These three works provide only a sampling of the *genre,* but they give a clear idea of one of Borso's foremost pleasures: being unreservedly admired by others. An outgoing, talkative, and entertaining man, Borso nevertheless concealed some very real complexities beneath his affable exterior. Pius II, who cannot be counted among his admirers, has left a convincing portrait:

> Borso was a man of fine physique and more than average height with beautiful hair and a pleasing countenance. He was eloquent and garrulous and listened to himself talking as if he pleased himself more than his hearers. His talk was full of blandishments mingled with lies. He desired to seem rather than to be magnificent and generous. . . . He bought as many precious stones as he could and never appeared in public without jewels. He collected rich household furnishings: even in the country he used gold and silver dishes.[4]

[2] B. E. M. Alpha G, 7, 21 (Lat. 120); Kristeller, *Iter,* I, 369; Fava and Salmi, 143-44; Fava, 253. Fava regarded this as a presentation copy, and identified Ludovico Argenteo as a minor figure in the chancellery, used occasionally by Borso for diplomatic missions. The MS. describes Borso's assumption of the powers of *signore,* and his reception of the Emperor Frederick III.

[3] B. E. M. Alpha M, 7, 21 (Lat. 82).

[4] See *Memoirs of a Renaissance Pope: The Commentaries of Pius II,* tr. F. A. Gragg, ed. L. C. Gabel [an abridgment] (New York, 1959), 114.

There is no flattery here. In fact, the Pope's description might cause a reader to wonder what others found to praise in this apparently egocentric, self-serving, duplicitous character. Yet even Aeneas Sylvius himself must have found something good to say about him, for it was he who played a major role in persuading a reluctant Frederick III to raise Borso to the rank of Duke of Modena, in 1452, and then delivered an oration on "the glories of the house of Este, the ability of Borso, and the exalted rank conferred upon him." [5]

"The ability of Borso." There are the key words. For, as Pius realized, one could easily fault Borso as a man, but he was unquestionably a shrewd and effective prince. The long scholarly debate about Borso and his regime in Ferrara has had to come to terms with this distinction, which in our time seems obvious enough. We take it more or less for granted that effective leadership at a high level is not at all incompatible—and may even have certain affinities—with character traits that are generally regarded as faults when they occur in private men. In recent history, political leaders have been known for their vanity, cruelty, love of ostentatious display, sexual deviations, stupidity, greed, mental instability. We know that our leaders are almost at best ordinary human beings, often indistinguishable in talent, taste, energy, intelligence, and humanity from their constituency, and some have considered this a virtue. Yet even while we realize, and may sometimes even exaggerate, the fallibility of our leaders, we continue to expect them to serve as models of the traditional virtues, exemplars of the prevailing mores, and exponents of an idealized vision of the status quo. I think that men of the *Quattrocento* reveal much the same kind of ambivalence about their rulers. [6] Every-

[5] *Ibid.*, 64.

[6] It may be useful to regard anti-signorial literature as a counterpart of the *speculum principis* genre. Theoretical attacks on the signories often reveal a striking awareness of the personal limitations of a particular

body, including the princes, knew perfectly well that they were ordinary human beings, and that what distinguished them from others was the ability to display their virtues and indulge their vices on a larger scale and with greater effect.

Thus, while a few were naive enough to believe that princes would or could be made to be perfect, i.e., to exemplify as well as articulate the highest aspirations of their society, there was much hope that they could become better, i.e., more responsive to the popular will, receptive to prevailing social and cultural norms, and so forth. One aspect of flattery is that it was an expression of such hope. If one told a prince how good and virtuous, as well as how powerful he was, often enough, he might start to behave that way. Court panegyrics may be regarded, at least in part, as an early attempt at "positive reinforcement," just as the Ciceronian rhetoric of the Florentine chancellors represents a functional analogue of eloquence in the service of civic ideals in a republican context.[7] The *speculum principis* literature,

---

ruler, an aspect which in its general formulation is of course an established tenet of Aristotelian constitutional thought, as well as an empirically obvious point in almost all cases. See esp. N. Rubinstein, "Florence and the Despots," 21-45; also the studies of P. J. Jones and D. M. Bueno da Mesquita previously cited, p. 44.

[7] I do not mean to suggest that flattery and the self-serving goals of the impoverished courtly humanist were not an essential consideration in his decision to heap praise upon his prince, nor do I believe that princes necessarily took such work seriously as anything other than useful examples of the subservience of the learned before the powerful. However, exhortations to virtue, whatever their ulterior motives may be, necessarily tended to carry with them the accumulated moral weight of ancient political thought and Christian teachings on proper exercises of power. In an age that looked to the past for its models of wisdom and authority, this alone must have had some persuasive impact. In the same way, I would suggest that though Florentine humanist chancellors obviously had a clear self-interest in praising republican values and condemning those of the despotisms, though they clearly stood to benefit from the preservation of the *status quo* (as most people in positions of power have traditionally done)

always popular at the courts, represents a more normative, less personal expression of the same aspirations that we find in these Borsian tracts. How else can one understand the perennial appeal of a work like the *Cyropaedeia* of Xenophon, of which the Este library had several copies? [8]

If Borso's subjects regarded him with ambivalence, there is certainly no evidence of the fact. By all accounts he was immensely popular. Scholars who have found his learning meager, his tastes conventional, his rule severe, his judgments vindictive, his love of display vulgar have had difficulty reconciling themselves to that perfectly obvious fact. But for the people of Ferrara between 1450 and 1471 Borso— unlike Niccolò III and Leonello—apparently represented precisely the model of a just, able, and enlightened ruler.

their case for the republic turned out to be more than a series of self-serving rationalizations or claims based on ancient rhetoric. Indeed, this case came to be a civic credo, a system of beliefs or, in Hans Baron's terms, a "civic humanism." Thus, as Kristeller has suggested, in "The Moral Thought of Humanism," reprinted in *Renaissance Thought II: Papers on Humanism and the Arts* (New York, 1965), 47, there is a close functional tie between civic humanism on the one hand and what might be called despotic humanism on the other. In fact the distinctions between these could be tenuous enough that it may be misleading to equate civic humanism with republicanism, for in their own ways the humanists of the court were trying to influence the *signori* in their management of civic life and values. For another view, see E. Garin, "The Humanist Chancellors of the Florentine Republic from Coluccio Salutati to Bartolomeo Scala," in *Portraits from the Quattrocento* (New York, 1972), 1-29; first published in Italian in his *La cultura filosofica del Rinascimento Italiano* (Florence, 1961).

[8] See, e.g., B. E. M. Alpha G, 6, 2, where the work is translated by Matteo Maria Boiardo who, it should be recalled, was also the translator of Herodotus. For that MS., see *Iter,* II, 607, where Kristeller says it is "apparently" in the Vatican Library as part of the T. De Marinis Bequest. However, efforts to find it there were unsuccessful, and it may still be in Florence. For full description see T. De Marinis, *La legatura artistica in Italia nei secoli XV e XVI* (Florence, 1960), II, p. 50, (n. 1458), where it is described as the presentation copy for Ercole I, and dated 1491.

His faults were minor and peripheral, his strengths and virtues were immediately apparent. Unlike Niccolò, who had been a successful statesman, Borso did not defy the morality of his contemporaries. Indeed, he was a bachelor and appears to have led a celibate existence. Unlike Leonello, he disliked the company of scholars and intellectuals, and preferred to spend his time on hunting, fishing, and politics, probably in that order. He was engaging and sympathetic where Leonello had been somewhat aloof and aristocratic. These differences in style help to account for his popularity. But even more important is the fact that by the standards of his time, Borso symbolized and stood at the head of an exceptionally prosperous and successful state.

For Borso, succession to the many and varied powers, privileges, and properties of the Marquess of Este was plainly a windfall. Nothing could have seemed less likely than the death of Leonello at the age of 43. Moreover, not only did Leonello himself have a legitimate heir, the young Niccolò who had been born in 1438 to Margherita Gonzaga, but there was also the legitimate son of Niccolò III's final marriage to Ricciarda da Saluzzo, Ercole, and his younger brother Sigismondo. Upon Leonello's death, then, Niccolò was only twelve years old, and Ercole was nineteen. Though both had the advantage of legitimacy, neither was in a strong position to press his claims. Niccolò, who naturally enjoyed strong support from the ruling family of Mantua, had no base of support within Ferrara. On the contrary, his extreme youth and his close ties with a generally friendly though rival state significantly diminished his appeal. Ercole, though older, was still a minor. Like Niccolò, he had no partisans in Ferrara, and was very much an unknown quantity there, having spent most of his youth in Naples, where he was assured a good courtly education and could not become a threat. Borso, in contrast, was in his prime. At 37, he had long since absorbed some of the rudiments, if not the refinements, of a humanist education. For twenty years, more or less, he had been acquiring and polishing military and political skills through long campaigns with the ablest *condottieri* in Italy, and periods of residence in places like Venice, Milan and Naples. He had held numerous important *condotte*, and was a respected general. In 1445, after a peripatetic career in the fields and courts of Italy, he had returned to Ferrara to assist Leonello in the management of the Estense territories.[9]

Though he avoided prolonged absences from the state for the rest of his life, Borso never overcame the restless activism of his soldier's career. He traveled constantly throughout the Ferrarese, moving from one to another of the country houses, palaces, and rustic retreats for hunting and fishing that his father had built or improved. It certainly did no harm politically to make personal appearances throughout Este lands on a fairly regular basis, but in these constant travels the political motive appears clearly secondary to Borso's keenest passion: the hunt. Hunting may not have been the alpha and omega of Borso's existence, but it certainly was his favorite activity after 1445. We shall have more to say later about the scale on which Borso came to practice this genteel substitute for war. Suffice it to say now that it accounts for the major part of his peregrinations.

His active and robust personality helped make him a popular favorite among the people even during Leonello's reign, and Borso had other conspicuous virtues as well. He was deeply religious, attended mass every morning, and scrupulously observed the festivals.[10] His philanthropies were directed toward convents and monasteries, and he

[9] The only reliable comprehensive study of Borso is the monograph by G. Pardi, *Borso d'Este, Duca di Ferrara*, in *Studi Storici, vols*. xv, xvi (1906-7), 3-58, 134-204, 241-88, 377, 416; vol. xvi, 113-70. The later study by A. Lazzari, *Il primo duca di Ferrara, Borso d'Este* (Ferrara, 1945) has very little to add.

[10] Pardi, *Borso d'Este*, xv, 149-53.

founded the great Certosa of Ferrara, which became a bulwark of the religious life of the city for centuries, and remains the site of its principal burial ground.[11] His religious observance carried over into his private life to an unusually high degree, and he was known for his moral uprightness. To these estimable qualities, Borso added the formidable assets of his eloquence, his natural bonhomie and courtesy, his impressive stature and handsome face, and his sumptuous taste in clothes and jewelry. The latter seems hard to accept as an asset, for we live in an age in which differences in status are supposed to be expressed outwardly only in the subtlest possible ways. Our leaders carefully follow, rather than attempting to define, fashions and styles. But in the Renaissance, as in most other periods, elegance and magnificence were more than perquisites, they were traditional princely virtues, valued expressions of authority and power, as all of the humanist authors who praised Borso's glorious appearance well understood. Even Aeneas Sylvius observed that as early as 1446 Borso had a great following in Ferrara and was regarded as "quasi deus" by the people.[12] Immediately upon Leonello's death at Belriguardo, the entourage of citizens, courtiers, nobles, and, significantly, dependent princelings acknowledged Borso as the new *signore*. That done, the entire assemblage rode in to Ferrara, where Borso was officially "elected" according to the carefully preserved communal rite, and with obvious popular enthusiasm. As the anonymous diarist says:

[11] See *DF*, 70; also *Ant.Est*. II, 224. Mr. Charles Rosenberg, a doctoral candidate at the University of Michigan, is studying Borso's patronage of the Certosa, and several other monuments.

[12] Quoted by A. Lazzari, *Il primo duca di Ferrara, Borso d'Este*, 17-18. The passage, written in 1446, reads: "In sero venit frater eius admodum pulcher Borsius nomine, quem Ferrarienses quasi deum calunt." For additional references to Borso in Aeneas' correspondence, see R. Wolkan, ed., *Der Briefwechsel des Eneas Sylvius Piccolomini*, in *Fontes Rerum Austriacarum* (Österreichisches Geschichtsquellen; Vienna, 1918), 4 vols.

The illustrious prince *messer* Borso da Este . . . entered
Ferrara with a splendid and magnificent company . . .
with the entire populace acclaiming him: *"Viva, viva*
the illustrious *signore messer* Borso, a *liberal* signore."
And thus, with the will of the *popolo* of Ferrara,
he was made *Signore* of Ferrara, Modena, and Reggio. . . .[13]

His election was subsequently ratified by Pope Nicholas V,
who confirmed him as papal vicar.[14]

Borso did not rule by appearances alone, though. From
the beginning of his reign, he revealed a deep and continuing interest in the internal development of his state.
Perhaps because of his personal attachment to the countryside, this concern manifests itself in particularly interesting
ways. Irrigation, flood control, and land reclamation projects
had long been a concern of the *signori* of Ferrara. Indeed,
such activities would have been less urgent if the city had
developed as a mercantile and industrial center. Instead,
Ferrara went in the direction of continued feudal land-
holding patterns, supported an expensive monarchy and
a nobility of birth and wealth heavily dependent for its
continued prosperity on revenues from land rents and agricultural revenues. Crops and livestock had to be protected,
boundaries and rights of way clearly established, new
acreage had to be brought under cultivation. This meant
the extensive use of agrarian labor, not just for farming,
but also for digging drainage ditches, filling in marshland,
building and maintaining dikes and levees, transporting
materials and establishing new settlements, cutting brush,

---

[13] *DF,* 33: "Lo illustre principe messer Borso . . . intrò in Ferrara
cum splendida et magnifica comitiva . . . chiamante tuto il populo: viva,
viva lo illustre signore messer Borso, signore liberale; e così, cum
voluntade del populo di Ferrara, fu facto Signore. . . ." *Liberalità* was,
of course, one of the princely virtues.

[14] *ASM, ASE,* Cancelleria, Casa e Stato, xxv, no. 21.

fencing out predators, and the like. It was not uncommon in the fifteenth century for the great landowners, like the Bevilacqua and Bendedei families, to undertake such projects on their own. Mario Zucchini, in his recent and useful book *L'Agricultura Ferrarese attraverso i secoli,* has discovered some notable examples.[15]

According to communal records, Leonello was the first to import professional hydraulic engineers to deal with the numerous problems involved in managing the Po and its tributaries. A decree dated 6 February 1442 summons the engineer Antonio Marin from Grenoble for this purpose.[16] There are other hints of Leonello's interest in this area. But under Borso, it took on much greater importance. Zucchini points out that one of Borso's heraldic symbols was the *paraduro,* which is actually a kind of stockade fence used in flood control. Considerable drainage and reclamation work was done during Borso's reign, often on lands granted by him as fiefs to members of his court such as the *referendarius* Ludovico Casella, the humanist professor Baptista Guarini, the counsellor and cameral official Prisciano Prisciani.[17] River diversion projects also occupied his attention,

[15] (Rome, 1967), 79, 83. Zucchini points out that the major works of territorial defense and land reclamation are unknown for the period before Borso: "Ed è proprio durante il dominio di Borso che si hanno notizie e riferimenti" (p. 85). See also the same author's articles "Gli Statuti e l'agricoltura ferrarese," *Rivista di storia dell'Agricoltura,* i:1 (1961); "Statuta Communis Ferrariae ad Offitium Argerum," *ibid.,* ii:2 (1962); "Pomposa nella storia dell'agricoltura ferrarese," *ibid.,* iii:3 (1963), which I have not been able to consult.

[16] *L'Agricoltura ferrarese,* 84, Zucchini cites a decree of Leonello's dated February 6 ,1442.

[17] Cf. Zucchini, *L'Agricultura ferrarese,* 85-6. For Borso's confirmation of old grants or conferring of new feudal titles to lands in the Ferrarese, see the remarkable series of Catastri delle Investiture in *ASM, ASE,* Camera. There is a five-volume manuscript index to this immense collection of volumes in which were recorded transactions involving grants of land by feud, "Livello," and other contractual arrangements. The series

sometimes with enduring results. Such projects were also undertaken frequently by Borso on the vast private lands of the Estensi. It should be noted that massive efforts such as these were directed invariably toward the lands of the great feudal lords or other courtiers of substantial wealth. If lesser landowners or agrarian workers benefited from them, that was entirely coincidental. The idealized images of rural handicraft visible in the Schifanoia frescoes recall the miniatures of similar scenes in Flemish books of hours. They evoke the pastoral simplicity, but not the servile misery, of

covers the entire central period of Ferrarese history under the Estensi. The *registri* are arranged in chronological order. Within each volume, there is an index, arranged alphabetically by recipients of grants. Often a *registro* will also include a table of contents, also usually in alphabetical order. Without studying these systematically (which should be done, and would yield rich rewards for the economic, agrarian, and perhaps demographic history of Ferrara), I have gone through the major portion of the collection dealing with the *Quattrocento* and can offer the following tentative generalizations: As one might expect, the vast majority of the donations appear to go to the great noble families of the Ferrarese *contado,* whose claims stretch back over centuries. Names like Costabili, Negrisola, Trotti, and others from the old nobility are common. It is extremely rare for an artist or man of letters to have his services acknowledged by a grant of land, especially a big one, by any of the Este *signori,* unless the recipient also happens to come from an important family in the local gentry, such as the Boiardi or the Ariosti or the Prisciani. However, there are occasional references of grants to such figures as Michele Savonarola, Cosimo Tura, Francesco Ariosto. See for the latter Vol. FG, f. 171, grant of lands and houses dated February 20, 1470; Vol. FG, f. 140, for Tura; *ibid.,* f. 85 records M. Savonarola's release from payment of feudal dues on certain properties (August 16, 1460). For Pellegrino Prisciani, see Vol. FG, f. 318; for Feltrino Boiardo, Vol. BC, f. 61 v°. But such rewards to what might be called men of culture were few and far between. They were rarely if ever conferred on men of less than the highest or most valued talents, and as often as not may in any case be interpreted as rewards for services other than artistic and literary ones, especially if the recipients are Ferrarese noblemen or diplomats, and not merely men of letters.

the Renaissance laborer. In fact, there is no basis for even suspecting that the life of the agrarian laborer in the Ferrarese changed fundamentally during the three centuries of Este rule.

Of course, the extent of Borso's personal involvement in the management or supervision of these kinds of initiatives is unknown, but there is no reason to believe that it was extensive. He had a large, growing, increasingly populous and complex state to rule, and a very full round of amusements and pleasures to pursue. Accordingly, to reconcile and moderate some of these demands upon his time, he became somewhat more of an administrative innovator than his predecessors. Not the least of his abilities was that of overseeing and staffing a bureaucracy of able, intelligent, and devoted people, an administration that was fully capable of managing even the most sensitive tasks of government on a day-to-day basis.

Among the first and most important steps taken by Borso and directed at rationalizing and expediting the process of signorial government was a major revision of the statutes of 1287. These had been revised previously, first in 1320, then under the regency in 1394, and again in 1420. All of the previous redactions were executed by one or two men (usually notaries) appointed for the purpose, who were called "statutarii." Borso, revealing his politically and bureaucratically sound instinct for broadening representation, appointed an entire committee of eight *statutarii,* whose work would in turn be passed upon by two highly accountable experts, jurisconsults serving as a committee of review. These were called "revisori" and "approvatori." Borso's committee included ordinary guildsmen, as well as a notary, a lawyer, and three "pettifoggers." The rewritten statutes which they drew up were adopted, appeared in a printed edition in 1476, and continued in force until the monumental revision of 1534, which in turn formed the basis of all successive editions up to the end of the sixteenth century.[18]

The criminal law, comprising book three of the code, continued most of the harsh provisions of the Obizzan statutes. Borso prided himself on his evenhanded approach to justice, though by more recent standards he appears to have fully shared the vindictive and retributive notions enshrined in the law codes of all Italian cities of his time. In one of the Schifanoia frescoes, Borso appears beneath an arch on which is inscribed in Roman letters the single word "Iusticia." In his own lifetime, Borso had a statue of himself erected by the commune in front of the Palazzo della Ragione. The statue presented him enthroned, presumably dispensing justice, and bore an inscription by the court poet Tito Vespasiano Strozzi, stressing Borso's love of justice.[19]

Law, as a recent observer remarks, "is supposed to be a codification of those lasting human values that a people agree upon."[20] Thus, when historians make statements about Ferrarese law such as that "punishments are out of proportion to the crimes," they are making an anachronistic and somewhat misleading assessment of a past society, from the point of view of their own personal values and standards.[21] There is nothing particularly illegitimate about that

[18] See W. Montorsi, *Statuti Ferrariae,* anno *MCCLXXXVII* (Ferrara, 1955) cxxxviii-cxxxix; also Pardi, *Borso d'Este,* xv, 25-29.

[19] The statue was later moved to the site where a late copy now stands, in front of the palace, opposite to the façade of the cathedral. See R. Albrecht, *Tito Vespasiano Strozzi, Ein Beitrag zur Geschichte des Humanismus in Ferrara* (Leipzig, 1891). The inscription reads:

Hanc tibi viventi Ferrara grata columnam
Ob merita in patriam princeps iustissime Borsi
Dedicat Estensi qui dux a sanguine primus
Excipis imperium et placida regis omnia pace.

Here, too, there is the evident emphasis on justice and peace.

[20] C. A. Reich, *The Greening of America* (New York, 1970), 117.

[21] For example, see Pardi, *Borso d'Este,* xv, 28.

—as long as one is aware that that is what one is doing— but it should be clear that such evaluations lead us astray from an understanding of those "lasting human values." In Ferrara, what was valued was a peaceful, honest, and obedient life, pursued according to the tenets of traditional Christian morality and ethics. Minor deviations from this norm often involved a fine. More serious infractions—and these were many and varied—were discouraged, but never prevented, by confiscations, banishments, mutilation, a whole spectrum of methods of execution, and some or all of these sanctions used in concert. Under the law, thieves and murderers were hanged or, like rapists, decapitated; counterfeiters were burned, sodomists hanged and then burned, traitors hanged and then quartered. Instruments of torture were reserved for crimes of a special order, such as the murder of a priest, incest, or the acts of some particularly vicious or notorious criminal, and were used prior to execution. Punishment was supposed to serve an exemplary and deterrent, as well as perhaps an entertainment, function and so was generally carried out in the public square, with exceptions for great dignitaries whose humiliation would be a stain on nobility in general. It was that, and only that, that an aristocratic evildoer was spared. In this sense, justice may be said to have been impartial, though in every other respect it naturally favored the rich, who could hire lawyers, suborn public officials, and draw upon their power and prestige in other, more subtle ways.[22]

All the evidence suggests that Borso was a firm believer in a strict application of the criminal law as an instrument

[22] There is no adequate study of the *gentil'uomo* as a criminal, except of course in relation to such broader social issues as magnate disorders viewed as an expression of a feudal ethos constituting a problem in urban development. Even here, serious work has often been limited to Florence in the period of the Ordinances of Justice (1282). The question deserves further study.

of social and political control. This is of course particularly evident in cases of treason or *lèse-majesté,* as I have shown.[23] At the same time, it should be noted that the *signore* was not usually directly involved in the administration of justice.[24] For this, he had an entire administrative system under the *podestà,* an office which he in effect controlled, but which it was not in his interest to appear to control too completely. For in the rare cases of popular dissatisfaction with a *podestà* or one of his subordinates, the *signore* was insulated from blame, and could simply remove the official in question and appoint somebody else. If, on the other hand, such officials were regarded as just, the *signore* got much of the credit.[25]

This judicial machinery had survived nearly two centuries by the time Borso inherited it, and there appears to be nothing extraordinary about Ferrara's version of the judicial system under a *podestà.* Such administrative rationalizations and refinements as Borso was able to make in the governmental structure of Ferrara occurred rather in the more informal and personal area of his own administrative staff. Here, of course, there were no public expectations to be met or rigid traditions to be respected. Yet even here Borso cannot be said to have undertaken a major revision

[23] See my "Crime and Punishment," pp. 122-25.

[24] There are very rare exceptional cases in which the *signore* intervenes personally, and this almost invariably constitutes a violation of normal juridical procedures. However, the provocations under which such acts occur are usually so great, or their rationalizations so convincing, that no popular dissatisfaction results. See, e.g., the case described in "Crime and Punishment," in which Ercole personally orders the execution of a craftsman who murdered his partner over some trivial quarrel.

[25] The discussion of Tommaso da Tortona above, p. 58; also Ercole's actions in replacing unpopular *Giudici dei Savi,* pp. 215-17, and the discussion of the hated *podestà* Zampante in "Toward a Reinterpretation," 273-74. Cf. A. Piromalli, *La Cultura a Ferrara al tempo di Ludovico Ariosto, Biblioteca di Cultura* XLV (Florence, 1953), 135-55.

of the structure of the Estense bureaucracy. The *cancelleria* and the *camera* continued to administer princely diplomacy and finance, respectively. What Borso did was to alter the relationships between himself and various officials. Increasingly, court notaries and chancellors became mere functionaries, civil service bureaucrats who executed commands from above. Instead of drawing his personal staff of advisers and confidential agents from this tier of the administration, Borso assembled a kind of "kitchen cabinet," comprised of trusted personal friends, most of whom were not trained in the law. These men became the ranking bureaucrats of the Este administration. They had easy access to the prince, they claimed executive powers over the rest of the staff, they assisted in the formation as well as the implementation of policy, and they got the big territorial grants.[26] The title "ducal secretary" comes to carry a great deal more weight than many more sonorous and traditional titles around the court. This remained true from Borso's reign on through the sixteenth century, and it serves to explain why the men who bore this title were already important figures before they acquired it.

Another of Borso's administrative innovations was the Consiglio di Giustizia, instituted in 1453. It will be recalled that, according to the researches of Filippo Valenti, the Estensi had occasionally and from time to time attempted to constitute some sort of consultative council, to act in an advisory and legislative capacity, and that this was called the *consilium domini marchionis*.[27] Its main period of strength was during the regency of Niccolò III, and in the *Quattrocento* there are only rare and sporadic traces of it,

[26] See, for example, the grants to the Costabili, in *ASM, ASE,* Camera, Catastri del Investiture, Vol. CD, ff. 141 v°, 172 v° 179, 258; Vol. EF, f. 106, 117, 299; Vol. FG, f. 142; Vol. KL, f. 57 v°, 147; Vol. BC, f. 92, 126, 177; etc.

[27] See Valenti, "Consigli di governo," 20-24.

and these are limited to very precise and narrow judicial matters. The Consiglio di Giustizia, as its name implies, was constituted to deal with a more specific area of signorial affairs. Not surprisingly, it was in effect the formalization of a group of curial officials which was already in existence, and had in fact a long and important history. The court had from the beginning included some officials called judges, who concerned themselves with the legal problems of the princes themselves, and rendered advice on other matters. They may—though this is not clear—have actually sat as judges in matters directly involving the Estensi. Occasionally, one of these officials appears to have been appointed as *vicarius domini marchionis,* but without the plenipotentiary role this title involved under other regimes. According to Valenti, it was Borso's elevation to the title of Duke that prompted the formation of the new council, as a mark of dignity, and in imitation of the procedure followed by the Visconti when they became dukes. This view is perfectly correct. Not only does the decree constituting the council openly state that this is being done "curie nostre ad dignitatem," but it fits the pattern of faithful imitation of Milanese administrative techniques which should by now have become evident to anyone familiar with the work of Caterina Santoro.[28]

As a duke, now recognized as sovereign by imperial decree and papal appointment as well as popular election under the laws of Ferrara, Borso enjoyed more complete authority than that of his predecessors, and his new magistracy, the Consiglio di Giustizia, formalized the new

[28] See esp. *Gli Uffici del Dominio Sforzesco* (Milan, 1953), pp. xv-xxxi, which considers the administrative system of the Sforza. It is striking how closely the structure of the Sforza regime, both in Milan and in the provinces, mirrors that of the Estensi. Indeed, the differences seem negligible, although further and deeper study of Ferrarese administrative institutions could reveal more profound differences. See Appendix I, below.

powers. It served as a court of original jurisdiction for cases referred to it by the Prince, as a court of appeal from all lower courts, and as such, as a supreme court from which there was no further judicial appeal. It was also, perhaps mainly, to be an advisory body to the duke. Whether the *consiglio* actually fulfilled all of these statutory obligations will almost certainly never be known, for all of its records down to 1598 are lost. But there is no doubt that this was another step in the gradual piecemeal bureaucratization of the ducal household under Borso (a tendency continued by his successors).

A further step in the formalization of the ducal administration occurred around 1463, when the first mention of the *Consiglio Segreto* appears. This, too, is a leaf from the Visconti book. In the context of Ferrara, the word *segreto* is best understood as "confidential" or "private," for there was nothing secret about it in our sense of the word. Most of the *consiglieri segreti* were learned in the law. They do not appear to have functioned primarily as a corporate body, but rather as a mutable group of individual problem-solvers who exercised the highest level staff duties between the Duke and the administrative offices of the court.[29]

Thus, Borso was the nucleus around which there revolved a number of different particles. There were the private secretaries, often able and learned men, who handled a great deal of the diplomatic correspondence, offered political advice and judgment, and provided much of the intellectual tone of the court. Then there were the secret counsellors (usually three), who proferred specialized legal advice. At another remove were the highest officials of the *cancelleria* and the *camera,* with their staffs of scribes and notaries. Generally present, though less active professionally were the courtiers in the narrow sense—men who were present for

---

[29] See Valenti, "Consigli di governo," 29-33; but cf. also n. 5 to Appendix I, below.

the purpose of paying court or "courtesy." All of these are more fully described in Appendix I. They might be there in token of feudal duty or service, as ambassadors to or diplomatic agents of the Duke, as official petitioners or favor-seekers either on their own account or as representatives of a particular town or region.

In addition, there were personal favorites of the Duke, companions-in-arms, hunters, heralds and musicians, and a wide variety of specialized as well as general servants, petty functionaries, and retainers.[30] Finally there were Borso's relatives, each of whom had his or her own entourage, though of course on a much smaller scale. Clearly the servicing, provisioning, staffing, transporting, housing, and maintaining of the court constituted Ferrara's biggest and most important industry. It is easy to understand why a rather elaborate managerial structure had to be created to control the process.

An establishment as large and multifaceted as the Este court depended not only on a rationally organized system of control. It also required real competence from its officials. There was room for mediocre talents in various areas, and the court unquestionably had its share, but there were many other positions at home and abroad that required men who could handle very exacting responsibilities. This meant that the relatively small pool of talent available within the ranks of the traditionally powerful noble families was inadequate both in quantity and quality. The administrative system was therefore open to ordinary citizens, some of whom shaped extremely distinguished careers at court. The entire configuration is structurally and functionally anal-

[30] For the differentiation of social and occupational roles within the Este court, see the antiquarian studies of G. Campori cited above (p. 121), and also L. A. Gandini, "Usi e costumanze alla corte di Ferrara," *passim;* occasionally useful in this respect is K. Chledowski, *Dwor w Ferrarze* (Łwów, 1907) [German tr. *Der Hof von Ferrara* (Berlin, 1913)].

ogous to the emergence of a *noblesse de robe* in sixteenth-century France. The most conspicuous example of this tendency under Borso—his *referendarius,* Ludovico Casella —was one of the few men of the court for whom we have extensive records.

Casella was born in the Polesine di Rovigo, and spent the major part of his life at the courts, first of Leonello and then of Borso d'Este. Though not strictly speaking a humanist— he produced no works of literature or scholarship—he was a man who combined with his administrative duties a keen and enlightened concern for cultural and intellectual matters. Rather early in his career he appears in Decembrio's *De Politia Litteraria,* as one of the cultivated men of affairs at the court of Leonello. By the time Borso came to power, he had had many opportunities to see this able and learned young secretary in action, and decided to make him his *referendarius* or, first secretary of the chancellery. In this post, Casella operated as a virtual prime minister, and Borso came to regard him as practically an *alter ego* in the execution of day-to-day affairs of state.[31] Their correspondence reveals a remarkable communality of understanding and respect.[32] The common citizen and the noble duke came in time to be close personal friends. Casella on at least one occasion gave a dinner in his house attended by Galeazzo

[31] See esp. *ASM, ASE,* Cancelleria, Carteggio di Referendari, Consiglieri, Cancellieri e Segretari, Busta 1, 2A. In diverse ways the letters preserved here reveal Casella's importance as the top administrator in Borso's government. I intend to deal with these sources more specifically in a future study.

[32] *ASM, ASE,* Cancelleria, Carteggio di Referendari, etc., Busta 1, see for example letter of September 5, 1462, which, in the most familiar terms, colloquially and personally, conveys general news of the court, describing recent visitors, events at court, the condition of the horses, etc. It is interesting to note that in writing to Borso Casella uses the vernacular, while in addressing his colleagues in the chancellery, he almost always writes in Latin.

Maria Sforza, Ludovico Gonzaga and his son, and Borso. The diarist comments that it was a worthy meal (*degno pasto*).[33] Though it was not common for citizens to entertain dukes, this is only one of a number of instances when it occurs in Ferrara.[34] Invariably, the hosts are men of wealth, who have been greatly enriched by virtue of loyal service to the house of Este.

Casella, however, was more than a successful and able opportunist, though he rose from the level of a notary to the second highest office in Ferrara. The range and depth of his interests and sympathies won him the respect and admiration of all elements of the population. No one begrudged him the extensive benefactions he received from Borso, for he was generous in his treatment of others. Apart from his constant technical services to Borso, he provided the one continuing and reliable link between the Duke and humanists such as Ludovico Carbone, Michele Savonarola, Tito Strozzi, Pellegrino Prisciani, and others. In this area, as in the rest, Borso trusted Casella's judgment completely. As a result, it becomes as difficult to distinguish between self-serving flattery and genuine admiration of Casella during his own lifetime as it is in the case of a princely Maecenas. He was constantly receiving commendatory epi-

[33] *DF,* 44.

[34] This occurs more frequently under Ercole. The diarists tend to take notice of such events, which suggests that they were not common. However, there is evidence that several ordinary citizens acquired enormous wealth in Ferrara, and not only through service to the Estensi. During Borso's time, the richest man in Ferrara was reputed to be Bartolommeo Pendaglia, a nobleman who made his fortune in commerce. Under Ercole, Filippo Cestarelli and Giannone Pasqualetti also acquired great wealth through commerce, and the former also achieved an important position at the court. See *DF,* 276, n. 7; also the list in Caleffini's chronicle, cited in Appendix I, note 3. Such evidence as there is suggests that the acquisition of great wealth opened the doors of the highest courtly society to any citizen of Ferrara.

grams, letters of fulsome praise, and other testimonies of the undying affection of people who may well have wanted something.[35]

Events after Casella's death in 1469 enable us to make a surer judgment. In the first place he was given a state funeral on a scale comparable only to those of the Este dukes themselves. For the official period of mourning, all activity stopped in Ferrara by ducal decree—classes in the university were suspended, shops closed, artisans prohibited from working, the law-courts recessed, "so that *in its entirety* [*generaliter*] all the *popolo* should go to accompany the body of Ludovico to [the Church of] San Domenico of Ferrara, for even his ducal Lordship would be there." A solemn procession then accompanied Ludovico from his house to the church, where his body was placed on a large tribunal in the central nave. Borso led the procession, weeping. He was accompanied by the Venetian *visdomino,* his brother Sigismondo d'Este, Niccolò di Leonello d'Este, Alberto d'Este, and several ranking courtiers. This group was followed by the rectors of the university, and then the people of Ferrara, "grandi e piccoli," including an enormous contingent of clergy. Each of the brothers Este and the accompanying grandees held one of Ludovico's relatives by the hand and all were dressed in mourning. Having completed their lugubrious mission, the company stood in silence for over an hour, while Ludovico Carbone delivered a eulogy of his good friend. The diarist pays the rarest kind of tribute:

[35] Almost all of the letters addressed to Casella that are listed in Kristeller's *Iter* that I have seen may be interpreted in this way. But see also the grossly adulatory and flattering poems addressed to Casella by such important humanists as Carbone and Guarino. A selection may be sampled in a MS. of the Biblioteca Marciana in Venice (MS. Marc. Lat xii, 137 [4451]), f. 35 v°, 38; also Marc. Lat. xii, 135 (4100), f. 36, where Baptista Guarini actually offers his services, saying, "Tibi magna ferrem, si modo possem."

The death of this man strongly grieved the entire
popolo, because he was greatly liked by every man for
being a good speaker, and for his handsome appearance: he had a good word for everyone and nobody
ever went away from him discontented. He was indifferent to worldly goods and display. He was very
learned in poetry, and in matters of state he knew all
that it is possible to know. He was a refuge for the
poor; the duke loved him so much that that is why he
personally accompanied the body, for the House of
Este never before went with the body of any subject;
and the more so as Ludovico was not a man of gentle
birth. . . . I cannot describe the grief of the *Signore,*
because he loved him more than any brother.[36]

Casella's will gives some reflection of his character. Borso
himself was named as executor. The entire estate of the
referendarius was bequeathed to his widow for her lifetime.
Upon her death, all of it was to be turned over to the
hospital of Santa Anna.[37]

Two fitting memorials to this remarkable figure survive.
One is the presentation copy of Ludovico Carbone's funeral

----

[36] See *DF,* 59-60: "La morte di questui dolse forte a tuto il popolo,
perchè lui era sumamente da ogni homo amato per essere bello par'latore,
bello de aspetto: dava ad ogni homo buone parole et mai malcontento
alcuno da lui non se partiva; non curava de roba nè de pompe. Costui in
poesia doctissimo, in facti de Stato ne sapea quello che fusse possibile a
sapere; costui refugio de poveri homini; costui fu amato somamente del
prefacto duca, et per essere andato lui in persona al corpo se pol presu-
mere, perchè la Casa da Este ad alcuno suo subdito 'mai non andò a il
corpo; et tanto più che dicto Ludovico non era gentilhomo. . . . La
dolgia che ne have il prefacto Signore non te dico, perchè lo amava più
che fratello che lho havesse.

[37] Earlier legislation had required that a small donation (at least five
scudi) from every estate of a deceased Ferrarese citizen be turned over
to the Ospedale di Sta. Anna (see *ASCA,* Deliberazioni del Maestrato,
L, ff. 52-54.

oration, dedicated to Ercole d'Este. It is the humanist's own translation, and with its handsome illuminations is one of the modest glories of the Biblioteca Estense.[38] The other is another presentation manuscript of a funeral oration, by Baptista Guarini. The original is in Latin, and it is accompanied by an Italian translation, probably by the author. This manuscript, too, is decorated with an illuminated frontispiece, including a miniature of Casella lying in state.[39] The view that Renaissance despotisms were closed aristocratic societies that systematically excluded and looked down upon all men of diverse origins must somehow explain away these kinds of evidence if it is to survive. I do not believe that it can do the former, or that it should do the latter.[40]

Among other things, Ludovico Casella's funeral reveals the humanity of Borso d'Este. It demonstrates, further, that even when Borso was at his most human, even when he was reacting with grief to the death of an intimate, he did things on a very grand scale. This has some bearing, I think, upon the significance of Borso's well-known vanity. Most impor-

[38] *BEM,* MS. Alpha P 6, 6 (Ital. 96), *Orazione funebre per lo magnifico referendario Lodovico Casella.* For this MS. see Fava, 81; Fava and Salmi, no. 66. Another copy is reported in the Biblioteca Concordiana in Rovigo, MS. 519.

[39] *BEM,* MS. Alpha J 9, 43 (Lat. 1269), *Baptistae Guarini in clarissimum et amplissimum virum Ludovicum Casellium Gloriossissimi Ducis Borsii Referendarium Funebris Oratio.* I shall discuss these MSS. further in the future article on Casella.

[40] I am suggesting that Ferrara under the Este dynasty offered opportunities for new men which were not unlike those available to citizens of new or increased wealth in Florence. For evidence, see Caleffini's list of new "zentilhomini," cited in Appendix I, n. 3. Indeed in some ways Herculean and Borsian Ferrara may have been a world more open to social and (in its limited way) political advancement than Medicean Florence. For the subject of *novi homines,* see the articles by M. Becker, "An Essay on the 'Novi Cives' and Florentine Politics, 1343-1382," *Medieval Studies,* xxiv (1962), 35-82; and *idem,* "Florentine 'Libertas', Political Independence and 'Novi Cives', 1372-1378," *Traditio,* xviii (1962), 393-407.

tant, of course, is that it illustrates the social openness of the Ferrarese high administration, a point which nonetheless requires further investigation. Indeed, the question of the real and intended functions of Borso's manifest gift of showmanship is central to an understanding of his style and his values as a despot.

In the long course of Borso's lordship over Ferrara, two events stand out above all others. These are Borso's investiture as Duke of Modena and Reggio, near the beginning of his reign, and his investiture as Duke of Ferrara, near the end. On the surface, both of these events would appear to possess purely symbolic significance. We are inclined to take such titles rather lightly, knowing that they were bought with hard cash, that they were the product of political calculation and self-serving diplomacy on the part of both buyer and seller, and that sonorous titles can provide considerable gratification to certain types of ego. But there is much more to it than that.

While it is true that the rights and privileges of a duke under the Holy Roman Empire were no longer in the fifteenth century what they had been in the distant past, the title itself constituted a far from negligible political asset. Domestically, it unquestionably increased Borso's prestige, for it projected an objective index of his stature in the community of European princes. It also placed an additional *imprimatur* on his legitimacy, a fact that meant much for the second consecutive bastard *signore* to come to power in the presence of legitimate heirs. By the same token it catapulted him into a new relationship with the other Italian rulers.[41] He was now, apparently if not really, the virtual equal of the Duke of Milan, and the superior of the *Marchesi* of Mantua and Urbino as well as the myriad princelings of

[41] The implications of this change are explored by E. G. Gardner, *Dukes and Poets*, 70-75, and by G. Pardi, *Borso d'Este*, pt. v ("La politica estera").

the Romagna. There is no doubt that Borso wanted to use his new status as a diplomatic counter in extending his territories. Indeed, a large part of his diplomacy appears to have been directed toward this goal—generally without exposure to serious military risks—which nonetheless eluded him. In general, it appears that he took a conservative and prudential stance when it came to military action, while seeking aggrandizement in less tangible, but apparently equally satisfying, ways.

His investiture in the duchy of Modena by Frederick III in 1452 is a case in point. As the correspondence of Aeneas Sylvius reveals, Borso made extensive efforts to arrange this event well in advance of the Emperor's arrival, though it took some hard bargaining at the last minute actually to get the title.[42] But in this, Borso had the upper hand, for the Emperor had come as a guest to his court, along with an enormous company of German knights. Borso received them with great pomp, lodging the entire company at his expense, loading the Emperor down with all kinds of presents, and even arranging for a formal welcoming oration by the humanist physician Girolamo da Castello, and a presentation of a glorious manuscript by Menghius Blanchinus (Fig. 6), the commentary on Sacrobosco's *De Sphaera.*[43]

[42] *Der Briefwechsel des Eneas Sylvius Piccolomini*, III, 59-60, is the letter from Aeneas to Giacomo Tolomei announcing the forthcoming imperial journey through Italy and the passage through Ferrara.

[43] The proceedings are described in detail in *DF*, 34-36. Sabbadini, *Vita di Guarino Veronese*, 161, also mentions a Latin poem prepared for the occasion by Janus Pannonius, who studied at Ferrara in this period (see also Bertoni, *Guarino da Verona*, 70-71, *et al*). The astrological tables of Blanchinus, subsequently published at Venice in 1495 and again in 1526, survive in the original presentation copy in *BAF*, Ms. Cl. I, 147: *Federico iii Romanorum Imperatori SEP Augusto. Astrologiae Tabulas Dicat Ioannes Blanchinius Ferrariensis I. V. D. Borsiique Estensis Ducis Primi Procurator Generalis ac Pro Gratissimo Optatissimoque munere concedit idem imperator eum agnatosque suos aquile Caesareae insignibus nobilitari.* The minia-

After a stay of ten days, the Emperor and his party moved on toward Rome, but Borso had made his mark. In May he came to Ferrara again on his northward journey. By this time Borso's influence with Frederick had grown to the point where he was not only asked to intercede with him on behalf of the Florentines, the Venetians, and the Milanese, in relation to a diplomatic problem, but was even able to induce him to attend the wedding of his *fattore generale,* Bartolomeo Pendaglia (Fig. 7), a wealthy merchant who was marrying a daughter of one of the Costabili. After spending a week in the city, Frederick invested Borso with the symbols of his new office in a great public ceremony, which culminated a period of lavish festivities. As Borso led his retinue out to the great tribunal that had been built for the purpose in the piazza, the populace burst out into cries of "Duca, duca." Dismounting, he kneeled before the Emperor, who was dressed in robes and jewels with an estimated value of 150,000 ducats (a figure which, like all numbers in the chronicles, must be taken *cum grano salis*). After the speeches Borso received the symbols of his new office, and the Emperor then proceeded to confer knighthood on fourteen of Borso's allies and associates.[44]

The first ducal investiture, then, strengthened Borso's hand both politically and diplomatically in Ferrara, throughout the rest of his territories, and abroad. It gave a stamp of approval to him after the first two years of his reign, years during which he had advanced or initiated construction on new public works such as the *campanile* and new

ture on the frontispiece portrays the author presenting the work to the Emperor, with Borso and courtiers watching.

[44] See A. Lazzari, "Borso d'Este, Il Primo duca di Ferrara" (Ferrara, 1945), which develops this theme fully. The heightened importance of Borso's new role emerges clearly in the tone of such works as Flavio Biondo's *Borsius, sive de militia et iurisprudentia,* a work that survives in several MSS, but has been well edited by B. Nogara, ed., *Scritti inediti e rari di Flavio Biondo* (Rome, 1927; Studi e Testi XLVIII), 130-44.

walls and fortifications, and had arranged that one-half of the expenses of the university should be drawn from his private revenues. Thus he entered upon the central period of his rule with a degree of prestige, authority, and popular support probably never enjoyed by any previous Este prince. Under such conditions, with a populace traditionally inclined toward support of the ruling house, committed almost reflexively to hierarchical concepts of social structure, and adequately policed, it would have required truly flagrant abuses of his power for Borso to have been seriously challenged from within. And indeed, as we have seen, Borso—despite some appearances—used power judiciously. His efforts at modernization extended beyond bricks and mortar to the administrative and judicial systems, to education, land reclamation, and the revitalization of religious institutions. Those aspects of his personality that make him appear a trifler to modern eyes—love of magnificent dress, a passion for the hunt—had the opposite effect on his contemporaries, who could be impressed and intimidated by display, and who saw in Borso's prowess at killing animals evidence of his bravery, vigor, and peacefulness toward men.

In 1470, then, after two decades of peace and relative prosperity, the Duke, now in his fifty-seventh year, could look back with some satisfaction on his life. He had enjoyed himself, aggrandized and fortified his city, kept the faith, outlived such grand figures as Pius II and Cosimo de' Medici, held Milanese and Venetians at bay, crushed an aristocratic plot masterminded by outside agitators, and held on to his health, vigor, and good looks. Unlike many princes, he could continue as he had always done to walk in the streets of his capital, talking to the people, hearing special pleas, and being seen in the act of helping the poor. But in the *Quattrocento,* fifty-seven was a ripe old age, and the Duke was well aware that there were two rival claimants for succession, both of whom were busy drumming up support.

For Borso, the choice between half-brother and nephew cannot have been an easy one. In June of 1470, on Pentecost, when Borso reformed his *Consiglio Segreto,* both Ercole and Niccolò di Leonello were appointed to it, though Ercole also retained his position as governor of Modena.[45]

The following January, Borso made a mistake which, had it been one of a series of such miscalculations, would have cost him dearly. As it was, it created only transitory uneasiness, and gives us a nice example of how extreme an Este prince's folly had to be to cause him real trouble. Borso decided that he should have a mountain, and gave the order that it be built, using wagons, ships, and carts to haul the earth. Forced labor was required of all the peasants. It is clear that a project of some evident use, no matter how disagreeable, would have been accepted by the people. But this seemed a futile aberration, and they complained bitterly. Not to have done so would hardly have been human. A mountain in January! The anonymous diarist reports:

> On account of this thing all the *popolo* suffered greatly, because it was of no use whatsoever, and the *contadini* could not work their lands by reason of this labor; and he had this mountain made where it is called Monte Santo; and the *popolo* complained about it greatly.[46]

[45] The early public careers of Ercole and Niccolò di Leonello may be followed through entries in *DF.* See pp. 304, 307. Also A. Capelli, "Niccolò di Leonello d'Este," *AM,* v (1870), 413-38, which contains biographical notices. On the reorganization of the *consiglio segreto,* see *DF,* 64.

[46] *DF,* 66: "[MCCCCLXXI, de Zenaro, lo illustrissimo duca Borso cominciò dare principio a fare una montagna de terra per forza de carri, navi et brozi et de opere manuali, che era una grande facenda;] del che tuto il populo se ne redoleva molto, perchè non era utile alcuno et li contadini non poteano lavorare le possessione per cagione de dicto lavoriero; et facea fare questa montagna dove se chiama Monte Sancto; et di questo il populo mor'morava molto." For the later history of the Monte Santo see the suggestion of F. Gibbons, "Ferrarese Tapestries of Metamorphosis," *Art Bulletin,* xlviii (1966), 409-11.

The whole thing savors of lunacy, unless one bears in mind
the generally manipulative and exploitative attitude toward
nature revealed in the works of Renaissance engineers, especially in regions like the Ferrarese, where human inhabitants had to overcome many serious obstacles. Accordingly,
it was not the work but the pointlessness of the work that
aroused indignation. A new fashion in landscape design, or
the mere fact that the land was flat may have been enough
to justify Borso's decision in his own view, but it clearly
did not suffice for anyone else.

Fortunately, the adverse effects of this bizarre episode
were soon outweighed by a stunning success. Borso was
invited to Rome, to receive the papal investiture as Duke
of Ferrara. This event, the apex of his career, aroused the
same fervent enthusiasm that his investiture as Duke of
Modena had produced eighteen years earlier. The best
account of Borso's journey, the splendid festivities in Rome,
and his tumultuous welcome back to Ferrara is preserved
in a Vatican manuscript written by Francesco degli Ariosti,
called Peregrino. It contains one work describing Borso's
trip to Rome, and another tracing the history of the duchy
(since 1452). A vernacular translation follows the original
Latin, and the entire work, written in 1471, is accompanied
by an autographed letter of transmittal by the author to
Ercole d'Este, dated January, 1479, from Ficarolo, where he
was serving as Captain.[47]

Borso had been trying to obtain this title for a long time,
but had met with real difficulties. Pius II had turned him
down, possibly in retaliation for Borso's minimal support
of the projected crusade against the Turks. But in Paul II,
Borso found a man more to his own taste. The new pope

[47] *BAV,* Chigiana MS. J, vii, 261. The text has been published and
adequately studied by E. Celani, "La venuta di Borso d'Este in Roma,
1471," *Archivio della Società Romana di Storia Patria,* xiii (1890), 361-
450.

was a Venetian, who was well aware of the danger Venice posed to the states of the Church. This in itself may have prompted his decision to strengthen Borso's hand. But in addition to that, as Celani has said, Paul "recognized in Borso a prince worthy of the Church." [48] After all, Borso's religious benefactions had been magnanimous, he had never betrayed the Pope, and there was even a kind of personal affinity between the two men—for Paul, who had been modest, charitable, and altogether unassuming as a Venetian cardinal, turned out, in one of those astonishing reversals of character that elevation to high office sometimes produces, to be a profligate, extravagant, and ostentatious pope.[49] With his love of display and his arbitrary and despotic behavior, it is almost as though he was trying to be a *signore* of the type of Borso d'Este, without having been schooled in the implicit restraints that successful secular princes well understood.[50]

[48] *Ibid.,* 372.

[49] *Ibid.,* 361.

[50] It is a theme of the present work and of some other recent studies of Renaissance despotism that successful *signori* generally manifest an implicit understanding of the limits of their power. In general it can be said that when *signori* forgot the lessons of experience, and overstepped the traditional restraints imposed by communal privilege, statutes, etc., they came to grief. When they remembered them, and operated within the traditional limits of dynastic sovereignty, they often managed to retain significant bases of support, and in the absence of severe economic or external political crises managed to maintain a stable *stato.* For an interesting recent study of this phenomenon, which bears some similarity to several aspects of Este rule in Ferrara, see the recent work of C. F. Black, "The Baglioni as Tyrants of Perugia, 1488-1540," *EHR,* LXXXV (1970), 245-81. Black makes the point that the Baglioni, though *signori,* were in some ways actually less capable of determining local policy than the Medici in Florence (p. 281): "In fact the Baglioni had even less chance of controlling internal events in their city than had either Cosimo, Piero, or Lorenzo Medici, since they had to contend with papal officials as well as the rest of the oligarchy. The Baglioni were *domina dominantium,* content to

Thus, the event was conceived to flatter and magnify both of these men. Borso arrived with an enormous retinue of hundreds of liveried attendants, all on richly decorated horses. For a month Borso and his entire party, numbering over 500 people, were sumptuously entertained in Rome as guests of the Pope, and on April 14, 1471—Easter Sunday —in the Church of Saint Peter, before an enormous crowd, Borso was installed as Duke of Ferrara and Cavaliere of St. Peter at a papal mass, and all of the symbols of office were conferred upon him. The next day, after receiving more honors and presents, Borso and his entourage paraded through Rome. Peregrino Ariosto provides all of the details of this remarkably open-handed affair, but we shall follow the anonymous chronicler of the *Diario Ferrarese* who says "I shall not relate the honors which were accorded to his *signoria* in going, staying, and coming back, for it would be too long." [51]

Three months later, the Pope died suddenly. And on August 20, Borso d'Este followed. He had been ailing ever since his return from Rome, and had suffered continually from a phlegmatic fever. He was attended at his deathbed by several clergymen. Despite the very acute political crisis produced by this event, which we will examine more closely later, his funeral was a typically magnificent and solemn Borsian pageant. He lay in state in the courtyard of his own *palazzo*. In death, as in life, he was dressed in cloth of gold, bedecked with a splendid necklace and bearing the ducal

---

leave normal government to the Signorelli, Corgna and others, provided they could be free to return from foreign engagements and hold social court in Perugia, reserving their tyrannical behaviour for their vicarial enclave. They were not dictators. . . ."

[51] *DF*, 67: "et il triumpho che fu facto per sua signoria, hora non posso scrivere, perchè longo il seria." Fortunately Francesco Ariosto's description provides all of the details of these events for interested readers. For this curious figure, uncle of the poet Ludovico, see now T. Ascari, "Francesco Ariosto Peregrino," *AAM*, Ser. v, xi (1954), 94-116.

sceptre and cap, a moving contrast with the surrounding platform and the benches for the mourners, all draped in black and brown. The procession included 850 people dressed in deep mourning, including 150 women. All the monks, friars, chaplains, and members of religious confraternities from Ferrara and all the surrounding regions were there, following the body as it was borne by the clergy of the city to the Certosa, where the Bishop of Adria, Borso's trusted counsellor Biagio de'Novelli, gave the eulogy, in the presence of the new duke and "all the rest of the people of Ferrara, all weeping and dressed in mourning." Before the interment, the cloth-of-gold and the jewelry were removed, and Borso was buried in a coarse red robe, despite his expressed preference to be buried nude. "To the people it seemed as though the Eternal God had died again." [52]

Borso's death, like his accession to power, is an obvious turning point in the political history of Ferrara. The extent to which the same may be said with regard to the city's intellectual and cultural development is more problematical, and no final assessment of Borso's rule can be attempted without considering his activities as a patron of the arts and letters.

It is worth inquiring whether Borso had the ability to make rational decisions as to his priorities in the fields of learning and the arts, whether he did so in fact, and whether the style of his patronage clearly reflects these priorities. Is it possible that Borsian patronage derives from a hierarchy of values and concerns in which self-glorification plays a conscious, calculated, and both politically and culturally significant part? Can it be that within this hierarchy of values (to express the matter more formally and structurally than is perhaps justified) advanced humanistic culture—the serious and disinterested study of ancient literature and

[52] *DF,* 70-71.

moral philosophy—played a distinctly minor and secondary role? If so, it would not necessarily mean that Borso lacked intelligence or taste, as some have alleged or implied. The explanation would then have to be found elsewhere.

First of all it must be remembered that Borso, unlike Leonello, had a second-rate humanist education, and that by training and early disposition he was cut out to be a *condottiere,* not a cultivated man of letters. During the years that Guarino was utterly transforming the intellectual and moral tone of the court, Borso was out in the field of battle. Upon his return to Ferrara he was, and surely recognized that he was, a relatively untutored and uncultivated accolyte of the circle around Leonello. For a proud, vigorous, and active man, this realization left two alternatives. He could either try to acquire the intellectual skills and graces necessary to compete with Leonello on his own terms, or follow his own training, character, and inclinations and continue to carve out for himself an entirely different and separate type of identity and image. He sensibly chose the latter course. In so doing, there was much to reinforce his choice. There was his simple and direct religious piety, which had traditionally correlated with a lack of positive interest in, if not of outright hostility toward, pagan thought and letters. There was his obvious pleasure at being a public figure, and at wielding power in direct and personal ways—hearing pleas, giving away money, taking part in processions and ceremonies. For Leonello, Marcus Aurelius might have provided a model. For Borso, Augustus would have seemed more suitable.

The comparison is not entirely fanciful, and may even be illuminating. Like Augustus, Borso allowed himself in a sense to be deified in his lifetime, and successfully controlled and dictated the terms in which he wanted to be seen by his contemporaries and future generations. That is to say that Borso, like Augustus, was a skillful manipulator of the available means of communication. He used all of these to the same ends: to appear magnificent, magnanimous, generous, rich, powerful, just, pious, and of course godlike. Like Augustus, Borso did this so effectively that it remains no easy task to develop a soundly-based conviction about him. But that this "institutionalization of charisma," in Weber's phrase, was one of his primary concerns seems certain.

Let us return for an example to the subject of coinage, which we have considered in the context of the earlier Estensi. Where Leonello had maintained the original system almost without change, minting only his own *quattrini* and *bagattini,* Borso eventually changed everything. The decisive event here was his coronation by Frederick III. Immediately after this event, the mint produced an entire new line of coins. There were golden *lire,* silver *grossetti* (*soldi*), and lesser coinage of silver and base metals. Surviving examples reflect a stylistic transformation which is even more important. The example of Roman imperial coinage, which had heretofore been used primarily in commemorative medals, now provides the basis for Borso's new money.[53] The ruler's image appears on almost every coin, in idealized profile.[54] In the most distant corners of the

[53] However there is evidence that Leonello, too, had had his coinage modelled on ancient examples. See Nogara, ed., *Scritti . . . di Flavio Biondo* (Rome 1927), 159-60, a letter dated February 1, 1446, from Biondo to Leonello, in which the author indicates that he has learned of Leonello's minting of 10,000 bronze coins in imitation of ancient Roman coinage. Biondo offers Leonello his writings on the subject: "nummos te ad decem millia aëneos vetustorum principum Romanorum more cudi curavisse, quibus altera in parte ad capitis tui imaginem tuum sit nomen inscriptum, etc." On the use of coinage as an instrument of propaganda in imperial Rome there is a vast literature, but see esp. R. Syme, *The Roman Revolution* (Oxford, 1939), and the useful views of M. P. Charlesworth, "The Virtues of a Roman Emperor," *Proceedings of the British Academy* xxiii (1937), 107. Also my "Augustus and the Art of Persuasion," *Amherst Review,* i:2 (1959), 1-6.

[54] V. Bellini, *Delle monete di Ferrara,* 121-30. For the tradition of

realm, and in the most trivial transactions, his presence is seen and felt. The symbolic value and significance of such apparently para-cultural objects cannot be easily dismissed. Indeed, one of the historic differences between republics and principalities which is still operative today is that republics use their coinage as memorials, principalities as testimonials.

Borso's cultural priorities, then, would appear to reflect a partially political concern for grandeur. This concern appears in every field, both in positive and negative ways. Consider for example the phenomenal growth of the university. In the course of Borso's reign, 584 degrees were awarded in the 19 years for which there are records, an average of 31 degrees per year. For the previous 19 years for which there are records, the total of degrees awarded is 132, an average of only 7 degrees per year.[55] The reasons for this are obvious. Borso heavily subsidized the university out of his own revenues. He made scholarships available to some students and took an interest in the hiring and recruiting of professors, in the administration of the university, and even its supplies and equipment. He understood the operation of the laws of supply and demand that then as now governed the academic marketplace, and was prepared to be generous when it came to recruiting or holding on to important professors.[56] But he cannot be said to have had a special concern for the *studia humanitatis*. Law and medicine were the fields in which he wanted his *studium* to excel, as the researches of Giuseppe Pardi have convincingly shown.[57] If these two areas could be developed, the institution would not only

portrait medals in Ferrara, see Gruyer, *L'Art ferrarais,* I, 583-650. Also P. B. Cott, *Renaissance Bronzes from the Kress Collection* (Washington, 1951), 160 ff; and the definitive catalogue by G. Pollard, *Renaissance Medals from the Samuel H. Kress Collection* (London, 1967).

[55] Pinghini, "La popolazione studentesca," 141-42.

[56] F. Borsetti, *Historia Almi Ferrariae Gymnasii* (Ferrara, 1735), I, 93-96.

[57] See esp. the author's *Titoli Dottorali conferiti a Ferrara* (Lucca, 1900).

acquire great prestige, it would also be serving a vital utilitarian function for court and commune alike. It is worth noting that these priorities are further demonstrated in Borso's actions upon the death of the university's administrator, Agostino Villa. Borso, learning of the event at his country castle at Fossadalbero, immediately instructed his chancellors in Ferrara that they appoint a committee of three to take over Villa's functions—a physician, a jurisconsult, and a nobleman—and that after ordering their appointment, the names should be made known to the rectors, professors, and students. So much for scholarship.[58] Borso controlled the university, just as he controlled virtually everything else.

Of course the thriving humanism of Guarino's and Leonello's Ferrara did not simply wither away. Borso needed men of letters at his court, and if they had not been there, he would have gone out and gotten them. But for Borso, the humanist was not a potential friend, companion, or teacher. He was a servant. As such, he was expected to perform a particular set of specialized functions, and for this he would be rewarded. A serious discussion of whether poets are superior to painters, such as the one resolved by Leonello in favor of the poets in Decembrio's *Politia Litteraria,* would hardly have occurred in the presence of Borso. If it had, he would have seen little difference between the two.

Borso needed the humanists because they had become a perquisite of office. One simply could not be a great prince in mid-*Quattrocento* Italy without having a squadron of humanists. They were the men who had to be ready to coin new verses to celebrate whatever was happening— arrivals, departures, births, deaths, coronations, weddings, visits, special events of all kinds. They were the men who had to write the words of praise that were both pleasing

[58] *Borso d'Este,* xvi, 129.

and politically useful. They were the men who had to think up the amusing allegorical displays for ceremonial entries, banquet centerpieces, cake decorations, and the like. They were the men who had to tell the painters what went where, making sure it all came out looking like the right passage in Ovid or Lucretius. The least common denominator of these courtly functions, then, may be summarized in two words—entertainment and propaganda.

With these values in mind, it is easy to see why Borso for the most part got the humanists he deserved—articulate, even eloquent, men whose strength lay in selling a product, rather than in developing a new idea. I have already mentioned several conspicuous examples, and there are many others, all of whom have received some scholarly attention. The major figures in this circle are Baptista Guarini and Ludovico Carbone. Guarini emerges as an important figure on the Ferrarese cultural scene after the death of his illustrious father Guarino da Verona in 1460. The latter had become relatively inactive in court circles during the 1450s, and had even contemplated leaving the city to which he had come in 1429. He had, however, retained his post as Professor of Greek and Latin, and maintained his close epistolary ties with distinguished humanists and many of his former students, who came to him from all over Europe. Upon the great old master's death, his son was appointed to succeed him. Baptista did well, and was handsomely rewarded "for his eminence and virtue, which have rendered him very dear to the court." The terse notation in the *Registro dei Mandati* is revealing.[59] Baptista was more the courtier than his father ever could have been. The ducal bonus is dated 1470, and may therefore have something to do with the previously mentioned oration on Casella. Guarini, despite his professorship, found time to take part

[59] Bertoni, *La Biblioteca Estense,* 149; quoted also by Pardi, *Borso d'Este,* xv, 118.

in several diplomatic expeditions, write elegant court verse, compose the well-known *De Ordine Docendi et Studendi,* and dabble in the classics.[60] The second generation of the Guarini family produced the courtier's range and versatility, but the price was a loss of scholarship and intensity. Baptista's career seems a good example of adaptation to environmental change.

Ludovico Carbone is the very model of the opportunistic courtly sycophant (Fig. 8). Born in the early 1430s, of a family of Cremonese origin, he came to Ferrara in his youth and studied the ancient languages under Guarino and Teodoro Gaza. Shortly after Borso's accession, the young Carbone became professor of poetry and eloquence in the *studium.* During this period he became what might be called the master of ceremonies of the court. In his later years he was to pride himself that no girl of good family had married without an epithalamium from his pen, nor had any important Ferrarese man or woman died without benefit of his eulogy.[61] Many of these poems and speeches are preserved, and they offer interesting glimpses into

[60] For B. Guarini, see the interesting references collected by Bertoni, *La Biblioteca Estense;* also the comments and translation by W. H. Woodward, *Vittorino da Feltre and Other Humanist Educators* (New York, 1963; first pub. 1897), 159-78; and the essay by T. Ascari, "Sul 'De Ordine Docendi ac Studendi' di Battista Guarino," *AAM,* Ser. v, xii (1954), 145-52.

[61] On Carbone's life and works see L. Frati, "Di Ludovico Carbone e delle sue Opere," *AF,* xx (1910), an inadequate discussion which should be superseded by a modern and comprehensive study. Carbone's *Facezie* were published by A. Salza (sometimes listed as Kader Salza), *Facezie di L. Carbone* (Livorno, 1900). More accessible samples of Carbone's work may be found in E. Garin, ed., *Prosatori Latini del Quattrocento* [La Letteratura Italiana: Storia e Testi] (Milan, 1952), 381-420, the funeral oration for Guarino; also K. Müllner, *Reden und Briefe die Italienischer Humanisten* (Vienna, 1899; rev. ed. Munich, 1970), 85-107, prints the same work, as well as Carbone's inaugural lecture on Lucan and Valerius; see also the new bibliography, pp. xxviii-xxix.

Ferrarese social life.[62] There was in Carbone something of the dilettante. He prided himself on his good taste and collected works of painting and sculpture, including portraits of Leonello and Borso. He also prided himself on his literary style and condemned the barbarisms of lawyers and Aristotelians. Far from being immune to the blandishments of court life, Carbone, like his master, coveted titles. He made enough of an impression on Pius II to receive from him the title of Count Palatine in 1459, ostensibly in reward for a flattering harangue. A decade later, we see him seeking confirmation of this title from Frederick III, from whom he also wanted to wring the title of Poet Laureate—according to his biographer, Ludovico Frati, Carbone had at least a quantitative claim to the title, for he had produced close to 200 orations and 10,000 lines of verse.

All of this courtly activity left relatively little time for scholarship, which must anyway have seemed a bothersome chore for this good-natured writer of ribald tales. And so it is especially interesting to notice that Carbone did train some reasonably competent court poets, including Ludovico Carro,[63] who carried on some of Carbone's activities after his death, which probably occurred around 1482. Nor was Carbone an insignificant scholar. A manuscript in the British Museum, dedicated to Alberto d'Este, a half-brother of Borso, in which Carbone presents his translation of Sallust's *Catilinarian* into Italian, reveals his linguistic and historical

[62] There are many MSS. containing bits and pieces of Carbone's *œuvre*, but the main sources, apart from those which have been published are *BAV*, MS. Ottob. Lat. 1153, especially, ff. 100-200 (microfilm in Univ. of Pa. Library); Vat. Lat. 8618, which includes the famous dialogue "Il Barco"; Vat. Lat. 8761, containing the same work. The Fondo Tioli in the Biblioteca Universitaria in Bologna has late transcriptions of many of the works included in the Vatican MSS. See also A. Lazzari, "Il dialogo di L. Carbone in lode del Duca Borso," *AF*, xxviii (1929), 125 ff.

[63] No significant work has been done on Lud. Carro, poet and physician to Ercole I. But see below, p. 258.

accomplishments. Written about 1464, it comes as an especially welcome addition to our knowledge of the humanistic culture of Ferrara because it provides new evidence of an interest in history—especially Roman republican history—there, and serves to confirm the growing awareness of the exceptionally important role of the vernacular in Ferrara at an early date.[64] Carbone's preface deals specifically with these questions, and offers enough new information on these subjects and Ferrarese attitudes toward them to merit publication in full as an appendix.[65]

A growing interest in history emerges in Ferrara during the last four decades of the *Quattrocento*. The court chroniclers become more precise, more thorough, and somewhat more personal. Antiquarian researches on Ferrara and on the Estensi are expanded by various writers and especially by Pellegrino Prisciani, who was not only the first official ducal historiographer, but who also served at various times as court astrologer, librarian, and diplomat, and was probably the most learned man in Ferrara in the last quarter of the fifteenth century.[66] Finally, there is an ongoing effort to collect and, where necessary, translate the works of Imperial and Italian historians for the princes, a tendency of which

[64] British Museum MS. Add. 22337: *Traductione di Sallustio Historiographo per Lodovico Carbone allo Illust. et. Gratioso messer Alberto da este.* The same prince also received a volume of poems by Filippo Nuvolone, *Ad illustrem et excelsum dominum Albertum Estensem*, Brit. Mus. MS. Add. 22335. Bertoni, *La Biblioteca Estense*, 12, regarded Alberto as an important bibliophile.

[65] See below, Appendix II.

[66] The only modern study of Prisciani is A. Rotondò, "Pellegrino Prisciani, 1435ca.-1518," *Rinascimento*, xi:1 (1960), 69-110. Many Prisciani MSS. survive, not only in the Archivio di Stato and the Biblioteca Estense in Modena, but also in the Vatican and Marciana libraries. For further references, see Kristeller, *Iter*, vols. I-II. This fascinating humanist, astrologer, courtier, antiquarian, historian, and diplomat deserves extended study.

the Carbone manuscript provides a typical example. To mention a few others, there is Niccolò da Lonigo's translation of Procopius, of which several magnificent manuscript copies survive;[67] and in the inventory of Ercole's library, almost every important historian appears, usually in the original and in translation, and often in more than one copy.[68]

This emphasis on the *volgare* is one of the most telling indicators of the transformation of Ferrarese culture under Borso. Leonello shared with his humanist friends a snobbish disdain for the vernacular, based at least in part on an assessment of its current expressive limitations. Borso, on the other hand, knew no Latin, a fact that does not seem to have caused him a moment's anguish. But it irked and embarrassed his humanists, who liked to parade their learning, and who saw in this Borso's only flaw.[69] They could

[67] See for example *BAV*, MS. Barb. Lat. 4085 (XLVI, 27), Procopius; *Historia belli Gothici . . . ridotta in vulgare de Maestro Nicolo da Lonigo* with a pref. to Ercole I (see Kristeller, *Iter*, I, 464); Bib. Marciana, MS. Ital. VI, 222 (6040); *BEM*, MS. Alpha H, 4, 2 (Ital 463), the presentation copy and one of the most magnificent codices in the Estense. Cf. Kristeller, *Iter* I, 384, Fava and Salmi, 179-80, Fava, 255-56. There is also a copy in the Biblioteca Ambrosiana.

[68] Bertoni, *La Biblioteca Estense*, 235-52.

[69] *BEM*, MS. Alpha G, 6, 12 (Ital. 1004): Carlo da Sangiorgio, *Storia del tradimento fatto verso il duca Borso da Gia. Lod. Pio ed Andr. da Varegnana* Cf. Kristeller, *Iter* I, 376; Fava and Salmi, 154. Dated 1469, illuminated frontispiece. Carlo da Sangiorgio was Borso's main scribe, and also served for a time as ducal librarian. See Bertoni, *La Biblioteca Estense*, 41-63, passim, 194. This MS. was published by A. Cappelli, "La congiura dei Pio signori di Carpi contro Borso d'Este," *AM*, II (1864), 367-416. The work begins with an explanation that it is written in Italian only because Borso cannot read Latin (". . . la fortuna inimica de ogni virtuoso hyomo non la voluto a li altri tuoi singulari ornamenti adiungere l'ornamento de le littere, il quale è più excellente che l'huomo havere possa" [p. 377]). Note similar remarks by Carbone below, p. 299. It will be recalled that the *Politia Litteraria* reflects extreme reservations about the use of the *volgare* as a literary or scholarly language. Protestations such as

not have guessed that out of this new climate, indifferent
to Latin, and hospitable to Italian, would come the three
greatest poets of the Italian Renaissance—Boiardo, Ariosto,
and Tasso.

It will be recalled that the library inventory of Niccolò
III listed 276 books. A similar list compiled for Borso in
1467 and published by Bertoni included only 148, which
suggests both poor custodial arrangements over the years,
and a low rate of replacement. From this low point under
Borso, the size of the ducal library more than tripled by
the end of the century. Although Borso was clearly not
an aggressive book collector, much less an avid reader, he
applied the same set of values and assumptions to books
that he brought to humanists, artists, clothes, horses, and
the like. He wanted them if, and insofar as, they contributed
to his own aggrandizement. Thus we find in the inventory
of Ercole's library no less than seven separate works listed
as "Laude del Duca Borso," not including another work
given as "Deificatio del Duca Borso." And thus we find
Borso taking a vital interest in the production of one particular manuscript, the celebrated Bible of Borso d'Este.[70]

In commissioning the *Bibbia,* which took an entire team
of miniaturists about eight years to produce, Borso planned
to create one of the most beautiful books in the world, and
he succeeded. Under the direction of the master Taddeo
Crivelli, the two great volumes of the Old and New Testa-
ments took on a timeless and ageless beauty. Every one of
a thousand pages is covered with ornamental illuminations

---

those of Carlo da Sangiorgio and Ludovico Carbone indicate that humanists in Ferrara still adhered to this viewpoint, and that counter-pressures
in favor of the *volgare* came primarily from the courtly circle of men
with scholarly or literary interests who were not professional academicians.

[70] After a long and complicated history the *Bibbia di Borso* resides in
the Biblioteca Estense. It was published in facsimile (Milan, 1937), 2 vols.,
with a preface by A. Venturi.

and miniature paintings. Saints and patriarchs, birds and animals, mythological creatures, Este symbols, all abound in a rich tapestry of leaves, branches, grasses, and flowers. This contrived and elegant naturalism is a perfect expression of Borso's magnificence, to which it catered and which it evokes. In other ways, the same concerns and qualities appear in the larger works of art created under Borso, some of which are considered in a subsequent chapter.

E. H. Gombrich has shown in another context that for the *Quattrocento* patron, the acquisition of paintings was cheap, relative to other forms of consumption.[71] What was true for Florence under Cosimo, where there was much competition for the best artists, was even more true of Ferrara under Borso and Ercole. Not only were non-Estensi sources of patronage comparatively meager and unstable, but the Estensi never bothered to conceal a literally patronizing attitude toward painters. They were craftsmen, mixers and appliers of color, men who worked with their hands. In general, they required neither special consideration nor special rewards, though the usefulness and attractiveness of their services was never denied. In part this hierarchical concept of the social role of the artist in Ferrara derives from the predominantly literary and even Platonizing tone of the Leonellan court.[72] In part it results from the structure of Ferrarese society. The artist would no more than anyone else presume to treat the *signore* as a client, or a mere employer. After all, the Estensi were not common citizens, bankers, or tradesmen. They were lords, and they required another kind of deference.

Given their dominance as consumers in the local market, as well as their pre-eminence in the social hierarchy, the

[71] "The Early Medici as Patrons of Art: A Survey of Primary Sources," in *Italian Renaissance Studies,* ed., E. F. Jacob (London, 1960), 279-311.

[72] Baxandall, "A Dialogue on Art from the Court of Leonello d'Este," 308-309.

Estensi were not even bound to honor their own commitments very scrupulously.[73] That they nonetheless usually did so illustrates their own general sensitivity to the implicitly contractual concepts upon which their peculiar prestige and popularity was and always had been based. An interesting exception is the letter from Francesco del Cossa, complaining of Borso's non-payment for the Schifanoia frescoes, and imploring the Duke not only to pay his bill, but to pay more than the insultingly and unsatisfactorily small sum agreed upon. It reveals the artist's sense of frustration, his own pride and sense of humiliation, and his total lack of recourse.[74] Whether Borso responded to Cossa's pleas with the "Iustitia" upon which he prided himself, and under the sign of which he had himself shown in those very same frescoes, we do not know.

Borso became a legendary figure in his own time, and the legend lived on after him. A great number of manuscripts in Italian and other libraries offer signed and anonymous verses in praise of this able, colorful, complex, figure. Even in these encomiastic writings, Borso's paradoxical character emerges. He is friendly but can be imperious; just but he can be arbitrary; generous but he can be vindictive and greedy; pious but he can enjoy the most secular pursuits; brave but he seeks nothing more than tranquillity and peace. There is no doubt that his achievements as a propa-

[73] There is much evidence that the dukes felt no strong obligation always to abide strictly by their financial commitments to artists. Francesco del Cossa's famous and bitter letter to Borso is a prime example, but it is not unique. (For a new translation, see D. S. Chambers, *Patrons and Artists in the Italian Renaissance* [Columbia, S.C., 1971], 162-64.)

[74] The letter is in *ASM, ASE,* Archivio per Materie, Busta 14 A. Published by A. Venturi, *Storia dell' Arte Italiana: La pittura del Quattrocento,* pt. III (Milan, 1914), 590-91. For complete bibliographical references to Cossa see now the monograph by A. Neppi, *Francesco del Cossa* (Milan, 1958), a volume published by the Cassa di Risparmio di Ferrara.

gandist—and therefore as a patron of a certain style of cultural production—were almost Augustan, the necessary changes being made. He sought and got great titles. Without ever appearing to be anything but a peacemaker, he played an active role in Italian diplomacy, protecting his interests and helping to inflame conflicts from which he might benefit. At the same time, he took some care to have his own territories properly administered and improved, and was obviously a master at giving the people what they thought they wanted. He was a great politician and a surprisingly good prince. Two decades after his death, people like Ercole Strozzi were already referring to his rule as the "golden age" of Ferrara.[75]

[75] Bib. Marciana MS. Marc. Lat. XII, 136 (4389), *Excellentissimae Reginae Helionorae Aragoniae ad Invictissimum Ducem Herculem Estensem Per Herculem Strozam EPICEDIUM.* See esp. f. 4 v°:

> Musarum phoebique choris Leonelle dicate
> Primus Nicoleo Sceptrum Regal tulisti.
> Mox solis insedit, fatis in regna vocatus
> Borsius, & patrie dedit aurea secula genti.

For an elegant discussion of the "aureum saeculum" theme, see now H. Levin, *The Myth of the Golden Age in the Renaissance* (Bloomington, 1969). The Marciana MS. is a presentation copy to Ercole, with decorated borders all in brown, denoting mourning. The work appears to be an unknown early poem by Ercole Strozzi. No other MS. but this one is cited by Kristeller, and the poem does not appear in the Aldine edition of the poems of Tito Vespasiano and Ercole Strozzi (1513). M. Wirtz, "Ercole Strozzi, Poeta Ferrarese, 1473-1508," *AF*, xvi (1906), 21-57, makes no mention of it. I intend to publish an annotated edition of the work at a later date. Another MS. commemorating the death of Eleanora is the *De Nobilitate Humani Animi* by Bartolomeus Gogius, BEM Campori, app. 134, Gamma. S. 6, 7.

Hercules Dux Ferrariae

Leonello inherited the Este *stato,* or regime, at the age of thirty-eight. Borso had been thirty-seven when he came to power; their half-brother Ercole, who had been an adolescent during Leonello's reign, and a young courtier and *condottiere* throughout most of Borso's, was almost forty in the summer of 1471 when Borso died. Thus not only were the three men who ruled Ferrara from 1441 to 1505 brothers, because they had one father, but there is also some importance in the fact that they all took office at the same time of life. They were young enough to be at the height of their powers, and likely to enjoy long reigns. They were old enough to have been raised under the influence of Niccolò III, to have had extensive experience in warfare, governance, and the life of the court, to have come to know their counterparts in the other Italian cities, and to have established bases of popular support for themselves in Ferrara. These factors in themselves are extremely helpful in accounting for the impressive administrative and political continuities that characterize Ferrarese government and social life in the *Quattrocento.* Though such continuities are important as well as impressive, it seems much more interesting to notice that each of these princes composed his own variations on the *leitmotif* of the popularly-supported despotism of the Estensi. Though ties of blood, of self-interest, and of real personal devotion bound them to one another, there is historical significance in the fact that these were deeply individual men, each of whom followed his own concerns and private passions while fulfilling the traditional duties of the *signore.*

Such a statement applies with special force to Ercole, whom historians have generally regarded as the most enigmatic and inaccessible of the Estensi. Though he ruled

Ferrara for thirty-four years, and presided over the most important cultural and artistic developments in the city's long history, though his wife and four of his children played important roles in diverse areas and he himself was intimately involved in the major military and political events of his time, no one has ever written a full scale biography of him.[1] Nevertheless, much has been written about Ercole, and even more about Ferrara in the time of Ercole, and the literature includes extremely varied assessments of the man and his regime. I do not believe that the evidence sustains either the view of Ercole as a cynical and bloodthirsty tyrant, nor the interpretation by which he emerges as the genuine cultural hero of the Estensi.[2] A responsible

[1] This astonishing situation should be corrected, the more so because so many good works exist treating specific aspects of the history of Ferrara in the Herculean period, and with particular characteristics of Ercole's regime. I hope that the present chapter suggests some fruitful lines of inquiry for further study of this subject. For other sources, see especially the fairly comprehensive bibliography given by Chiappini, *Gli Estensi,* 525-30. For other general discussion see now Chiappini, *Gli Estensi,* 144-210, sensible throughout, and particularly useful with regard to Ercole's diplomacy, and chs. 5-7 of E. G. Gardner, *Dukes and Poets in Ferrara,* which offers a competent narrative account of the major features of Ercole's rule. Of course, the fundamental sources such as Muratori's *Antichità Estensi* and Frizzi's *Memorie* remain valuable, as does the remarkable collection of documents assembled in the second volume of M. Catalano, *Vita di Ludovico Ariosto* (Geneva, 1930), a work that deserves the same high reputation among historians that it has always enjoyed with literary scholars.

[2] The negative view is sustained by A. Piromalli, *La cultura a Ferrara al tempo di Ariosto* (Florence, 1953), who while attempting to criticize in particular the social structure of Ferrara and the manipulative character of the signorial regime from a Marxist perspective, also finds great individual faults in the Estensi themselves. This results in the author's characterization of the family as manifesting a "mediocrità umana." I have discussed Piromalli's contribution—which incidentally has to do neither primarily with culture nor with the time of Ariosto—in "Toward a Reinterpretation," 271-74. For an almost diametrically opposite approach,

evaluation of this critical period in Ferrara's history, and of its chief protagonist, is somewhat more complex. For it to be convincing, or even intelligible, it will have to follow and emerge from a wide-ranging analysis.

Ercole, born in the lap of privilege, had a rather peculiar childhood even by the bizarre standards of his own time and place. Though legitimate, he was born so late among the myriad children of Niccolò III that he cannot have enjoyed sustained attention or affection from his father. At the same time, he was the repository of high political hopes. His birth anteceded that of any offspring of his half-brother Leonello, and he was the first legitimate male heir of Niccolò III. That made him a power to be reckoned with even in the cradle, especially for Niccolò's older bastards. At the age of two, Ercole was knighted by the Emperor Sigismund, as was his newborn brother, whom the Emperor held at his baptism, and who received the name of Sigismondo. These youngsters were raised at the court by their mother, Ricciarda da Saluzzo. In 1443, however, she returned to her ancestral home in the Piedmont, loaded down with clothes, money, and jewels, but leaving the boys with Leonello.[3] Under similar circumstances in less stable and

somewhat closer to the present study, see E. G. Gardner, *Dukes and Poets in Ferrara*. Chiappini, 154-58, takes a more balanced view.

[3] *DF,* 27: "A dì XXIV de Octobre, se partite madona Rizarda, molgiere che fu del marchexe Nicolò, et andete a Saluzo per stare, et portò con lei, tra roba, veste, dinari et zoje, che furno estimate ducati sexante milia." For Ricciarda's pompous and ceremonious return to Ferrara after Ercole's ascent, see *DF,* 80. Ricciarda had not seen her children in 27 years, according to the chronicler. She was escorted to the outskirts of Ferrara by a company of 200 nobles, who complemented her own retinue of 70. At the city gates, she was met by the 500 leading ladies of the city, and escorted to her suite in the palace. While taking note of the chronicler's chronic tendency to exaggerate, it is worth observing that he admires Ercole for this display: "E se mai a persona fu facto honore, pensa ch'il prefacto Signore lo fece a la sua madre."

legally scrupulous despotisms, such an act might have been tantamount to signing their death warrants. In the Ferrara of Leonello and Borso, however, it meant that the administration of the court would have to see to it that the boys were maintained in a manner befitting princes of the House of Este, that their education be advanced in the traditional ways, and not least that they be away from Ferrara, so as not to present political opportunities to themselves or anyone else. Considering their importance, the choice of a place presented a delicate problem. On the one hand, they could not be packed off to a trans-Alpine court, like some bastards from a collateral line of the family.[4] On the other hand, the Lombard and Tuscan courts were too close, and offered too many opportunities for intrigue. It seemed natural to arrange that the boys would grow up in Naples, where Borso too had spent much time. In fact, he was there for most of 1444, and it was from Naples that he returned to take up residence in Ferrara in 1445. In the fall of that year, Ercole and Sigismondo were sent away to the Aragonese court of Naples, where they were raised as companions to the young prince Ferrante. In a very real sense, Naples was their second home. Ercole's long sojourn there unquestionably affected his sense of his role and power, and his particular interests and enthusiasms, more than has generally been acknowledged.

Little information has come to light on Ercole's early Neapolitan years. That he had a thorough military and chivalric education is certain. He even acquired a solid reputation in dueling and jousting, and was in later years sought after as a *condottiere*.[5] As he grew older, Borso began to take notice of him. Having decided not to complicate the dynastic

---

[4] The pages of Muratori are full of examples of minor offspring of the family who had careers of this sort, but see the especially interesting discussion of Francesco, the bastard son of Leonello, in E. H. Kantorowicz, "The Este Portrait by Roger van der Weyden," 367-80.

[5] A fact that has always been well known (Cf. Gardner, *Dukes and*

situation further by marrying and producing legitimate children of his own, Borso knew that he would have to develop as a successor either Ercole or Niccolò, the son of Leonello, who, though Ercole's junior by only seven years, was of course his nephew. Both men would eventually come forward as claimants to the duchy. While Borso had to reach some decision as to whom he would favor, he had to do so in such a way as to prevent a crisis before his own death. He managed to do this by conferring certain privileges on both men, without committing himself to an explicit political testament. However, it is perfectly clear that after 1460, when Ercole returned to Ferrara, he was increasingly able to gain Borso's confidence. In 1469, while serving as governor of Modena, the second city of the realm, Ercole was able to put the finishing touch on his powerful influence on Borso by revealing a plot which was intended to bring him to power. The incident bears some scrutiny, both as a crucial step in Ercole's ascent, and as an example of responses to political unrest under the Este regime.

As I have shown elsewhere, the most real danger of violent attempts against the authority of the Estensi rulers came neither from townspeople nor outside enemies, but from rival claimants within the family.[6] There are occasional instances of palace plots under Niccolò and Borso, but some

---

Poets, 158-60), but see now the correspondence between Lorenzo de' Medici and Ercole concerning military matters, indexed in P. G. Ricci, and N. Rubinstein, *Censimento delle lettere di Lorenzo di Piero de' Medici* (Florence, 1964), the texts of which will soon be published in a new edition of Lorenzo's letters under the general editorship of N. Rubinstein. Ercole also fought for the Venetians early in his career, and of course for the Neapolitans too. Professor M. Mallett is currently investigating the *condottieri,* and he informs me (private communication) that Taddeo d'Este appears to him a prototype of the faithful *condottiere,* a "phenomenon which Venice was at great pains to cultivate." Taddeo's son, Bertoldo II d'Este, who was killed as a Venetian *condottiere* in the Morea in 1463, may serve as another example.

[6] See "Crime and Punishment," 122-27.

of them may well have been staged. So it would appear, at least, in the case of the execution of Uguccione dell' Abbadia, the principal secretary in Borso's chancery, who was secretly decapitated one night in 1460.[7] His crime was failure to inform the Duke that one Pietro Paolo, an acquaintance of his, had been going around saying that he wanted to murder Borso. Given Uguccione's silence, the same Pietro Paolo told Borso that his friend had heard of his intent, and done nothing about it. The hapless secretary's defense against this obviously contrived charge was that he had not taken Pietro Paolo seriously, considering him "puocho savio." In the wake of the execution, Uguccione's very considerable estate was divided up among the Duke's intimates, and his family dispersed among remote prisons.[8] The incident would seem to reveal more about ducal methods of maintaining the absolute fidelity of associates than about social unrest in Ferrara.

In 1469, however, a more serious attempt to unseat Borso was nipped in the bud. Some members of the house of Pio, the lords of Carpi and traditional allies and vassals of the Estensi, plotted—in retaliation for an alleged insult—either to depose or murder Borso, and to replace him with Ercole. Again we are dealing neither with a plot against Este rule *per se,* nor with popular discontent, but with an instance of the magnate *vendetta* combined with interstate intrigue. The Pio faction gained support from Borso's enemies in other cities, and then sought Ercole's complicity. Ercole, however, did not commit Uguccione's folly. Instead he

[7] Cf. "Crime and Punishment," 123, and the references to this incident in *DF,* 43; *Libro dei Giustiziati,* BAF MS. CL. I, 404, f. 4 v⁰.

[8] *DF,* 43, indicates that the main beneficiaries of this event were Cristoforo da Roseta and Tomaso da Milano, both ducal chamberlains, and other courtiers such as Alberto del' Assassino, Galazzo degli Ariosti, Bonvicino delle Carte, Niccolò Galuzzo, Lorenzo Strozzi, "el conte Lorenzo," *et al.* Uguccione's children were allowed to retain only enough money to repay their father's outstanding debts.

revealed the general lines of the plot to Borso, who instructed him to play along and learn the rest of it. After Ercole had done so, he then arrested all of the principals and sent them, under guard of 400 horsemen, from Modena to Bondeno, from where they cruised down the Po to Ferrara. There, they were given a proper trial and sentenced, some to execution, others to life imprisonment, all to confiscation of goods by the ducal *camera*. A month later the sentences were carried out. The two brothers Pio, who were actually nephews of Borso by virtue of his half-sister Margherita's marriage to Galasso Pio, were decapitated in a splendid public ceremony, and so was one of their chancellors. The other conspirators were spread among various dungeons, whence many escaped, were ransomed, or were eventually freed.[9]

Among the contemporary accounts of this series of events is that of Carlo da San Giorgio, an important court secretary and ducal librarian. Written only a few weeks after the events, it was rapidly translated into the *volgare* so that Borso could read it. Despite its predictable bias, it adds considerable detail to the chronicler's account. We learn, for example, the suggestive fact that when the prisoners were brought into Ferrara, they had to wear hoods over their faces, to prevent the outraged populace from recognizing individuals and tearing them into "mille pezzi."[10] This would have been an expression of popular enthusiasm which, while flattering to the Duke, would have set a perilous precedent.

---

[9] See "Crime and Punishment" 123-24; *DF,* 60-62; *BEM,* MS. Alpha G, 6, 12 (Ital. 1004), which is Carlo da Sangiorgio's *Storia del tradimento fatto verso il duca Borso da Gia. Lod. Pio ed Andr. da Varegnana, MS. cit.;* and above all the study by A. Cappelli, "La congiura dei Pio, signori di Carpi, contra Borso d'Este," *AM,* ıı (1864), 367-416, who published Carlo da San Giorgio's account.

[10] Cappelli, 377-78.

Several months later, Borso appointed Ercole as head of the *consiglio segreto,* and made Niccolò di Leonello second in command.[11] Ercole was now governor of Modena, and chief of the most important political body within the court. That his duties were revolving more toward the central administration of the duchy is underlined by the fact that a few days later Borso also appointed an able new *capitano* for Modena, Luchino Marcello.

When Borso died in the following summer, Ercole's succession, while smooth, and fully supported by the communal government and the traditional *parlamento,* was bitterly resented by Niccolò and his Gonzaga partisans. An early plot was nipped in the bud, and Niccolò with about 85 of his followers were declared rebels, and punished by banishment and confiscation of goods and feudal privileges. At the same time, two of Niccolò's men were hanged for treason after attempting to suborn the Ferrarese captain of the stronghold of Ficarolo. Ercole made one attempt to rid himself of this persistent menace at the end of 1471, when Niccolò Ariosto was sent to Mantua to arrange for Niccolò d'Este's assassination. He managed to bribe one of Niccolò's men to poison the leader, but at the last minute this agent revealed the plot, and Niccolò Ariosto was lucky to escape with his own life. For his pains, he was soon made governor of Reggio, where his famous son Ludovico was born three years later.[12]

It was not until September 1, 1476, that Niccolò di Leonello finally made his real move, the biggest attempt at a *coup* in fifteenth-century Ferrara. That summer Ercole's wife, Eleanora of Aragon (the daughter of his childhood friend Ferrante whom he had married three years earlier, and who had already given birth to two daughters, Isabella

---

[11] *DF,* 64; for the *Consiglio Segreto* and other administrative bodies, see Appendix I, below.

[12] Gardner, *Dukes and Poets,* 125-27, gives a good account of the incident.

and Beatrice), produced a male heir, Alfonso, named for his maternal great-grandfather, Alfonso the Magnanimous, whom Ercole may have remembered almost as a father. Niccolò resolved that under these circumstances he could afford to wait no longer. Accordingly, on a Sunday afternoon, having learned from an informer that Ercole was leaving the city that morning for his palace of Belriguardo, Niccolò invaded Ferrara with an armed force of at least 650 men. Catching everyone completely by surprise, they quickly took over the main square, and began shouting, "Vela, vela!" to arouse the *popolo* in support of Niccolò, who had appropriated his father's *impresa,* the sail. More concretely, Niccolò also rode around promising lower taxes, and a reduction of one-third in the price of grain. He also released all prisoners in the *Palazzo della Ragione.*[13]

But he could do no more. Shortly after becoming duke, Ercole had built the elevated passageway from the palace in front of the *duomo* to the *castello,* and the terrified duchess with her company and her infant heir now crossed over to that imposing citadel.[14] While the *veleschi* continued to mill around the square, swaggering and carousing, the *popolo* held its peace and refused to be stampeded. Meanwhile the news went out to Ercole, who immediately rallied

[13] For slightly different but remarkably close accounts of these events see *DF,* 91-92; Zambotti, *Diario,* 15-19; U. Caleffini, *Croniche facte per . . . Ugo Caleffino notaio ferrarexe, BAV,* MS. Chigiana I, 1, 4, ff. 63 v⁰-67 r⁰, in some ways the best account, by an able and productive Ferrarese notary and chronicler. He has been studied, but not sufficiently, by A. Cappelli, "Notizie di Ugo Caleffini notaro ferrarese del Secolo XV, con la sua *Cronaca in Rime di Casa d'Este,*" *AMP,* ii (1864), 267-312. The paraphrase made by G. Pardi from the late copy of Caleffini's Vatican chronicle in *BAF,* published as *Diario di Ugo Caleffini, 1471-1494,* vols. i-ii of the series *Monumenti* of the *Deputazione Ferrarese di Storia Patria* (Ferrara, 1938-40) is of very limited value.

[14] See, e.g., *DF,* 91: "Et Madama et messer Sigismondo se ne andorno in Castello Vechio, et non ge havea munizione alcuna necessarie al vivere."

his men for a return to the city. But as he was approaching the walls, another messenger reached him with the fantastic report that Niccolò had a force of 14,000 men, and that three German students had already been executed in the *piazza* for refusing to say "Vela, vela." [15] Now alarmed, Ercole retreated to assemble more troops in the *contado*. But his brothers Sigismondo and Rinaldo, who were still in the city and could see how precarious Niccolò's position was, launched a counter-attack, crying, "Diamante, diamante!" Niccolò retreated, and the *popolo* rallied to Ercole's emblem, the diamond.

The reprisals against the first captured *veleschi* were, the chronicler says, "una crudel cosa da vedere." Eventually, Niccolò and many of his followers were captured at various points around the city, and imprisoned. The next day, Ercole made a ceremonial entry, "cum grande alegreza del popolo." [16] By September 3, the reprisals were well under way. Seventeen men were hanged from the windows of the Palazzo della Ragione, and five more swung from the battlements of the *castello*. More followed over the next few weeks. The most important of course were Niccolò himself, and his cousin Azzo. Because of their status of nobility, they were spared public humiliation, and were instead beheaded

[15] This comes from Zambotti, *Diario,* 16.

[16] See *DF,* 92: "Et lo giorno seguente fu facto grande alegreza dal popolo di Ferrara et fu facto faluò et tri giorni processione. . . . Et lo seguente giorno, a hore XVI, intrò dentro da Ferrara dicto duca et fu ricevuto cum grande alegreza dal popolo." In later years, Ercole's emblem, the diamond, came to be memorialized in many ways. The façade of the Palazzo dei Diamanti, designed by Biagio Rossetti, was constructed using 12,600 identically-cut, diamond-shaped stones. And one G. L. wrote the song "O triumphale diamante" (Paris, Bibl. Nat., MS. Rés. Vm⁷ 676, No. 67, ff. 76v-77) to these words: "O triumphale diamante, nobile e lucento/Colona di forteza et de vigore" (communicated by Prof. Lewis Lockwood). On the reverse of a portrait medal of Ercole by an anonymous artist, a shower of diamonds falls from heaven.

in the castle. Ercole, whose sense of family pride equaled his desire to enforce the law of treason, had Niccolò's head sewn back on, and gave him a dignified funeral, including a pompous procession to the Church of San Francesco, where his body was placed in the ancient family tomb.[17] Though the reprisals went on for a time, the last serious external threat to Ercole's regime had now been extinguished.

These events show that in dealing with organized threats to his regime, Ercole used all of the traditional, time-honored sanctions available in the Italian city-states. To have done anything less would have meant at best to invite charges of weakness or incompetence, and in effect to encourage other potential revolutionaries. Very little, then, can or should be made of the severity, even cruelty, of the punishments. They were normal by the standards of any other Italian city, and relatively mild in comparison with some.[18] What seems especially useful to notice is that they were legal. Indeed, according to the statutes, every one of Niccolò's men could have been executed. Instead, only the uppermost echelon of his leadership was put to death, a number probably amounting to three or four percent of the expeditionary force. Ercole's apparent restraint here probably reflects his awareness that he would have to continue to maintain acceptable relations with the Marquess of Mantua, who had sheltered Niccolò and given him much support. He knew that Niccolò had other important, though covert, allies as well. He knew, too, that a *signore* appears great

---

[17] All the chronicles describe this, but the most detailed and interesting is given by Caleffini, *MS. cit.,* ff. 65 v⁰-66. Cf. also Chiappini, 145-54.

[18] See the remarks offered by J. Larner, *The Lords of Romagna: Romagnol Society and the Origins of the Signorie* (London, 1965), 165: "Criminal justice compensated for the ineffectuality of the police by dealing out occasionally draconic sentences."

not by force alone, but by a judicious combination of severity and clemency. His handling of this affair reveals mastery of this art.

In other ways, too, Ercole was always eager to demonstrate his generosity for political ends, particularly by rewarding his favorites with extensive territories, houses, and tax exemptions. The *Catastri delle Investiture* in the Archivio di Stato in Modena provide dramatic evidence of this policy, which Ercole merely continued.[19] But in addition to routine largesse which was expected of a great feudal lord, Ercole also consistently tried to appear open-handed in other ways. Thus, immediately upon taking office, he announced a series of acts calculated to buttress his popularity. Some taxes were waived, prisoners were released, sentences commuted, grazing rights extended, fines canceled. The *popolo* was delighted. A few days later, Ercole moved to strengthen his position further. He confirmed the statutes, gave bonuses to many officials, renounced his monopoly on the sale of salt, canceled the tariff on imported wheat, took over payment of the salary of both the podestà and the judge of appeals, and enacted many similar "belle gratie." [20]

Such acts were undoubtedly well-advised, and backed by strong political motives. But they were in no sense alien to Ercole's character. Indeed, the pleasure of being magnanimous in public was one that he relished all his life and indulged at every opportunity (Fig. 9). It is closely related

---

[19] See the discussion of the *Catastri delle Investiture* above, p. 136, n. 17.

[20] *DF,* 73-74. Ercole seems generally to have tried to combine the use of carrot and stick. At the same time that he was introducing these reforms, designed to increase his popularity and acceptability in the presence of another claimant from his own family, he also established an armed bodyguard, the first such force of which we have record in *Quattrocento* Ferrara: "Et tenea continue 25 fanti armati di tutto arme, dì et nocte, suso la sala dove manza sua Excellentia, per esser più sicuro."

to—perhaps even the product of—the most striking single aspect of his personality, his piety. For Ercole was a Christian prince in ways that far surpassed the gaudy behaviorism of his father, and had little in common with the cultivated Christian Platonism of Leonello or the vigorous institutional philanthropy of Borso. Unlike his predecessors, whose piety, though real, took relatively conventional and routine forms, Ercole really lived the Christian religion. Indeed, he came closer to being a religious fanatic than any other male member of the Este family, including all the bishops and cardinals.[21]

Just as the panegyricists of Borso's court praised his elegance, majesty, and sumptuousness, his justice, and his political acumen, so the writers of Ercole's circle focus on his piety, and trace his other virtues back to that one. Thus the treatise *De triumphis religionis,* by the Bolognese humanist Giovanni Sabadino degli Arienti, a work I shall have much occasion to discuss later, finds Ercole's religious piety expressed in terms of "magnanimity, fortitude, magnificence, liberality, munificence, justice, clemency, affability, mansuetude, prudence, temperance, continence, chastity, love, charity, hope, and faith." [22] Arienti's treatise shows

[21] Ercole's religious zeal is well known, though opinions have varied as to how it influenced his policies. Gardner, *Dukes and Poets,* suggests that Ercole's devotionalism increased during his life, and tended to override other tendencies toward cruelty or sensuality. There is no evidence for that. L. Lockwood, "Music at Ferrara in the Period of Ercole I d'Este," in *Studi Musicali,* I (1972), 101-31, (a new journal published by the Accademia di Sta. Cecilia in Rome), considers his "deep personal religiosity, amounting almost to fanaticism," as one of the motivating factors in Ercole's effort to make Ferrara into an important musical center, and presents convincing evidence.

[22] *BAV,* MS. Vat. Rossiano, 176: *De Triumphis Religionis Ad Illustrissimum Principem Herculem Estensem Ferrariae Ducem Compatrem suum Colendissimum Ioannes Sabadinus Argenteus bononiensis,* f. 2 (hereafter *DTR*). Sabadino says these virtues are like grass and plants sprouting in the sun: "come lherbe e le piante al sole Magnanimita, Fortitudine,

how these qualities find expression in Ercole's life, and how they follow from his basic piety. If we were dependent on just this single source for evidence on this point, the matter would be debatable. But in fact, this work has remained unknown, while Ercole's piety emerges from many other sources as well.

What has to be understood is how this obviously deep Christian piety came to be expressed in historically significant ways, not from Arienti's point of view, but from ours. With this in mind, it will be useful to consider the problem in relation to three distinct areas of ducal activity where major innovations appear: administration of charity, patronage of the arts, and celebration of religious festivals. Other topics could also be considered, but these three relate especially well to the theme of despotic style.

The period of Ercole's rule produced a remarkable series of changes in the administration of charitable works in Ferrara. The most interesting of these involved the Duke himself. Every morning, for example, before hearing mass, Ercole personally dispensed charity to a dozen paupers, who got some money as well as other necessities. Ercole also instituted the *ventura,* an annual solicitation of foods, in which he and his company went through the streets of Ferrara, knocking on doors and seeking their "ventura," or good luck. They accepted any kind of food, which was then turned over to the poor. Though this became a custom, he took everyone by surprise the first year:

> 1473, on the fifth day of January, and it was a Tuesday, the most illustrious duke Ercole, as an improvisation, in the midst of a terrible snowstorm, and accompanied

---

Magnificentia, Liberalita, Munificentia, Iustitia, Clementia, Afabilita, Mansuetudine, Prudentia, Temperantia, Continentia, Castitate, Amore, Charytate, Speranza, e Fede. Queste divine virtute fano in tua Excellentia uno collegio a questa etate. . . ."

by the illustrious messer Sigismondo, messer Alberto, and messer Rinaldo, his brothers, and many noblemen and citizens went through the city of Ferrara seeking his fortune. The first evening [he went] on foot, with the sounds of trumpets, singers, and pipers. And the second evening, which was the sixth day of the afore-mentioned month, the Feast of the Epiphany, on horse-back. He got the following things, and he would have had much more, had the people known of his coming and had it been good weather, so that people could have gone to the country for things to give him to do him honor. But it is enough that his excellency was seen so willingly.[23]

The list that follows is nothing to be ashamed of. In later years, once people were prepared for this event, the yields grew, but even in that first snowy winter one sees a reflection of the abundance of Ferrarese agriculture, husbandry, and wildlife. To cite just a few items from a long list, Ercole received 1,823 capons, 276 large cheeses, 54 heifers and beef cattle, and assorted game birds, pies, marzipan and other confections. It is clear, even from the diarist's attitude, and apart from the tangible tribute, that Ercole's appearance was much appreciated. He was not only honoring the people by his presence, but giving them a chance to acknowledge and recognize his benevolence and their own prosperity. By institutionalizing a form of humility he enhanced his dignity and power.

Some of his other charitable acts had the same effect. Most notable among them was the custom he adopted—it may have been a traditional ducal prerogative—of washing the feet of the poor on Maundy Thursday. He also instituted a kind of banquet for the poor at the Easter season, which made a great impression. In these events, he was evidently

---

[23] *DF*, 83; cf. "Toward a Reinterpretation," 277.

presenting himself as a secular, earthly analogue to Christ himself, perhaps a more modest aim than that of the "divine" Borso. Eventually, these dinners grew to be huge ceremonial functions, held in one of the largest halls in the palace. Sabadino describes one:

> At the end of the great hall was the head table, where there were thirteen poor citizens who were reduced to the status of paupers. One of them was a priest who sat in the middle, in most holy and divine memory of Christ at the Last Supper; and the others up to the number of the apostles. The other tables were placed along the sides of the hall, and at them sat all the other assembled poor. At the first table [was] Your Excellency; at the others your sons and your brothers; according to the established order of your Religion they served the seated poor.[24]

The meal was most elaborate. There were all kinds of fish, including sturgeon, trout, and other river and ocean species, prepared in different ways, and served with white wines. There was boar, and other roasted meats served with red wines. Finally, there were fancy desserts of all kinds. The finest table linens and silver serving vessels were used throughout. After the banquet, the entire group moved into another room, where, joined by the nobility of Ferrara, the Estensi washed the feet of the poor with warm and cool water, taken from beautiful vases, then dried them with delicate towels. At one of these sessions, in 1497, there were fourteen "religiosi indiani" who received the same treatment.[25]

---

[24] *DTR*, f. 87 v°.

[25] *Ibid.*, f. 90 r°; a reference to another occasion in which Ercole ministered to the needs of the poor also mentions Indians, this time only eight (f. 86 r°). The term here probably means Indians from India who had been converted by Italian friars and were visiting Italy and making the

Ercole also extended his patronage to poor-relief in more systematic ways, though these too were invariably religious in inspiration and structure. The establishment of philanthropic religious confraternities during his rule reflects his encouragement of such organizations. There were at least eight such bodies in existence by 1505, but only one of them clearly antedates the Herculean period. The most relevant for present purposes is the Scuola di San Martino, established on April 1, 1490, for the purpose of aiding the "poveri vergognosi" of Ferrara. The statutes of the confraternity survive in a handsome manuscript in the Biblioteca Ariostea in Ferrara (Fig. 10).[26] The document shows that poverty had become a serious problem in Ferrara, and explains this in terms of the recent Venetian war. Even those who used to live comfortably are now among the ashamed poor, and there is a general awareness that these worthy people need help:

Considering the multitude of poor citizens of Ferrara who, whether because of the wars or owing to other worldly misfortunes, have gone from prosperity to want, and lack anything to cover their bodies or sate their hunger—people who formerly were accustomed to live civilly as *homini da bene*—certain good men, inspired by God, have, so as to keep dishonesty from many and prevent the want that is generally borne from such poverty, and also to redeem with charitable

pilgrimage to Rome. There are indications that such Indian friars were not unknown in Venice, which was probably the most usual port of entry. Ferrara would have been a logical stopping place for them in the course of their journey.

[26] *BAF,* MS. CL. I, 346, *Capitoli della compagnia chiamata la scola de' poveri vergognosi sotto la protezione di S. Martino,* cod. mem. in-4º, ff. 10, dated 1491. On the frontispiece is a handsome miniature showing St. Martin giving aid to a mendicant. In the background is a mountain, which may be the artificial "Monte Santo" of Ferrara, discussed previously.

and merciful deeds the many and enormous sins against God that are done by the impious . . . with the consent and approval of the most illustrious prince the Duke Hercules and the Duchess Eleanora his consort, . . . instituted and ordained a company called the school of the ashamed poor, under the name of the glorious protector of the poor, Saint Martin. . . .[27]

The confraternity itself was organized conventionally, in analogy with Christ and the twelve apostles. Thus, it was to be comprised of one priest and twelve laymen, who formed a self-perpetuating body. The initial group included a very strong representation of ducal secretaries and Ferrarese noblemen. They had exacting duties, and their honesty was rigorously controlled.[28] The group was for-

---

[27] *BAF,* MS. CL. I, 346, f. 3 v°-4 r°: "Consyderando: La moltitudine de poveri citadini de ferrara li quali, si per le guerre, si etiam per altri infortunij del mondo de stato di prosperita esser venuti in necessita & miseria extreme. & non haver pur de coprirse le carne. & satiare la fame di solo pane: che volta civilmente come homini da bene solean vivere: per obsistere etiam a molte dishonesta e manchamenti che ti tal poverta sogliano nascere: & anche per redimere con elemosyne & opere di misericordia li multiplici & enormi peccati che da limpii contra dio creatore son facti: acio per li severi & iusti iudicii soi insiema con peccatori li iusti non periscono: O lo quanti boni homini spirati da dio dal quale si sancti desiderii & iuste operatione procedano deliberorno con la benefictione de lomnipotente dio col consentimento e parere de li Illmi. principi duca Hercule & duchessa Eleonora sua consorte, & con lauctorita de Monsignore Reverendissmo patriarcha . . . instituire & ordinare una Compagnia chiamata la scola de poveri vergognosi sobto el vocabulo del glorioso protectore de poveri San Martino, la quale non attendi ad altro che a cerchare ogni adiutorio & elemosina da ciascuno signore secondo lor descretione, per distribuere per la occurentia de tempi a detti poveri vergognosi per li modi, via, & forma di sobto saran notati."

[28] *Ibid.,* ff. 5-8. Thus the statutes require that the members of the confraternity collect alms in locked boxes that can only be opened in the presence of the Prior, and that all funds thus collected be distributed *in toto* at the end of each week. They also require that each of the members attend confession at least three times a year, and specify the times

bidden to retain its collections. Everything had to be given away within a fixed time, except for special bequests. All gifts to the poor had to be anonymous. The group must have established itself, for we find that in 1500 "the twelve apostles" built a chapel in the Church of San Domenico.[29] The proliferation of such organizations in late *Quattrocento* Ferrara reflects not only growing social needs, but an increased and religiously based sense of social responsibility, emanating directly from the court of Ercole.

Ercole's piety also finds expression in his decisions as a patron of the arts. This emerges unmistakably in many areas, but perhaps most of all in music. Instrumental music

---

and places for this. Moreover, the list of the initial members of the confraternity indicates that every effort was made to recruit from the highest levels of Ferrarese society. It includes Giovanni da Santo Stefano, Antonio da Corregio, Severo (a ducal secretary), Conte Gerardo Bevilacqua, Aristotele di Bruturi (another secretary), Nicolo Bendedeo (a high court official), and Antonio da Leuti, Bartolommeo Barbalonga, Giovanni Machiavelli, one Paulo *pictore,* Hieronymo del Coniugo, Bartolommeo Bermia, and Nicolo di Coadi.

[29] Zambotti, *Diario,* 307, however, gives the impression that the chapel derived its name from a chapel with frescoes depicting the Twelve Apostles, and was actually the private chapel of the Pasqualetti family. Even so, it may be significant that this theme was revived and painted in a major new chapel in Ferrara so close to the time of the founding of this important confraternity, which has counterparts in many other cities. Zambotti, 221, also gives useful evidence that the confraternity was founded as a result of the Lenten sermons of Frate Mariano da Genazzano, of the Eremitani, a popular preacher of the time, who enjoyed special favor from Ercole and Eleanora: "Frate Mariano, predicatore famosissimo e eloquentissimo, predicò questa quarexma, e lo duca con tuta la Corte andava a le sue predice. E fece la compagnia de San Martino per li poveri vergognoxi, che se ha dispensare dinari e altre robbe." Mariano was a well-known figure in Florence, where his thinking was obviously shaped by the twelve Buonomini di San Martino, founded in 1442 by St. Antoninus. Other similar, though later, fraternities in Northern Italy are discussed by B. Pullan, *Rich and Poor in Renaissance Venice* (Cambridge, Mass., 1971), esp. 221, 229-30, 267-68, 373-74.

had long been part of court life. Cameral records reveal payments of trumpeters and other instrumentalists dating from the period of Niccolò III, and there is evidence that the tradition goes back much earlier. The presence of an occasional singer or lutanist also appears in the records, for the earlier *Quattrocento*. But such musicians were used primarily for the official functions of the court, or for modest secular entertainments. Instrumentalists preceded the *signore* during processions, heralded arrivals and departures, provided fanfares, and perhaps also gave concerts. The singers may be assumed to have functioned as soloists, often accompanying themselves on the lute,[30] though Leonello is known to have had a chapel choir.

Against this background, Ercole's discriminating patronage of musicians and composers in Ferrara appears as a radical departure from precedent. His years at Naples, an important musical center in the 1440s and 1450s, clearly gave him even more than an understanding and appreciation for music. It must have been there that he became reasonably proficient in it himself, both as a singer and player. After his foot was badly injured during the battle of La Molinella in 1467, when he was fighting as a *condottiere* for the Venetians, he probably became even more serious about music. The injury was to trouble him for the rest of his life—he walked with the aid of a cane—and from time to time it severely limited his mobility (Fig. 11). In any case, evidence is mounting that Ercole's well-known interest in music was not only more serious, sustained, and systematic than has ever been recognized, but that it appeared early, indeed at the very beginning of his reign. Moreover, it can now be stated without any doubt

[30] Such in any case is the impression presented by L. F. Valdrighi, "Cappelle, concerti, e musiche di Casa d'Este del secolo XV at XVII," *AMP,* Ser. III, vol. 2 (1883), 415-65, a work which, though full of defects, is in this case confirmed by many sources. See above p. 99.

that this was no mere quantitative change, but represents a new departure in Ferrarese music, for Ercole went beyond secular and ceremonial music to cultivate sacred, polyphonic music.[31]

One should not underestimate the importance of this decision. It means that Ercole would have to compete financially for the most sought-after musicians and composers, and that he would have to do so in a market that included such lavish and potent consumers as the Duke of Milan, the King of Naples, and, above all, the papacy. It meant that his ambassadors would have to add to their other duties those of identifying musical talent and recruiting new singers for the court. It presupposed, or at least required, the presence of an audience potentially capable of serious interest in and attention to music, and thus assumes musical professionalism of a new kind.

The painstaking research of Lewis Lockwood is now beginning to reveal precisely who these new singers were, and how Ercole recruited them as well as providing much more detailed and useful information about them. His work for the first time demonstrates why a composer of international stature, such as Josquin des Prez, would have written for Ercole such innovative and influential works as the famous mass, *Hercules Dux Ferrariae,* and the *Miserere.* From Lockwood's study of the growth of Herculean patronage of music, Ercole's ability to attract such eminent figures emerges as a natural consequence of policies rationally formulated and pursued, and not as a peculiar windfall.

The *De triumphis religionis* furthers our knowledge of this aspect of Ercole's activities. Sabadino describes Ercole

[31] All serious students of Renaissance music will now want to consult the important article of L. Lockwood, "Music at Ferrara," who makes and skillfully elaborates this point. Lockwood's footnotes, incidentally, provide the best available bibliography of the musicological literature of Renaissance Ferrara, as well as offering new documentary material.

going to Mass and hearing the "optime voce" of the "dignissimi Musici" while he himself follows the proceedings in a beautifully illuminated book, in front of which he kneels throughout.[32] But most importantly, Sabadino not only provides absolutely conclusive evidence for Lockwood's argument that this commitment to music starts at the very beginning of Ercole's reign, but reveals something about the precise nature of Ercole's innovations:

> What shall we say of your Excellency's religion, a thing even wonderful and worthy of Heaven? Just when you were made Duke, on August 21 in the year 1471— when your dignity and wealth grew—your spirit, always magnanimous, [alsò] grew with sacred prudence toward the higher things of Religion. You formed two musical choruses of expert singers, one of twenty-four young boys, and the other of more than that number of very expert professionals who instructed the lesser ones. And thus every day, wherever your ducal Highness happened to be, you heard Mass celebrated in the best song. And on festive days it was sung with the organ. You followed this procedure for ten years, until the bellicose fury of the Venetian princes disrupted your Excellency and your *popolo*. Then, as a result, you did away with the choir of young boys, and combined the two choirs into one, and that is how it has been to this day.[33]

[32] *DTR*, f. 92 r°: "Facta questa divina elymosina chel peccato extingue come Laqua il foco: tua Excellentia va ad audire solemne Messa celebrata da optime voce deli toi dignissimi Musici, existendo tu con uno tuo libro ornatissimo avanti devotamente a quella genuflesso, sempre come narrato habjamo."

[33] *Ibid.*, ff. 84 v°-85 r°: "Che diremo de tua Excellentia anchora cose mirande e degne del cielo, dela tua religione? Che essendo tu creato Duca correndo li anni dela salute mille et quatrocento septanta uno et giorni vintiuno de augusto, e cresciuta la dignitate con le richeze, l'animo tuo

Thus it appears that Ercole was actually able to begin his musical patronage on an even larger scale than obtained at the time which has generally been regarded as the heyday of music during his regime. It was only the Venetian war which forced some economies in this area. It is also notable that Sabadino's discussion stresses Ercole's cultivation of sacred vocal music, emphasizes the quantitative side of Ercole's effort, and explicitly relates the entire field to the Duke's celebrated piety.

Ercole's overwhelming religious concerns may also be traced to his patronage of the visual arts. On a small scale, many manuscripts on religious themes survive to attest to this concern.[34] From this point of view, the mere fact is significant that a treatise such as that of Sabadino degli Arienti was written. Ercole also encouraged miniaturists to exert great efforts on the adornment of missals, musical texts, and other devotional works.[35] In fact, during his reign, in which printing makes its first appearance in Ferrara, the work of the illuminator comes to be applied to a gradually decreasing range of subjects, among which items of religious interest occupy an increasingly important place.[36] The library

---

sempre magnanimo con prudentia sancta crescette ad cose più alte de religione. Facesti duo chori in la musica de periti cantori: uno de vinti-quattro Adoloscentuli, e laltro de magiori de tanto numero peritissimi che Insignavano a li Minori. Et cosi ogni giorno, dove la tua ducal Alteza si trovana, audivi in optimo canto Messa celebrare. Et li festivi giorni quella con lorgano se cantava. Questo ordine dieci anni servasti, sino chel bellico furore delli principi Venetiani la tua Excellentia, et il tuo populo turbarono. Diche alhora il choro de li Adolescentuli deponesti facendo de duo Musici chori uno. Et cosi sino al presente giorno hai observato."

[34] See Bertoni, *La Biblioteca Estense,* esp. Appendix III.

[35] G. Gruyer, *L'Art ferrarais,* ii, 436-43. Gruyer noticed the slow decline of miniature painting in Ferrara in the Herculean period, but did not associate this with the correlative rise of the printed book, as most later scholars have done.

[36] The first printing press in Ferrara was started by a Frenchman named André Beaufort (also known as Andrea Gallo, Andrea Belforte

of Eleanora, of which we have an inventory, is dominated by religious books, and the reciprocally reinforcing fervor of this couple is of more than passing relevance.[37] In fact, sixty of the seventy-four books listed in the inventory are demonstrably religious in character, and at least half of the remaining fourteen may have concerned religious subjects.

On a larger scale, Ercole is responsible for a vast amount of church building and redecorating in Ferrara, but unlike the secular elements of the Herculean addition, most of the visual evidence of this extensive undertaking disappeared centuries ago. However, some of Biagio Rossetti's façades still remain, and so do the outer structures of an impressive number of churches built at the end of the *Quattrocento,* though some of these now serve more mundane uses as garages, warehouses, and even, in one instance, a cinema.[38]

Gallicus, Andrea de Francia, and Andrea Francigena), in 1471. On the early history of printing in Ferrara, see G. Antonelli, *Ricerche biblio- grafiche sulle edizioni ferraresi del secolo XV* (Ferrara, 1830), who offers a catalogue of Ferrarese *incunabula;* also Gruyer, *L'Art ferrarais,* ii, 501-38. Ferrara offered an atmosphere receptive to the early introduction of printing. Indeed, Gruyer gives evidence that the art would have been introduced somewhat earlier than it was had it not been for the pre- occupation of the *savi* with reconstructing certain dykes in the early 1470s. See Carbone's praise of printing in a letter to Borso d'Este reproduced by R. Hirsch in *Printing, Selling, and Reading, 1450-1550* (Wiesbaden, 1967), 40.

[37] See Bertoni, *La Biblioteca Estense,* 220-33. Of 74 titles given in the inventory of Eleanora's library, only six are not demonstrably religious in character, and of these four have to do with family history and affairs. The only clearly secular books of general interest in Eleanora's library were a printed translation of Pliny and a manuscript of Caesar's *Com- mentaries.*

[38] See esp. G. Medri, *Le Chiese di Ferrara nella cerchia antica* (Bologna, 1967), a work that offers saddening support for the historical conserva- tionist. On Rossetti's churches, the best source is B. Zevi, *Biagio Rossetti, architetto ferrarese: il primo urbanista moderno europeo* (Turin, 1960), a major contribution to the history of Ferrarese construction in the Renaissance.

Sabadino lists, among Ercole's claims to *magnificentia* in the adornment of the city, his financing of religious foundations, and actually enumerates many of the monasteries and churches that were major beneficiaries of Ercole's support and gives in round figures the sums spent on each. For the construction of the residence of the Augustinian canons regular, for example, Ercole is said to have spent 4,000 ducats. For that of the order of Carmelites, he spent more than 2,000 ducats, "con grande splendore." Sabadino cannot even list them all. After citing a large number specifically, he simply lumps the rest together: "And you generally either adorned, or started, or repaired all the other Churches and holy places in a most devout way, a stupendous thing, to the entire glory of the highest and most glorious prince, the omnipotent *signore* God." He adds that the sounds of the masons' hammers and the other workmen who are doing these labors can be heard around the world.[39] Small wonder that Ferrara in the 1490s became a kind of Mecca for the religious, a city of new monastic and lay foundations, a city in which such mystics as Suor Lucia da Narni were persuaded to resettle, a city in which vanities were burned, sumptuary laws enforced, public morals carefully watched.[40] Small wonder that Girolamo Savonarola,

[39] *DTR*, f. 65 v°: "gia per tutto el Mondo el sanctissimo suono delle pietre dal martelli percosse per li muranti maestri, et da li molti Intagliatori de li molti et varij marmi per ornamento de li edificii et spirituali." For comments on the relationship of ideas of magnificence to building, see R. A. Goldthwaite, "The Florentine Palace as Domestic Architecture," *AHR* lxxvii:4 (Oct., 1972), 977-1012, esp. 989-92.

[40] See L. Chiappini, "Ercole I d'Este e Girolamo Savonarola," *AF*, ser. ii, vol. vii, pt. 3 (1952), 45-53; *idem*, "Un bruciamento delle vanità a Ferrara," *AF*, same volume, 57-58. There are numerous ducal as well as communal decrees from the period attempting to legislate standards of dress and other aspects of public morals, a fact that suggests not only a high level of religious and moral concern for these subjects, but also an increasing degree of difficulty in preserving standards of public order and deportment.

after having left Ferrara in disillusion with its worldliness as a young friar, admired and praised the zealous Duke who consulted him in anxious and soulful letters.[41]

It is evident that religion in the Herculean court was very much a part of everyday life. At the same time, it yielded many special moments as well, periods of heightened awareness and exalted celebration which this period of Estense rule in Ferrara produced. Thus, for example, the chronicles give evidence of a dramatic increase in the number of religious processions in this period.[42] There were processions for all sorts of things. If the Duke was sick, processions were ordered to pray for his recovery; when he recovered, a procession thanked God for His goodness. An immense religious procession signaled the victory over Niccolò di Leonello. The great holidays, such as St. George's Day, Corpus Christi, Easter, and so forth, invariably called for processions as well.

Ercole also took a great interest in the state of the Church in his territories. He had decreed in 1476 that nobody might seek an ecclesiastical benefice without ducal permission, so that the high churchmen of Ferrara during his reign were invariably men he respected and approved.[43] They were predictably severe in enforcing good doctrine, undoubtedly with full ducal support. Indeed, the Grand Inquisitor of Lombardy was based in Ferrara, and on at least one occasion

---

[41] This subject has been explored by A. Cappelli, *Fra Girolamo Savonarola e notizie intorno a suo tempo* (Modena, 1869), where most of the relevant correspondence is published.

[42] These are listed by G. Pardi in his index to Zambotti, *Diario,* 415.

[43] Zambotti, *Diario,* 36. It has been suggested by L. Lockwood (private communication) that one major purpose of this move was to make lesser benefices available for the musicians for whom Ercole was competing against the papacy and the Sforzas. Lockwood cites numerous references in the diplomatic correspondence between Ercole and his emissaries in Rome to the need for this and related powers of appointment, and for that reason.

acted severely to make an example of a suspected heretic.[44] In some ways, though this subject merits study on a much larger scale, it appears that Church and State were almost inextricably intertwined in the Ferrara of Ercole I.[45]

Nevertheless, though it gives us many clues, and helps to explain some apparent paradoxes, religion should not be taken to be the golden key that explains Ercole's every action. This duke was a man of deep passions, many of them directed toward God no doubt, but not a few directed elsewhere as well.

In 1478, for example, the list of appointments to high offices, usually released early in January, did not appear until March 16. The chronicler Zambotti offers an explanation: "He did not give them [the offices] out during the festivities of last Christmas, as is the custom, because he spent every day playing [i.e., gambling] with one Abbram, a Jew who had much money, and the Duke was the winner." [46] Zambotti's explanation does not seem convincing, for it would hardly have taken nearly three months to announce the forty or fifty names involved, even if the card

---

[44] See *ibid.,* 28.

[45] This is not to suggest that Ercole did not have his differences with a succession of popes, until the marriage of his son Alfonso to Lucrezia Borgia, the daughter of Alexander VI. Indeed, Ercole was excommunicated by Sixtus IV, an act that had little practical significance. Ercole's relations with the papacy are particularly well narrated by E. G. Gardner, *Dukes and Poets.* The point I make here is simply that Ercole took if anything an even more active role in the religious affairs of Ferrara than any of his predecessors.

[46] Zambotti, *Diario,* 45: "Lo illustrissimo duca nostro distribuì li officii soi, e non li dette a le feste de Nadale passate, como solea, per havea ogni dì attexo [a] zugare con uno Zodio Abbram, il quale ha molti dinari, e lo duca hè remaxo vincitore." L. Lockwood informs me (private communication) that the same Abbram was a frequent card playing companion of other members of the Este family, and was even known to have accompanied some of them on boat trips on the Po for that purpose.

game (if that is what it was) had gone on for three or four weeks without interruption. But the point is that it seemed eminently plausible to an informed contemporary observer that Ercole would drop all of his other interests indefinitely once he became interested in a good game of cards. The incident would be revealing if this quirky, idiosyncratic intensity did not appear in other ways. Consider for example his *penchant* for the odd pastime—perhaps not lacking in sexual significance—of riding around the streets with members of the court throwing raw eggs at the young girls who came to their windows to look.[47] Consider the unconventional means he chose to show the *popolo* he had recovered from his long illness during the Venetian war— he simply shaved his beard.[48] Consider the grandiose project

---

[47] *Ibid.,* 44, 60. Ercole himself took part in the great egg-fight of February 1, 1478, which lasted for an hour in the great Piazza, ". . . e tuti quelli se ritrovòno in Piaza, forno caregi de ove rotte." The events of February 12, 1479, may in part be explained as a northern Italian version of the Tuscan snowball fight, according to Pardi. It is clearly an activity associated with the annual season of carnival, and follows several nights of masked balls and precedes yet others. "Lo excellentissimo duca nostro insieme con messer Zoanne Bentivoglio e messer Sigismondo e messer Raynaldo da Este, con circa quaranta di soi cortexani, andonò per la citade con un cesto de ove ciaschaduno e con le coracine, immascheradi e con camixe bianche, tragando a le fenestre a le zovene." After proceeding to the Piazza where a pitched battle was waged with the remaining eggs, the courtiers started aiming their missiles at Eleanora and her ladies, who had come out on a portico to watch but quickly took refuge indoors. For some astute suggestions as to the political and cultural significance of such ritualized and institutionalized forms of misrule as the carnival, the *ventura,* and the egg-fights and snowball fights for which Herculean Ferrara provides much evidence, see now N. Z. Davis, "The Reasons of Misrule: Youth Groups and Charivaris in Sixteenth-Century France," *Past and Present,* No. 50 (February, 1971), 41-75. In addition to providing much useful comparative data, Davis' notes offer a virtual annotated bibliography of the sociological and anthropological literature bearing upon these kinds of events.

[48] Zambotti, *Diario,* 133; the same information in Sanudo, *Commen-*

he conceived as his own memorial. A gigantic marble column was brought from somewhere in the Veronese to the banks of the Po near Ferrara in the early 1480s. Then war intervened, years passed, and the immense stone was never moved. In 1499, Ercole finally succeeded in having it laboriously transported into the city at communal expense. It was set up in the great *piazza* which Rossetti had designed to form the nucleus of the addition. Though Ercole Grandi had designed an equestrian statue of Ercole for the top of the column, somehow this work was never done, and in later years Ludovico Ariosto was set upon the heights, where he remains today.[49]

This episode is noteworthy because it shows that Ercole was just as vain, as concerned for his own glorification, as Niccolò III or Borso, and because it suggests that beyond this element of continuity, the way in which Ercole did things, even if his attempts sometimes failed, differs by an order of magnitude from the scale common to his predecessors. For Ercole, no discreet statue mounted on a modest column would do. It had to be the biggest. The same difference in scale carries over into his patronage of painters, his treatment of the poor, his contributions to churches, his extension of the city, and, perhaps most conspicuously of all, his introduction of entertainments into the lives of courtiers and *popolani* alike. Lavish balls, jousts, tourneys, dinnerparties, masquerades, hunting and fishing expeditions, cere-

---

tarii della Guerra di Ferrara tra I Veneziani e il Duca Ercole d'Este nel 1482 (Venice, 1819), 42.

[49] For this project see Gruyer, *L'Art ferrarais,* i, 526; cf. Zambotti, *Diario,* 286: "La colona grande nova, che hera suxo la riva de Po, fu liurà de condure hozi (March 4, 1499) in suxo la piaza de Tera Nova con grandissima spexa e bello inzegno, perchè hera grandissimo pexo per essere lunga pedi 20½. . . . La colona, dapo'che la fu conducta de Veronexe, he stata anni quindexe suxo la ripa del Po al porta de San Polo. . . . Suxo dicta colona se ge ha a mettere il duca Hercule a cavalo, de bronzo, con belli intagli."

monial entries fill the chronicles of these years.[50] Vast sums
were spent on these entertainments, not only by the Duke,
but by members of the court and men desiring to make their
way in Estense circles.[51] Ercole's personal life style was so
extravagant, compared even to Borso's, that it is no surprise
to find him hiring himself out as a *condottiere* at an age
and stage in life that his predecessors had regarded as a
good time to take things somewhat easier (Fig. 12). Increasingly he was forced by these heavy expenses to levy
heavy taxes and forced loans, to borrow more and more
often from Jewish bankers, and ultimately to try to effect
some economies. Generally speaking, Borso appears to have

[50] All three of the major Ferrarese chronicles for Ercole's reign give
much useful material on these kinds of events, but by far the most
copious and accurate information generally appears in the *Diario* of
Zambotti, not only because he was a personage of some stature in the
court, and therefore an eyewitness to many of the events he relates, but
also because he was keenly interested in the pageantry, luxury, elegance,
and display which comprised an essential element of Ercole's style. The
same may be said, though to a lesser extent, of Caleffini, whose interests
tend to run more strongly toward economic and political matters. Least
helpful in this area of the social world of Ferrara is the anonymous *Diario
Ferrarese,* which—more than the others—reflects a non-courtly, bourgeois
point of view. Additional materials confirming the reports of Zambotti
and the others also appear frequently in the correspondence of foreign
ambassadors to Ferrara, in letters of members of the Este family, and in
such encomiastic MSS. as Sabadino's *De triumphis religionis.*

Both Zambotti and Caleffini often state the cost of various spectacles,
the value of gifts or works of art, and similar kinds of data. More detailed
and reliable information on Estense patronage is available in the records
of the ducal *camera,* and a good part of this has been studied by such
scholars as A. Venturi, and now L. Lockwood, in the area of musical
patronage. A detailed study of the financial registers for the entire
Herculean period is needed.

[51] It is again Zambotti who notes the efforts being made by other mem-
bers of the Herculean circle to engage in prestigious forms of display.
See, e.g., his notices on the behavior of Borso Pendaglia, pp. 29, 317; of
Lodovico Muzzarelli, pp. 308, 346; *et al.*

managed to live fairly well within his very substantial income. For Ercole that was impossible. One may well ask why.

By virtue of his office alone, Ercole was a much more exalted figure than his brothers. He was the first of the Estensi to assume signorial powers with all of the titles and privileges to which a ruler of Ferrara could possibly aspire. The recognition and authority that Borso devoted his career to building up could be taken almost for granted by Ercole. He might still win honors worth savoring, such as the Order of the Garter, which he received from Edward IV in 1480, but these were merely icing on the cake. They could add little to his legal authority and nothing to his power. Being a duke, however, entailed different kinds of obligations from those of a marquess. It required maintaining a much grander public style, which included the maintenance of larger and more prestigious diplomatic missions, more elaborate receptions, hospitality, and departures for important visitors, the fulfilment of greater popular expectations of generosity and display, bigger dowries, and so forth. At the same time, Ercole had by far the largest family to support since Niccolò III had ruled Ferrara. The marriage to Eleanora brought in some capital, perhaps quite a lot, since the marriage agreement negotiated by Sigismondo d'Este called for a penalty of 100,000 ducats in case of a violation by either side. But soon she had two daughters, Isabella and Beatrice, and both of them soon needed dowries themselves. A number of other children followed.[52]

In addition to his own nuclear family, Ercole had a sizable court to maintain at ducal expense. In addition to his brother and half-brothers, there were the great noblemen, and of course the hundreds of servants of all sorts, and the vast

---

[52] The best work on Eleanora d'Aragona is that of L. Chiappini, *Eleanora d'Aragona, prima duchessa di Ferrara* (Rovigo, 1956), with many documents.

establishment of houses, horses, and the like. Even in Borso's time this was a large operation, but under Ercole parts of it had probably doubled. How could the Duke hope to keep pace with such escalating expenses without a comparable increase in his revenues from the land? There were several ways. Alongside the inevitable increases and extensions of taxes, there were frequent levies on an *ad hoc* basis, to meet some particular need. These were sometimes presented as forced loans, but they were not repaid.[53] Such extraordinary taxes were raised during the Venetian war, during the construction of the Herculean addition, and at other times.[54] The sale of court offices and titles, which Ercole was probably the first to institute at Ferrara, also became a new and important source of revenue.[55] The growing population of

[53] For the *prestanze* and other *ad hoc* fiscal techniques see P. Sitta, "Saggio sulle istituzioni finanziarie del ducato Estense," *AF* III (1891), 193-96. Other sources of income available to the Estensi are discussed in the same work, 135-85.

[54] *DF*, 199: On the same day as Ercole declared a surtax on sales of meat, raising that tax to the highest level since the Venetian War, he also declared a special levy for the new walls. The outcry against what must have been regarded as excessive spending for defense was clearly impressive: "In dicto giorno fu dato principio a doverse scodere li danari per fare fornire le mure nove de Ferrara, cum tante bestiame cridi et maledictione che è una maraviglia, facendo pagare preti, frati, remiti, terreri, forastieri, et fachini et ogni altra persona." The clergy was frequently taxed along with everyone else in Ferrara, as the above passage shows, but specific monasteries or orders were often exempted from particular levies. See *ACSF*, Registro dei Proclami Ducali, A, 7, 10, f. 90, where the laborers of the *monaci certosini* are exempted from the *cavalzellanaria,* probably because of their works in the fields or hydraulic projects. Ercole also tended to grant exemptions from local taxes when a particular region was engaged in public works, especially land reclamation. It is possible that exemptions were more or less routinely granted to certain favored groups of religious (cf. Proclami Ducali, cit. 12, 1, f. 196).

[55] This is merely a suggestion, which will require much further research. But see Caleffini for January 5, 1486, and December 24, 1485, esp.

the city also meant more income from property taxes, taxes on consumer goods, and the like. However, Sitta's estimate of Ferrara's population at 100,000 in the late fifteenth century cannot be taken seriously. At its height, the city may have numbered 30,000.[56]

On this basis, the dukes had to manage their two major expenditures—the court and defense. Sitta's findings suggest that except in wartime, which was rare, the figures spent on these items increased gradually throughout the fifteenth and sixteenth centuries, from a base figure of about 20,000 *lire marchesane* in 1434 to about 120,000 *lire* in the late sixteenth century.[57] Throughout this period, the Estensi tried to build up an industrial base in Ferrara. The guilds, no longer in any sense a political threat, were encouraged to reorganize and function effectively.[58] The dukes occa-

---

f. 229 v°, who reports that at the beginning of 1486 Ercole sold all offices "universaliter" to the highest bidders.

[56] Here I follow K. J. von Beloch, *Bevölkerungsgeschichte Italien* (Berlin, 1937-61), II, 108-21, who offers an educated guess based largely on urban construction.

[57] Sitta, "Saggio sulle instituzioni finanziarie," 120-30.

[58] Among the early acts of an incoming Este *signore* was the confirmation of guild statutes, whereby the privileges and prerogatives of the guilds were confirmed in return for the proper statements of allegiance. But there is also evidence that the Estensi recognized the usefulness of the guilds as instrumentalities in maintaining public order and economic well-being. See, for example, the statutes of the leather-workers, *BAF,* MS. Statuti, 43, f. 1: "Illustrissime princeps & excellentissime dux: A la vostra Ducale signoria expone la Università et homini de larte di pellacani de la cita vostra de ferrara vostri fidelissimi servituri. Che essendo da multi anni in qua sta epsa arte male gubernata & desfavorita da alcuni officiali et etiam da alcuni potenti citadini, che hano messo le mane in epsa arte totaliter devorata et destructa, e necessario volendola redrizare, reformare et renovare lo Decreto et ordinamento de quella etiam per la varieta di tempi che hano facto variare il modo del lavorare, come in ogni altro exercitio accade." The Biblioteca Ariostea possesses a *fondo* of guild statutes consisting of 47 MSS., and there are others in other *fondi.* Although some of these are of later origin, many date from the fifteenth

sionally offered fiscal and even financial support to entrepreneurs in tapestries, majolica, and cloth.[59] Indeed, Ferrarese textiles were protected by tariff within the Este state,
and the tiles and *terra cottas* of the city eventually attracted
more than local attention. Included within the vast gamut
of taxes elaborated by the ducal exchequer and the communal treasury were the state monopolies. These imposed
a kind of hidden tax, awarding to the *camera* both the
ordinary profits and the mark-up that could be added because of the absence of competition. At various times, this
applied to a wide range of functions and commodities,
including glass-making, salt, soap, skins, leather, and occasionally wheat and bread. Finally, of course, the dukes could
borrow from banks, though they were sometimes obliged
to pawn some of their valuables to do so.[60] To keep this
avenue of credit open, the Jews of Ferrara were accorded
generally good protection, and lived peacefully with their
neighbors.[61] When threatened, they usually received ducal

---

century, and include not only statutes and confirmations of privileges, but
also matriculation records stretching over centuries. It is worth noting
that almost all of the statutes are those of the so-called lesser guilds, a
fact that fits in nicely with our interpretation of the effects of the Obizzan
suppression of the guilds (Ch. I above, esp. n. 34). I am indebted to the
late Dott. Ireneo Farneti for bringing these MSS. to my attention. Since
they are little known to economic historians, it is useful to cite the
references to them in P. Sitta's inadequate discussion, "Le Università delle
Arti a Ferrara," *AF,* viii (1896), 5-204. The first fifty pages (and esp.
pp. 57-78) of Sitta's monograph bear upon our period. The work as a
whole, though helpful, is certainly less precise than the same author's
piece on financial institutions.

[59] See G. Campori, *Notizie della maiolica e della porcellana a Ferrara
nei secoli XV e XVI* (Pesaro, 1879); Sitta, "Le Istituzione finanziarie," 139.

[60] Zambotti, *Diario,* 92: See also the sources on the Jews of Ferrara
given above, pp. 124-27.

[61] Balletti, "Gli Ebrei e gli Estensi," *AM,* Ser. v, vol. vii (1913), 11-13.
Balletti discovered, especially in the archives in Reggio, abundant documentation of both legal guarantees and favorable popular attitudes toward

assistance. Thus, when a lynch mob attacked a Jewish bank in response to rumors that the bankers had killed a little Christian girl in order to crucify her, Sigismondo, the Duke's brother, intervened on horseback to try to calm the mob. The Duke then appeared, and decreed that everybody should go home immediately, "a la pena de la forcha," because "his Lordship wanted to study the matter himself, and because no one should molest Jews or their houses." One member of the mob answered that it was a duty to kill these "pessimi Zudei," whereupon Ercole drew his sword, and the villain fled. The chronicler significantly adds that Ercole was afraid that there might be disorders in which the bank would be sacked, and that it contained as collateral goods belonging to "citizens and gentlemen, and also to the House of Este." [62]

It should be remembered that Ercole was also a professional soldier, and had a reputation comparable even to that of Federigo da Montefeltro. His income as a *condottiere* reflected the prevailing high opinion of his abilities. Thus, when he agreed to serve as Lieutenant-General of the League of Naples, Milan, and Florence, his stipend was set at 50,000 gold ducats in peacetime and 80,000 in wartime.[63] In accepting this arrangement, he was turning his back on the time-honored Venetian alliance on the one hand, and on his traditional liaison with the papacy on the other. For Ercole, personal religious belief and decisions as to political alliances clearly existed in separate compartments. Indeed, his cynicism and manipulative tactics in diplomacy would

---

Jews. All scholars have agreed that Ercole generally speaking maintained favorable conditions for the Jews of Ferrara, perhaps out of reluctance to allow the founding of a *Monte di Pietà*.

[62] Zambotti, *Diario,* 92;

[63] The other diarists say nothing about this event. The anonymous diarist's entries for 1481 are perfunctory, and Caleffini spends most of his section on May of that year describing heavy rains and floods in the *contado*.

have cast doubt on his piety, had he lived in a less super-stitious age.

A force that entered often and deeply into his life, the semi-pervasive role of religion in the despotic style of Ercole I d'Este could nevertheless be excluded entirely. If its pres-ence or absence were entirely a voluntary matter, we could be confident that he was perhaps mainly a *poseur* in matters of religion. Instead, his passionate credulity sometimes in-truded on situations in extremely direct ways. Thus in 1478, when Ercole betrayed both his papal and Neapolitan alle-giances to head the Florentine forces in the Pazzi War, he had visions of his sainted ancestor, the beatified Beatrice d'Este, crying aloud from her tomb.[64]

Generally speaking, though, Ercole managed to maintain a fairly rigid operational distinction between his religious and secular interests. The point is worth underlining, be-cause we tend to think only of modern societies in terms of the isolation of religion from daily life. But in fact this has often been true. For many rulers throughout European history at least, the gods simply had to receive their due mainly by means of ritual and ceremony. Their portion might be large, but once it had been provided, one could go on to other things. To be sure, one had to pay a small addi-tional price for the privilege of compartmentalization, and that was the psychic cost of some measure of guilt. (Ercole's vision of Beatrice d'Este is an especially nice example.) But religion itself even offers compartmentalized ways of coming to terms with one's guilt, and most people can live with a fair amount of it in any case. Such considerations help in understanding the almost jarringly "modern" juxtaposi-tions of secular and religious, pagan and Christian, mystical and cynical, savage and civilized, comic and serious that

[64] *Ibid.,* 155.

characterize the Herculean period.[65] A demonstration of this extremism of contrasts lies in another of the areas in which Ercole appears as a major innovator—the secular theatre.

Dramatic performances took place in Ferrara from the earliest days of Ercole's reign, but they did not at first command a notably high position in the scale of ducal patronage. Moreover, before the Venetian war, the performances were all devoted to sacred subjects. This was nothing new. As early as 1449 a play of St. George slaying the dragon had been publicly performed in the piazza, which had been decorated to resemble a forest.[66] In 1476, the same place provided the backdrop for a play representing the legend of St. James.[67] Five years later two scenes from the Passion of Christ were presented in the chapel of the ducal palace, with the aid of some complicated stage machinery and the ducal choir.[68] But it was not until after

[65] An editorial in *The New York Times* (November 3, 1970) may serve as an example of how the erroneous commonplace that compartmentalization is a modern phenomenon has permeated public consciousness: "It is a disquieting feature of modern high-technology societies that men with various kinds of expert knowledge compartmentalize their work and their private moral standards. They evade the moral implications of what they do in their daily jobs because they consider their work problems as purely technical or professional." This seems to me to be a very exact description of the diplomacy of Renaissance princes in general, and Ercole d'Este in particular.

[66] *DF,* 27. For the history of the theatre in Ferrara, see G. Pardi, "Il teatro classico a Ferrara," *AF,* xv (1904), 3-27; F. Rositi, "La commedia rinascimentale e le prime traduzioni alla corte di Ercole I," in *Pubblicazioni dell' Università Cattolica del Sacro Cuore: Contributi del' Istituto di Filologia Moderna* [Serie: Storia del Teatro] (Milan, 1968), i, 1-59; also the recent little book by E. Scoglio, *Il teatro alla corte Estense* (Lodi, 1965); and the more general survey by A. Stäuble, *La commedia umanistica del Quattrocento* (Florence, 1968).

[67] Zambotti, *Diario,* 11.

[68] E. Scoglio, *Il teatro alla corte Estense,* 38, 119.

the war, in 1486, that secular plays came to be given in
Ferrara. It is true that a comedy by Francesco Ariosto
Peregrino, the *Iside,* or *Isis,* had been read in the presence
of Leonello in 1444, and that the texts of Plautus had long
been known, admired, commented upon, and translated by
humanists in the ducal circle.[69] But no actual performance
was given until March 25, 1486, when the *Menaechmi* was
performed in the great courtyard of the ducal palace.

All the circumstances surrounding this production indicate that Ercole intended to make an impression with this
new and unprecedented revival of classical comedy. The
Marquess of Mantua came especially for the performance,
and the production was arranged in the usual Herculean
grand manner. There was a new stage, with five houses
painted as backdrops, and a galley with sails. A special platform was built opposite the stage for the Duke, his distinguished visitor, and the entire court. The rest of the courtyard was filled with spectators (Zambotti implausibly esti-
mates 10,000), who watched in amazed silence until the end,
when they applauded happily. The play lasted four hours,
ended with a round of fireworks, and cost over 1,000 ducats,
equivalent to one-fourth of the annual tribute due the
papacy, or the annual salaries of three important professors.[70]

[69] Scoglio, 36-37. The *Isis* is preserved in *BEM,* MS. Alpha Q, 7, 32
(Lat. 1096), which also includes an important elegy to Duke Borso. The
play has been amply studied, and full bibliographical notes are given in
the article by T. Ascari, "Francesco Ariosto Peregrino," *AAM,* Ser. v,
vol. xi (1953), 101.

[70] A good description is given by B. Zambotti, *Diario,* 171-72: Fu recitata
la comedia di Menichini, che fu beletissima e piacevole, in lo cortile novo
de la Corte ducale, suxo uno tribunale novo in forma de una citade de
asse con caxe depinte. . . . E durò insino a l'avemaria, zoè 4 hore, e infine
fu facto fogo in un arboro o zirandola, che in uno medemo tempo butò
più razi de foco in aere, alti, con gram strido e vampa stupendissima.
E cusi cum letitia, applauso e commendatione se finì la comedia, dove
intervene de le persone dexemilia a vedere con taciturnità." Noted also by

What Ercole had discovered was a harmless form of entertainment which could be attended by thousands of his subjects, and which therefore increased his stature not only with court and *popolo,* but even with the learned. In the comedy, Ercole had found an almost ideal expression of ducal magnificence.

Such performances therefore became a staple of Ferrarese life, the second element in the combination of bread and circuses upon which Ercole tended to rely. A few months later, in January, 1487, Niccolò da Correggio's *Cefalo* had its first performance, also in the outdoor theatre of the ducal courtyard. That these performances took place outdoors in the bitter chill of the Emilian winter should alert us to the semipolitical purpose they served. Correggio's play, Plautan in style and Ovidian in inspiration, was offered as part of a court wedding celebration. The Marquess of Mantua was again present, as were a great number of other dignitaries, citizens, and members of the academic community. In the wake of the destructive and demoralizing war, which had ended in the Peace of Bagnolo, such events contributed substantially to the restoration of Ercole's popularity. So did religious dramas.[71] By the end of Ercole's reign, most of the major plays of Plautus had been performed at least once, some works of Terence had made their appearance, the labors of Hercules had been presented in pantomime, and the Passion of Christ had also received due attention. Theatre had taken its place along with music as a major cultural interest of Ercole's. And unlike music, it offered manifest political dividends. It brought some of the gaiety of the court into the lives of the citizenry. This made

---

Caleffini, MS. cit., ff. 230. These performances usually occurred around the beginning or end of Lent.

[71] Scoglio, *Il teatro alla corte Estense,* 21; cf. Zambotti, *Diario,* 11, 88, 205, 206, 348-49. For the comedies see *ibid.,* 171, 178, 179, 180, 220-21, 215, 324-25, 321, 326, 329-31.

a difference, because one major characteristic of Ercole's rule by contrast with Borso's is an increased distance between duke and people, a fact that requires attention.

Ercole shared Borso's purposeful cultivation of the image of Augustan majesty. The medals struck in his honor by Sperandio, Baldassare d'Este, and others reveal an ever grander and more elevated classicism than Borso's. Herculean coinage carries forward the tradition of a majestic representation of *imperium*.[72] The painted portraits of Ercole—those which survive and those known only from verbal descriptions—reveal, in addition to this cultivated image of majesty, a sense of remoteness, detachment, and augmented psychological distance (Fig. 13). The famous portrait by Dosso Dossi in the Galleria Estense in Modena gives the best, but not the only, evidence of this.[73] The subject is dressed in ceremonial armor. Unprepared for combat, he is nevertheless protected from the world. His strong, serious face is set in a resolutely inscrutable, mask-like expression. He seems watchful, on his guard. To say that he appears defensive might not be too strong. There is no fear in his gaze, but one senses mistrust, even suspicion. He looks like an appropriate recipient for such works as the manuscript book *De Venenis,* which the Ferrarese physician Baptista Massa d'Argento presented to him after a series of lectures on the subject at the *Studium* (Fig. 12).[74]

[72] G. Gruyer, *L'Art ferrarais,* I, 583-651; and the medals listed by G. Pollard, *Renaissance Medals,* esp. 163.

[73] See the newly found descriptions of other portraits of Ercole below, pp. 256-57.

[74] See *BAF,* MS. Cl. I, 352, *Proservanda salute opusculum edidit de venenis et morsibus veneosis in felici gymnasio ferrariensia.* Massa's preface contains an interesting correction of Aristotle's view that all men desire to live, and thereby provides an unusual reflection of a certain degree of social consciousness in Herculean Ferrara. To this physician, it is absurd to suppose that all men want life, for there are many poor people for

Ercole was not incapable of lowering his guard, and he obviously did so in the company of his courtly favorites while hunting and fishing, or attending balls, jousts, and snowball fights.[75] But he was clearly an aristocrat who lacked the common touch. No one praises him for his accessibility or dwells on his popular appeal. Unlike Borso, who moved around just as much, Ercole was criticized for his constant peregrinations, his absenteeism from Ferrara.[76] The disapproval connotes a sense of loss because of psychological, not physical, distance. When Borso was in the city, he circulated casually and openly among the people; he had a kind word for everyone. People called him jovial; today they might say "casual." He was a man at peace with himself, a man whose sense of well-being somehow communicated itself to others. Ercole seems to have had none of this sunny affability. He could be moody and withdrawn. His natural taste for privacy was easily indulged by the ambitious counsellors and secretaries who carried out his decisions, and (probably often) even made them. When Ercole appeared in public, it was usually in a ceremonial way. Whether in elegantly entertaining the poor, seeking his *ventura,* attending a spectacle, or intervening to save or

whom life is merely a burden (f. 1): "Me pare, Illustrissimo Signore, che la natura voglia che ogne humana cretura appetisca e desidri el vivere longo. Ita che naturalmente luomo sta desideroso de vivere e star longo tempo ne la presente vita, como etiam e sententia di . . . Aristotele nel suo de generatione . . . Benche molte fiate vediamo lo opposito. Cioè multi essere piu cupidi de la morte che del vivere longo, e specialmente quilli che se ritrovono essere in extrema pauperta e grandissima miseria."

[75] Zambotti, *Diario,* 383-88, where Ercole's acts are listed by the editor G. Pardi for evidence of all of these activities. Cf. N. Z. Davis, in n. 47 above.

[76] Observers even sensed his psychological distance. Caleffini, for example, in his entry for May 20, 1484, comments disapprovingly on Ercole's constant musicianship during a period when his populace was starving and in wartime (f. 212).

condemn some miserable soul, he seemed to be exploiting his sense of occasion rather than reaching out toward other human beings. Missing from these events, even the self-consciously silly or comical ones, is the impression of spontaneity. The extent to which, even in mass societies, such differences in temperament are quickly and keenly sensed by an entire population is remarkable. In a small city like Ferrara, where the ruler's *persona* had long been one of the few subjects of genuine interest, and where bureaucracy had not heretofore impeded personal communication between *signore* and *popolo,* it was a vast change to go from a friendly, accessible prince to an aloof, remote type like Ercole. The change is symbolized by Ercole's love of masquerades, despite the serious social tensions they produced.[77]

These observations on Ercole's despotic style are not meant to imply that he lacked concern for the welfare of his subjects. Indeed, by all the indicators we have used before —construction of public works and fortifications, attempts to control flagrant abuses of public standards of morality and civil order, charitable and philanthropic acts, flood control and land reclamation work, support for the university and the learned professions—Ercole at least rivaled and generally

[77] Though he often arranged for masked balls, and was basically not opposed to the custom of going *in maschera* during carnival, Ercole was obliged to recognize that this sometimes led to unusual forms of crime and disorder, and consequently decreed against the practice. See *ACSF,* Commissioni Ducali, CD, 9, 30, f. 8, a decree dated April 12, 1476, that women might not appear in public with their faces so covered that they could not be recognized. Violation brought a fine of 25 *lire.* Yet the duke himself enjoyed appearing *in maschera* during carnival (see, e.g., Zambotti, *Diario,* 131), but after the war masked persons were forbidden to bear arms (*ibid.,* 171). During the last years of his reign, Ercole forbade the practice (*ibid.,* 356). The prohibition against bearing arms was put forward repeatedly, which indicates how hard it was to enforce. See the decree of Eleanora dated July 23, 1486, in *ASM, ASE,* Cancelleria, Gride Manoscritte, Busta la.

surpassed his predecessors.[78] But there were counterweights, which offset the positive effects of these beneficent policies. At least one of these counterweights was the direct product of the relative remoteness from day-to-day contact with the *popolo*: administrative malfeasance. Ercole's willingness to delegate authority sometimes led to inadequate supervision of ducal and communal officials, especially those with financial and judicial duties. There is more evidence of both popular and ducal dissatisfaction with the performance of trusted subordinates under Ercole than in any previous period. Part of this recurrent discontent must be written off to the traditional Estean adroitness in assigning subordinates to carry out unpopular policies and then bear the consequences. But others indicate that Ercole was neither so thorough nor astute a judge of men, nor so careful and effective a supervisor, as Borso, Leonello, or Niccolò.[79] Not the sort to arouse constant devotion in others, he had no Uguccione Contrari or Ludovico Casella to take up his slack. His wife Eleanora, despite her notable piety and intellect, and her celebrated courage and effectiveness during the crises of the war, was not in a position to exercise these kinds of controls consistently. Thus, Ercole once had to make a public declaration that he was restoring to the communal treasury tax funds that had been erroneously transferred to the ducal camera by his hand-picked *giudice de' savi,* Iacopo Trotti. At the same time, he commuted certain taxes and waived certain punishments. Two days

---

[78] Eg., M. Zucchini, *L'Agricoltura ferrarese attraverso i secoli* (Rome, 1967), 90: "Il disseccamento delle paludi per la salubrità dell' aria e per la fertilità delle campagne venne intensificato dal Duca Ercole I, . . . applicando interventi sempre più efficaci." Similar statements could be culled from monographs dealing with any specific aspect of Ercole's regime, except perhaps diplomacy and day-to-day administration, in which he was relatively haphazard and reactive.

[79] Especially pertinent here are the views of Chiappini, *Gli Estensi,* 182-84.

before, he had relieved Trotti of his position and sent him away from the city, and he now appointed another trusted adviser, Bonifacio Bevilacqua, in his place, "because he was pleasing to the people." It is evident from the chronicles, especially Caleffini's, that the four Trotti brothers, leaders of a family long influential in ducal affairs, had come to be hated by the *popolo*. Whether or not Ercole collaborated with their schemes to defraud the commune is not known, but he clearly was not implicated in the public mind. This is not a unique case.[80] By the following November, no member of the hated Trotti was safe in Ferrara. Even Paolo Antonio, a former *consigliere* who had been imprisoned in Ferrara, had to be moved to a rural stronghold to avoid his being killed by the *popolo*.[81] But at that point, Ferrara faced its greatest crisis in nearly two hundred years. It was the fall of 1482, and Venetian armies stood at the gates of the city. Enemy troops had broken through the walls of the great park, or *Barco,* of Belfiore, and were slaughtering the abundant wildlife there. Ercole lay almost comatose, fighting for his life. So many people actually thought he was dead that Eleanora succumbed to public requests that he be seen by the people. For an hour, gentle-

---

[80] See esp. Zambotti, *Diario,* 119-20. It appears that the resentment against the Trotti family, and particularly against Paolo Antonio Trotti, Senior, the ducal secretary and prime minister, emanated as much from noble as popular circles. Paolo Antonio was held accountable for the diplomacy leading to the Venetian War. In the great confrontation of 1482, the nobles and emissaries of the citizenry were kept from outright rebellion only by the eloquence and coolness of the Duchess, who had to hear such grandees as Francesco di Rinaldo Ariosto and Rinaldo de' Costabili express their opposition to the Trotti in no uncertain terms. Two days later, Paolo Antonio was deported under armed guard, and it is clear that the diarist himself approved thoroughly of the action taken against him.

[81] *Ibid.,* 120; cf. Caleffini, MS. Cit., ff. 156 v°-157 v°, in which Zambotti's verdict is expressed even more forcefully, and Paolo Antonio is branded a "traditore."

men, citizens, and "plebei" were permitted to walk through the room where he lay, and the pitiful sight stiffened Ferrara's resistance to the threat of imminent destruction.[82]

In the aftermath of the war, popular discontent with ducal fiscal exactions reached a highpoint, and there was fairly rapid turnover in the position of Judge of the Twelve Savi. Only Bevilacqua won popular acclaim, and his demission after four years in 1486 may imply that he was not severe enough to satisfy Ercole's financial needs.[83]

This restiveness under increasing fiscal pressures, coupled with the impoverishment of a serious war, may also have some bearing on another expression of social dislocation: crime. For the period from 1482 to 1500, there seems to have been an appreciable increase in violent crime in Ferrara, most of it robbery with assault or, more commonly, robbery and murder. In a small city, where crimes against property were commonly punished by execution, there was not much point to leaving witnesses. And as we have already seen from other sources, there was more poverty in Ferrara now. For the first time in the century, there were many who lacked adequate food and clothing. The gulf between

[82] The best account of this strange event is Zambotti's, 119: ". . . la illustrissima Madama volgia fare ch'el popolo possa vedere la Excellentia del Duca . . . perche molti ge sono che credono la soa Excellentia essere morto, e per questo modo dubitano non essere inganati e dati in mano de altri. . . . E fece aprire tuti li ussi de le camere e anticamere dove hera la Excellentia del duca suxo il lecto, con una turcha, con la barba lunga, che a pena parlava e apriva li occhi, e teniva uno brazo e la mano aperta tocandola a tuti quelli che intrava. . . . Io steti sempre in uno cantone a vedere tale vixitatione, che durò più di una hora. . . ." Cf. Caleffini, f. 179 vº. It is not certain into whose hands the *popolo* thought it might be betrayed, but one suspects that people feared that the Trotti would turn Ferrara over to Venice at that point. The unrest, then, was inspired by fear that the Estensi would be overthrown.

[83] On the history of this important magistracy, see A. Maresti, *Cronologia et Istoria de capi, e Giudici de Savi della Città di Ferrara* (Ferrara, 1683) which is not altogether reliable and should be superseded.

rich and poor had grown both wider and deeper. Many of the more dramatic crimes look very much like amateurish and indiscriminate attacks by desperate men on the previously secure houses and persons of the privileged.

If economic and social problems are both more common and somewhat more sharply drawn in Ferrara at the end of the century, much of the woe that Ercole brought upon himself and his people was clearly produced by his own foreign policy. The first of the Estensi fully to repudiate the historic Venetian alliance by allowing his own marriage ties and ambitions for his children to produce a shift to a Neapolitan-Milanese-Florentine allegiance, he brought down upon himself the wrath of Venice and Rome alike.[84] In defying Venetian economic privileges in the Ferrarese, and raising the possibility of a hostile border where there had

---

[84] The most comprehensive discussions of Ercole's diplomacy are C. Piva, *La Guerra di Ferrara del 1482* (Padua, 1893); P. Negri, "Studi sulla crisi italiana alla fine del secolo XV," *ASL,* Ser. v, vol. L and Ser. vi, vol. LI (1923-4), 1-35; 75-144. Ercole's strongly Neapolitan orientation, the product of his formative years, is evident in the Hispanic names of his children— Alfonso (named for Ercole's father-in-law), Isabella, Ferrante. The marriages he arranged for his children (in Naples, Milan, Rome, and Mantua) reflect the lines of the new diplomacy. In the early phases (1470s and '80s) it might even have succeeded, had it not been for the assassination of Galeazzo Maria Sforza, a few months after the unsuccessful attempt by Niccolò di Leonello in Ferrara. That bizarre political crime meant a greater loss to Ferrara's security than any of the attempts from within which have been discussed here. Ercole had been systematically strengthening ties with Milan. Now the heir to that powerful ally was a boy of seven, his guardian a lady of no great acumen, and Milan was no longer in any position to appear as Ferrara's bulwark to her enemies. The Venetians, jealous of their salt monopolies on which Ercole was infringing, and covetous of the fertile Ferrarese *terra ferma* around Rovigo, were not slow to realize this. By 1482, the costly and destructive war was the result. Or, as Muratori put it (referring to Galeazzo Maria), "con esso lui morì la pace e quiete d'Italia [*Ant. Est.* ii, 235]." These and related events are more fully discussed by Chiappini, *Gli Estensi,* 155-68.

previously been a docile buffer state, Ercole exposed Ferrara
to the superior naval and land forces of a great power and
grossly misjudged the quantity and quality of the strategic,
tactical, and logistic support he would receive from his
allies. It was pure luck that Ferrara itself was not sacked
and destroyed like Carthage. While the Venetian forces were
pillaging the surrounding countryside, a modest contingent
of reinforcements arrived, and the enemy decided that the
risks of potential losses from street fighting were not justified by the potential gains. Eventually, papal adherence to
the slowly-developing league in defense of Ferrara guar-
anteed its ultimate success. Under the final terms of the war,
the *status quo ante* was restored, with minor exceptions.[85]
But it took time for Ferrara to recover its prosperity and
its self-confidence, for it had been badly hurt. Thus when
Ercole wanted to make the pilgrimage to St. James of
Compostela, in Galicia, thereby fulfilling the intent of his
father nearly eighty years earlier, there was popular opposition to his departure. In an elaborately contrived scene, a
weeping Ercole turned over the state to his brother and the
court officials, who tearfully vowed their allegiance and
fidelity. When Ercole got to Milan, the pilgrimage was
diverted to Rome, by order of the Pope, who suspected that
Ercole's trip through France would be used for political
ends.[86] If that was Ercole's intent, he appears to have kept
even his own trusted advisers in the dark. But given his
growing Francophile policies, the possibility cannot be
lightly dismissed. It must be remembered that this happened

[85] The terms of the Peace of Bagnolo are succinctly summarized by
M. Sanudo, *Commentarii della Guerra di Ferrara,* 141-44; E. G. Gardner,
Dukes and Poets, ch. VI, "The War of Ferrara," 165-211, is still the best
English account. More important is the work of C. Piva cited above
(n. 84), and G. Fuscaldo, *La Guerra di Ferrara, 1482-1484* (Ferrara, 1925).
The extensive bibliography on this subject may be sampled in Chiappini,
Gli Estensi, 526-27.

[86] The best account is that of Zambotti, *Diario,* 182-86.

only three years after the war, at a time when suspicions and intrigues were still running high.

Even if Ercole had originally formulated a more judicious foreign policy, and kept his territories safe from destruction, his reign would have produced significant changes from those of earlier *marchesi*. We have seen this by analyzing his own personality and concerns, and studying how these come to be reflected in the structure and function of the court. We have observed the growing gulf between wealth and poverty in Ferrara, and the increasing compartmentalization of functions and styles, both as reflected in the behavior of individuals and the structure and functioning of institutions. There is increased differentiation among groups, and increased specialization in the professional roles of individuals. Sub-groups, whether professional or social, seem to become more clearly defined, less open, more mutually exclusive. That is, Ferrarese society itself seems to become more differentiated and structured in functional terms. Professionalism, with its attractions and limitations, is on the rise.[87]

These are bold generalizations, and they must be approached with caution. At this point, they cannot be demonstrated statistically; but they grow out of some reasonable

---

[87] This kind of differentiation is characteristic of Ferrara in the late fifteenth century, and applies to all of the structures of society, including the university faculties, the guilds, and the structure of the court. It is a curious thing that the age which we associate with the ideal of the complete man (*uomo universale*), capable of excellence in all fields, should actually be an age of increasing specialization and professionalism. Could it be that scholars have been taken in by the educational treatises of the time, and that the idea of universality was one to which much lip-service was paid, but which may not have been taken seriously? If so, such a notion would be in some ways analogous to the contemporary American shibboleth about "liberal arts education," a concept that is now so deeply undermined by the specialistic and professionalistic tendencies of both scholars and students that it can hardly be taken seriously by any observer, even as a cultural myth.

evidence. Consider for example the position of the humanist at the court of Ercole I. On the one hand, there is the Ferrarese noble who writes; on the other, there is the professional man of letters, the rhetorician, orator, or court poet. He may come from anywhere, but he is not a *gentil'uomo,* he lives by his pen, and he is not primarily an academic. It can be safely said that the social history of humanism in *Quattrocento* Ferrara must be interpreted as the gradual decline of the second type of humanist in the court, and the growing ascendancy of the first. The Type II humanist in the persons of Guarino da Verona, Giovanni Aurispa, Teodoro Gaza, Antonio da Cornazzano, Ludovico Casella, and others had been on familiar terms with Leonello and his courtiers. Under Borso, most of them were still present in the courtly circle; and while he was not particularly interested in them, he had no wish to injure or exclude them, and they had a helpful intermediary in the increasingly powerful Casella. But members of this group, if they were at all good, became increasingly dependent on academic positions under Borso, and under Ercole even more so. That is to say, they took refuge in the structural world of another profession—because there was practically nothing for them to do at the court, whose own bureaucracy had been thoroughly professionalized. Notaries handled the routine business of *cancelleria* and *camera,* orators and counsellors from trusted local families handled more confidential ducal business, and Ercole's modest desires for the insights of men of knowledge were satisfied by vernacular books, and by clerics discoursing on religious subjects.[88] The frequent but trivial ceremonial orations the court required could easily be supplied by an academic hack like Carbone, working part-time. He, or someone like him, could be counted on to strike the right tone, without demanding much of his listeners by his speeches' intellectual content. From time

[88] See Zambotti, *Diario,* 87, 122, 155, 205, 221, *et al.*

to time, even lesser men, of whom the tedious Cleophilus was typical, turned in books of epigrams and other minor opuscules.[89] A competent but run-of-the-mill talent like Sabadino degli Arienti looks quite distinguished in the group of humanists in Ferrara who were not primarily professors in the *Studium*. This tendency was somewhat mitigated by the effects of Isabella's personality and patronage, but her impact was much more deeply felt in Mantua, after her marriage.[90]

Type I humanists, *per contra,* have extremely important roles to play in ducal administration and society. But they are noblemen, courtiers, diplomats, or provincial governors first, and men of letters second. They write poetry, study astrology, or compose histories, not as a means of livelihood, but because they have those talents and interests, and the energy, industry, and leisure to cultivate them. Under Ercole, the Type II, publish-or-perish humanists—"adversity's noblemen," in Charles Trinkhaus' phrase—produce not a single literary or scholarly masterpiece.[91] But the

[89] Octavius Cleophilus *Epigrammata, BAV,* MS. Vat. Lat. 5163, three books of courtly verse; *Georgius Merulla, Vicecomitum Estensisque Familiae Veteris Affinitatis Diuturnae Amicitiae ac mutui praesidii memoria* (Vat. Lat. 7703), with ded. to Ercole I; Pandolfo Collenuccio's *Bombarda* (Vat. Lat. 2934, vol. II, ff. 582-585), a dialogue dedicated to Ercole I, concerning the origins of the arts and sciences, and as vapid a piece of humanist dialogue as one is likely to come upon. For a list of the MSS. presented to Ercole I and preserved in the Biblioteca Estense, see G. Bertoni, *La Biblioteca Estense,* chs. 6, 7.

[90] The work of A. Luzio and R. Renier remains fundamental for an understanding of Isabella's impact on Mantuan and indeed Italian culture. See above all the article "La cultura e le relazioni litterarie di Isabella d'Este Gonzaga," *GSLI,* xxxv (1900), 193-237; but also the other articles cited by Chiappini, *Gli Estensi,* 528.

[91] For this phrase, its literary background, and its historical relevance, see C. E. Trinkhaus, *Adversity's Noblemen: The Italian Humanists on Happiness* (New York, 1940). It should be noted that even the most important translation of this period in Ferrara—Boiardo's version of Herodotus' *Persian Wars*—was written by a nobleman.

prosperous humanists of the gentry, with their high positions in the state, produce the works of Boiardo, Ariosto, Tito Vespasiano Strozzi, Ercole Strozzi, Niccolò da Correggio, Pellegrino Prisciani. All of these writers more or less directly reflect their courtly ambiance. They are rooted in the history and destiny of Ferrara, and deeply committed to the Estensi.[92] Yet though these roots and allegiances are reflected in their writings in a hundred ways, they are of secondary importance. Each of these authors would have had a secure position and a definite identity in the court had he never penned a line. They wrote to satisfy deeper urgings and strivings. Not dependent on learning for their livelihood, they were uncommitted to academic, Latinate humanism. Men of the world, as well as the court, they naturally preferred the *volgare*. By remaining gifted amateurs in the literal sense, they became the most genuine sort of professionals.

The philological, textual, and rhetorical traditions introduced by Guarino were now being continued in the university, which, however, does not appear to have grown substantially. Though the average number of doctorates awarded annually remained around thirty, there does seem to have been some qualitative improvement. There are, especially in the 1490s and the early sixteenth century, more eminent professors, like Leoniceno in medicine and Sadoleto in law.[93] And there are even some students who, like the

[92] For Pellegrino Prisciani, see above p. 167.

[93] Statements about the size of the university must be hedged with caution. Zambotti, *Diario,* 84, cites a gigantic snowball fight between 300 law students and the entire court. If his figure is only approximately accurate, it would suggest that at the very least the evidence on degrees granted is extremely fragmentary, or that most students left the university without having obtained diplomas. However, it is clear from the increasing number of students and scholars involved in one way or another in crimes of violence that the academic community in Ferrara was of substantial size in the 1480s and '90s; cf. "Crime and Punishment,"

Pole Copernicus, will make a name for themselves.[94] More-over, the *Studium,* though small, was a lively and active community. Faculty and students took part in public dis-putations, inaugural lectures were held in each faculty at the beginning of term and when a chair was newly filled.[95] Now and then there were bitter disputes over an intellectual problem, such as the vicious altercation between Leoniceno and Pandolfo Collenuccio over the reliability of Pliny.[96] Serious scholarship had its place in Ferrara, but that place

loc. cit. We know too that executed felons were sometimes turned over to the medical faculty for dissection. That the *Studium* was trying to set its house in order in the 1490s is evident from its revised statutes dating from that time, the original now in the Medical Library of McGill University in Montreal (MS. Ost. 7554, *Statuta Universitatis Scientiae, Medicinae, et Artis Civitatis Ferrariae*) a close version of which appears in F. Borsetti, *Historia Almi Ferrariae Gymnasii,* i, 364-437. The figure given here for the annual number of doctorates is based on the statistics compiled by C. Pinghini, "La popolazione studentesca dell'Università di Ferrara," 140-43.

[94] See esp. G. Pardi, *Titoli dottorali conferiti a Ferrara* (Lucca, 1900), and the more recent work by V. Caputo, *I collegi dottorali e l'esame di dottorato nello studio ferrarese* (Ferrara, 1962).

[95] Zambotti, *Diario,* is full of references to such occasions, as well as others such as pitched battles between students in various disciplines, or lunches offered by new officials or professors for their colleagues. The liveliest dispute between two distinguished members of the faculty occurred in 1477 when Ludovico Carbone, the poet laureate, and Matteo del Canale, a doctor of canon law and a recent alumnus of Ferrara, entered into a vicious personal diatribe against one another at the beginning of the year (see pp. 29-41).

[96] This controversy and its consequences are interestingly reviewed by L. Samoggia, *Le Ripercussioni in Germania dell'indirizzo Filologico-medico Leoniceniano della scuola ferrarese per opera di Leonardo Fuchs,* Vol. iv of *Quaderni di Storia della Scienza e della Medicine* (Ferrara, 1964), which includes a good bibliography; see also L. Thorndyke, *History of Magic and Experimental Science* (New York, 1953) vi, 593-610. On Niccolò Leoniceno (not to be confused with Niccolò da Lonigo, humanist translator of Procopius), see D. Vitaliani, *Della vita e della opere di Niccolò Leoniceno Vicentino* (Verona, 1892), an excellent monograph.

was seldom within the court. Its contribution had now become almost entirely and merely financial.

An overview of Ferrarese history from 1471 to 1505 suggests that the most Herculean thing about Ercole was his endurance. Coming to power at forty he ruled for thirty-four years. He survived serious and chronic illnesses, malicious and unpopular assistants, a major attempted coup, a disastrous war, and a great number of lesser vicissitudes. Despite an obvious concern for his standing with the *popolo,* traditional among the Estensi, he had shaken their confidence and then won back their affection and esteem. By the end of his reign, as his health and strength ebbed away for the last time, his regime had become unassailably strong, and his son Alfonso succeeded him with full popular acclaim. Yet this Phoenix-like *signore* who rose time and again from adversities has often been reviled by Italian historians. The reasons are obvious. He was an Italian prince in name alone. He knew no allegiance in politics other than to himself, his house, and (a distant third) his people. There was no larger aim or vision. In the *sauve-qui-peut* of late *Quattrocento* diplomacy he took no stands on principle, but chose to live by his wits and sail down the wind, no matter where it blew.

To many Italians, even then, it has seemed unnatural and perhaps even inhuman that Ercole allied himself with Charles VIII in 1494. Perhaps it was not exactly a sign of strength, but for Ercole no policy could have appeared a more natural or rational reflection of his priorities. The Estensi had traditional and close ties with the French, going back over centuries. They had close family ties with the Sforza, the chief agents of the French invasion. They had more to fear, as the recent past had shown, from their near neighbors the Venetians than from their old allies to the north. Indeed, if the French fully succeeded, Ferrara might cease to be a second-class power, and might regain her territories in the Polesine and Rovigo, lost in the Peace of Bagnolo.

Such views might not persuade anyone elsewhere, but they clearly won support in Ferrara. Its citizens knew well that there was little difference whether those who sacked, burned, and killed were called Venetians or Frenchmen. At a critical point, Savonarola's letters also influenced Ercole to maintain the French alliance, on the ground that Charles VIII was divinely inspired to redeem the evils of Italy. Yet the fact that in many parts of Italy Ercole was considered a traitor, and the Ferrarese were looked on as a nation of quislings, did not change the situation. In a period of general turbulence, Ercole's amicable relations with the dreaded French served to reinforce, not weaken, his signorial powers. Moreover, particularly in such an uneasy time, with Florence in total upheaval, Rome and the papal states full of intrigues and strife, Milan and Venice at loggerheads, the security of a stable, traditional despotism must have had even more than its usual attractiveness. From that point of view, the French invasion may be seen to have strengthened, perhaps even saved, the Estensi in Ferrara.

Ercole, at any rate, went out of his way to stay on the good side of the French. Their emissaries, such as Phillippe de Commynes, were received and treated like royalty.[97] French mores and styles were adopted at the court. By 1495, most courtiers and other citizens were dressing "alla Francexe."[98] Later the same year, the anonymous diarist was under the impression that Italians everywhere—*signori* excepted—were pro-French.[99] By the following spring, he can write, "The Ferrarese almost all universally adhere to

[97] Zambotti, *Diario*, 251.

[98] *DF*, 144: "In questo tempo in Ferrara, per Cortesani *maxime*, se usavano certe veste a modo de geleri . . . et berrette et scarpe a la Francexe. . . ."

[99] *DF*, 159: "Tuta Italia, *videlicet* li populi, gridavano ad una voce: *Franza, Franza, praeter* li Signori et Signorie."

and are partisans of the King of France, and many are dressed and shod and hatted in the French manner, above all the courtiers." [100] This was still true at the turn of the century. In later years, Ercole's grandson and namesake would marry a French princess, and Ludovico Ariosto would bring to its highest point the Ferrarese transformation of the medieval French epic into the limpid Tuscan *volgare* he might even have learned at the court of Ferrara. With the French invasion and all its problems there also came a renewed cosmopolitanism, a kind of literary "gothique flamboyant," which was to be Ferrara's most lasting contribution to European culture. Still it is somehow moving that in 1494, during all the cheerful acceptance of the French invasion, Ariosto's great forerunner Matteo Maria Boiardo, Count of Scandiano and a trusted gentleman of the court, gave up in despair the writing of his great saga with these last words:

> Mentre che io canto, O Dio Redentore,
> Vedo l'Italia tutta a fiamma e foco,
> Per questi Galli, che con gran valore
> Vengon, per disertar non so che loco. . . .
> Un'altra fiata, se mi fia concesso,
> Racconterrovvi il tutto per espresso.[101]

But Boiardo never wrote again. A poem had ended, and so had an era in the history of Italy. Yet the Estensi and

---

[100] *DF,* 171: "Ferrarexi quasi tuti *universaliter* tengono et sono partesani del Re di Franza, et molti ne vano vestiti et calzati et imbiretati a la Francese, et *maxime* tuti li curiali."

[101] *Orlando Innamorato,* Book III, Canto IX, verse 26:
> While I sing, O God Redeeming,
> I see all Italy with flame and fire disgraced,
> Because these French, with valor overweening,
> Have come, and to our land laid waste.
> Another time, if it's to me conceded,
> I'll see the whole tale back to you gets speeded.

their regime in Ferrara continued through the sixteenth century, adapting only in minor and outward ways to the vast changes that were occurring elsewhere. Ercole had established the constitutional, and in more ways the social, personal, and cultural styles for another century of despotism there. To achieve a clearer sense of the ideological and aesthetic components of these ongoing courtly traditions, it will be helpful to examine their characteristic expression in the important area of the visual arts.

VII Courtly Style in the Visual Arts

Almost every major museum of art in Western Europe and North America has an example of the "Ferrarese School" of painting.[1] As a result, many people interested in the art of the *Quattrocento* have an idea of what kind of art was produced in Ferrara, although that idea may be based on only a very few examples. This state of affairs tends to produce a combination of superficial and apparent familiarity on the one hand with profound and very real ignorance on the other. Such an unhappy situation can rarely if ever be changed by what one would assume to be the ideal corrective—a visit to Ferrara. The city has some well, and many indifferently, preserved monuments of the Renaissance,[2] but in the visual arts—architecture excepted —almost everything is gone.[3] Certainly the city's art mu-

---

[1] See R. Longhi, *Officina ferrarese (1934), seguita dagli Ampliamenti (1940), e dai nuovi Ampliamenti (1940-5)* (Florence, 1956), 236-38, for a complete index of places where works of the Ferrarese school are to be found. Longhi's book (hereafter *Officina Ferrarese*) is basic to an understanding of the stylistic development of native Ferrarese painting.

[2] The volume *Emilia e Romagna* of the *Guida d'Italia* series published by the Touring Club Italiano (Milan, 1967), 607-41, gives a good introduction to the remaining monuments. It may be usefully supplemented by G. Medri, *Chiese di Ferrara nella cerchia antica* (Bologna, 1967), and the fine work of B. Zevi, *Biagio Rossetti, architetto ferrarese: il primo urbanista moderno europeo* (Turin, 1960), hereafter *Biagio Rossetti*. For the surrounding region, see now the splendid guidebook by U. Malagù, *Guida del Ferrarese* (Verona, 1967).

[3] There are, of course, precious and notable exceptions, many of which are mentioned below. Perhaps others will come to light. One of the most intriguing aspects of the aftermath of the Florentine flood of 1966 was the discovery of significant works that had been covered over centuries ago. It is now to be hoped that, without the stimulus of further catastrophes, art historians may turn increasingly toward seeing their scholarship in the Renaissance period in archaeological terms, by rediscovering and reconstructing remains and fragments which have long since dis-

seum, housed in the famous Palazzo dei Diamanti, preserves a small representative collection reflecting local traditions in fresco and panel painting, and Cosimo Tura's celebrated organ panels may still be seen in the *duomo,* but even from these examples, one would never be led to think of the city of the Estensi as one of the greatest centers of Renaissance painting. That it was is one of the things I want to demonstrate in the following pages, which present new evidence to substantiate the claim.

The fact that the surviving remnants of Ferrarese painting are scattered over 125 cities and dispersed among more than 300 museums, galleries, churches, and private collections has constituted one of the major handicaps in the serious study of this school. The problem is not merely quantitative, for the greatest existing works of such painters as Tura, Francesco del Cossa, and Ercole de' Roberti are among those which are spread about from Ajaccio to Zurich. Indeed, parts of the same altarpieces have suffered in the same way, as the ingenious and painstaking reconstructions by Roberto Longhi have shown.[4] Only once, in 1934, was a sufficient number and range of paintings brought together

---

appeared. In the case of Ferrara, we have the interesting situation of a rather well preserved architectural nucleus and city plan (now slowly deteriorating under the press of industrial and urban development), with very little remaining of the other artistic forms in the city itself, at least as compared to other centers.

[4] See for example Longhi's partial reconstruction of the Roverella Altarpiece from panels in the National Gallery in London, the Metropolitan Museum, the Gardner and Fogg Museums in Boston and Cambridge; or his partial reconstruction of Cossa's Osservanza Altarpiece from panels in Dresden, New York, and Lugano. It is not essential to my argument that Longhi's reconstructions are correct (though I find them utterly convincing). It is important to realize that the dispersion has affected not only particular works, but even parts of particular works; and not in one case, but in many.

in Ferrara to enable historians of art to see a representative sampling of the surviving paintings together.[5]

The dispersion, which is of course characteristic of Renaissance painting in general, would have had a much smaller impact on the prevailing public and scholarly image of Ferrarese painting had it not been for two other aspects of the situation. The first has already been suggested: it is the absence, in Ferrara itself, of the kinds of extensive visual remains that still exist in and around Florence, Siena, Mantua, Urbino, Arezzo, and other towns. The result is that many people have assumed that great fresco cycles, apart from the very severely damaged Schifanoia frescoes, simply were not created in Ferrara. But it may well be true that the Estensi probably owned more square meters of frescoed walls than any other family in history, and almost certainly more than any Italian city except Rome, Venice, and Florence; and almost none of it survives. That this is so reflects primarily the systematic destruction of the remains of Estensi culture undertaken by the cardinal legates who succeeded Alphonso II in 1598, and it is one of the tragedies of Italian art history.[6]

The second reason is more complex, and perhaps more

[5] It was this occasion which produced Longhi's first essay, the original *Officina Ferrarese*, the foundation-stone for all subsequent attributional and stylistic analysis of Ferrarese painting. More important, perhaps, it produced a catalogue, compiled by Longhi, which listed and sought to identify all the works assembled for the exhibition. This catalogue appears in *Officina Ferrarese*, pp. 109-25.

[6] Most important to an understanding of this process are the works of E. Callegari, "La devoluzione di Ferrara alla Santa Sede," *R.S.I.*, XII (1895), 1-81; E. Prinzivalli, "La devoluzione di Ferrara alla Santa Sede secondo una relazione inedita di Camillo Capilupi," *AF*, x (1898), 121-333, with documents; and the less imposing summary by G. Pardi, "Sulle cause della devoluzione di Ferrara alla Santa Sede," *AF*, XXIV (1922), 113-41. For a brief summary, see L. Chiappini, *Gli Estensi*, 371-76.

speculative. It has to do with disjunctions in taste. The fact is that to many people today, there is something slightly repellant about many of the known works of the Ferrarese masters. We can admire their virtuosity, their technical brilliance, their fantastic inventions and imaginations, but we find it exceptionally difficult to enter into their world, to understand, let alone share, their moral or aesthetic values, to perceive traces of a coherent or articulable intellectual vision in their works, or even to understand what, if anything, they are trying to tell us. So it is attractive to speculate about why, for the most part, most Florentine painting still "works" in the twentieth century, while most Ferrarese painting, however exquisite, may safely be regarded as "provincial."

To some extent, the word "provincial" itself is significantly pejorative, denoting something rustic, narrow, illiberal, or parochial, as well as merely imitative of what is going on at the real center, the capital. The history of Italian art has sometimes been written in terms of a perhaps unconsciously metropolitan-provincial dichotomy.[7] From this viewpoint, Florence and Venice are generally viewed as the capitals, with a swarm of subordinate, derivative, and intellectually uninteresting artists churning out "provincial" work elsewhere. This approach is as untenable in the history of art as it is in the history of politics, business, or ideas. Italy in the fifteenth century was above all cosmopolitan. People in Ferrara knew, and cared, about what was happening in Florence, Milan, and Rome. The fact that unique and distinctive local and regional ways of doing things in all fields developed and were consciously cultivated and maintained does not give evidence of provincialism in the sense of "narrowness of mind, ignorance, or the like re-

---

[7] This point is made by B. Berenson, *Italian Painters of the Renaissance* (London, 1952; first pub. 1907).

sulting from provincial life without exposure to cultural or intellectual activity,"[8] but merely of devotion to local modes. What has to be analyzed, then, is how these local modes developed as they did, whether in Florence, Cremona, or Ferrara. To maintain this awareness is no easy matter, for we automatically and naturally think in terms of "Italy." But in the *Quattrocento,* it is essential to think of an Italy of capitals, each of which spawned its own provincialism (in the first sense) in its hinterland, even though they were not immune to outside influences.

A more serious, though related, aspect of what I have called a disjunction of taste, is a consequence of what I take to be the general truth that most of us no longer like, though we may admire, the courtly tradition and its products and artifacts. Courtly love, for example, tends to elicit ridicule, if not contempt, from the young, when one dares to tell them about it. The literature of chivalry is assigned in required courses, and one supposes that people struggle through it, but how many nowadays read Ariosto or Spenser, or even the Arthurian legends or the *Chanson de Roland* for the sheer joy of it? The same disjunction applies to our experience of visual arts from a courtly *milieu,* whether it be Renaissance or Rococo. Works that were created for the solid burghers of Florence or Venice, with their acute sense of societal and human reality tend to make much more sense to us—seem more accessible and intelligible—than works produced for a small circle of *conoscenti,* who tend to communicate in the complex and private language of symbols and allegories, whether literary or figurative.[9]

[8] See the appropriate entry in the *Random House Dictionary of the English Language* (New York, 1966).

[9] This point is nicely made by G. Getto, "La corte Estense di Ferrara," *Letteratura e critica nel tempo* (Milan, 1954), 229. To the extent that this private language takes iconological and iconographic form in the work of Dosso Dossi, see now the interesting interpretations of F. Gibbons, *Dosso Dossi* (Princeton, 1969). Another case in point is that of the

I have referred to "something slightly repellant" in much remaining Ferrarese painting, and that is surely related to what has just been said. Stylistically, this quality takes the form of a kind of late international Gothic proto-mannerism, a striving for extreme technical accomplishment combined with coolness and detachment. It is in a sense the artistic counterpart of the courtly ethos of perfect self-control and effortless excellence. It produces a result totally compatible with the values and interests of a small aristocratic élite— an art that is highly decorative, inventive, and sophisticated, and both intellectually and visually complex. In these respects, it is comparable not only with court painting in Mantua, Padua, and Urbino, but also with what might equally well be considered the court painting of Medicean Florence in the late *Quattrocento*.

Iconographically, the same kind of limited accessibility is built into the greatest works of Ferrarese—though of course not only Ferrarese—painting. In general, and especially in the works produced for the court, it is an art conceived by, and intended for, the learned and for those with whom the learned agree to share their secrets. Thus, many of the altarpieces represent the patron saints of important individuals or families, and in secular painting, recondite classical allusions, complex allegories, and mysterious em-

celebrated frescoes in the Sala dei Mesi in the Palazzo Schifanoia, for which see the ingenious interpretation of A. Warburg, "Italienische Kunst und internazionale Astrologie in Palazzo Schifanoia zu Ferrara," *Atti del X Congresso di Storia dell'Arte in Roma* (Rome, 1922), 179-93; and in G. Bing, ed. *Gesammelte Schriften* (Leipzig-Berlin, 1932), II, 465-81. An interesting recent addition to the analysis of courtly art is M. Levey, *Painting at Court* (New York, 1971). Pp. 56-76 consider the court of Ferrara under Borso d'Este as a model of what Levey calls "Courts of Earth." Most of his discussion centers on the Schifanoia frescoes, and therefore some of the elements of his general interpretation of painting at Ferrara will have to be modified in the light of new evidence presented here, and in my *Art and Life at the Court of Ercole I d'Este: The 'De triumphis religionis' of Giovanni Sabadino degli Arienti* (Geneva, 1972).

blems are characteristic of the *scuola ferrarese*.[10] In an intellectual tradition that can be securely dated back to the period of Leonello, the Ferrarese painter was regarded as a skilled craftsman, accomplished in the manipulation of physical substances, but clearly the intellectual inferior of the poet or philosopher. Therefore the painter commonly functions as the executor of complex schemes concocted by bookish humanists who are trying to outdo one another in reviving the pagan mythologies.[11] Even while appreciating the genuine passion such individuals often undoubtedly felt for recapturing a seductive vanished past, one can also notice the golden opportunities here presented for the kind of self-congratulatory obscurantism, that joyful immersion in minutiae which has always served as a useful weapon for those who like to give scholars a bad name. No one who has tried to decipher some of these almost private languages will deny that they can be irritating as well as ingenious. However, my main concern here is not with the specific meaning of particular works, but with the general cultural significance of this particular style of artistic expression. For it too, like the elegant and detached style common to the major Ferrarese masters of the *Quattrocento,* may be considered as a visual reflection of the princely style of the Estensi. It is an iconography of *conoscenti,* of men familiar

[10] And it should be noted that it is this characteristic, too, which provides the strongest link between literary and artistic culture in Ferrara, a link that continues throughout the sixteenth century, and may even best be symbolized by the scene in Tasso's play, *Il Re Torrismondo,* where an actual emblem is brought out on the stage, and all of the principals stand around trying to guess what it might mean. In fact, we still do not know.

[11] Such of course was the role of Pellegrino Prisciani in concocting the astrological motifs for the Schifanoia frescoes (cf. Warburg, *loc. cit.*). See also the impact of the poem on the myth of Psyche by Niccolò da Correggio, discussed below, p. 258 ff., and the comments on the role of the painter expressed by Leonello d'Este in Decembrio's *De Politia Litteraria,* above pp. 118-19.

(or anxious to be regarded as familiar) with classical texts, ancient languages, and romances of chivalry, Christian enough to feel unassailably secure and righteous in the midst of Zoroastrian astrologies, human enough to be seen with jesters and paupers as well as courtiers and ladies.

Though the earliest beginnings of painting in Ferrara are unknown, the basic lines of development of the fifteenth-century school have now been established beyond reasonable doubt. Unlike most other important Italian cities that developed influential traditions in painting, Ferrara does not seem to have a major *Trecento* artist. The few traces of fourteenth-century painting that survive in the city, such as the frescoes in the convent of San Antonio in Polesine, and the charming Giottesque figures in the Casa Minerbi reveal the presence of foreign, probably Paduan, artists. Though there is now some evidence of complex fresco painting at Belfiore dating from the reign of Alberto I, it was during the reign of Niccolò III, especially during the last years, when Leonello's cultural interests became influential, that continuing and ambitious painting in Ferrara began.[12]

The artistic activity of the 1420s and 1430s took a twofold form. On the one hand, there was the decoration of the small but growing number of Estensi palaces and pleasure-houses; on the other, there was the illumination of manuscript books with miniature paintings. Both of these functions, which were to play a decisive role in the development of the Ferrarese style, were fostered by Leonello on a scale far greater than that of his father.

[12] For the beginnings of painting in Ferrara, see Longhi, *Officina Ferrarese,* 1-15, 175-79 (esp. comments on the Minerbi frescoes, p. 175). There is a vast bibliography on painting and are in general in Ferrara, but for the origins of the *Quattrocento* school see the old but invaluable study by A. Venturi, "I primordi del rinascimento artistico a Ferrara," *R.S.I.,* I (1884), 591-631. A new study devoted to the Minerbi frescoes is C. L. Ragghianti, *Gli Affreschi della Casa Minerbi* (Rome, 1970).

But Leonello, whose eclecticism was as impressive as his classicism, reveals the instincts of the collector as well as those of the patron. He loved ancient cameos and coins, medallions, plaquettes, and brooches. Under the learned and critical eyes of his revered teacher, Guarino da Verona, the new Marchese assembled a small but choice selection of these objects, which became the subjects of elaborate discussions between Leonello and his favorite companions.[13] This collection was important for two reasons. First, Ferrara had not been the site of an ancient city, and therefore had no Roman buildings, statues, or sarcophagi, which provided such natural sources of inspiration to artists in Rome, Pisa, and other cities; Leonello's newly acquired ancient *objets de vertu* could provide such a source for court artists. Second, Leonello's interests as a collector seem to have been directed mainly toward small, essentially personal objects, a fact that reveals his choice of scale, also reflected in the taste for illuminated manuscripts, small panel paintings, and, above all, medals.[14] The scant decade of Leonello's rule reveals a new and growing interest in these forms, which share certain common features, not the least of which is their personal, private character. This is no art for the masses, but for the privileged few who are permitted to hold these things in their hands, who know enough too read and interpret them and to appreciate their affinity with the style of ancient princes. Furthermore, they all lend themselves admirably to portraiture, which may be seen as the reification of that flattering self-image that rulers generally learn to like and expect from their subordinates.

Leonello is the first of the Estensi of whose appearance

---

[13] Venturi, 593, makes the point that Niccolò III too had an interest in such antique objects, but suggests that what in him was simple curiosity became in Leonello a lively and cultivated affection.

[14] See G. Gruyer, *L'Art ferrarais à l'époque des Princes d'Este* (Paris, 1897), I, 34-46; 583-650, and the appropriate entrees in Pollard, *Renaissance Medals*.

we have a reasonably firm idea. His enthusiasm for the work of Pisanello becomes intelligible in the light of his love of detail, small things, and elegant portraiture in paint and metal. During his lengthy stays in Ferrara, in addition to painting and casting numerous portraits of Leonello, Pisanello also worked on some of the decorations for the great palace of Belriguardo, and influenced a number of medalists, painters, and goldsmiths who worked for the Estensi during the 1450s.[15] That Leonello also acquired some paintings by Roger van der Weyden for his study at Belfiore, a small palace outside the northern walls of the city, seems quite compatible with these tastes.[16] It was through these examples that oil painting was introduced in Ferrara, though it has been suggested that the first documented examples by a native artist are Tura's paintings (1469) for the chapel at Belriguardo.[17]

Apart from Pisanello, who was the sole painter of the 1440s to be memorialized by court poets such as Tito Vespasiano Strozzi, Basinio Parmensis, and Guarino, most of the local artists seem to have been engaged in relatively mundane tasks of decoration. Many years ago Adolfo Venturi discovered that the commissions of many obscure individuals of whose work no identifiable trace remains were paid to paint furniture, playing cards, clothing, banners, and coats

[15] A. Venturi, "Il Pisanello a Ferrara," *Archivio Veneto*, xxx (1885), 410-20; *idem*, "Orme di Pisanello a Ferara," *L'Arte*, xxxvi (1933), 435-44; *idem*, "I Primordi," 600-606; *idem, Pisanello* (Rome, 1939); and the many recent works on Pisanello by such scholars as R. Brenzoni, B. Degenhart, E. Sidona, and M. Fossi-Todorow Todorow.

[16] On Van der Weyden's work for the Estensi and the much-debated question of his possible presence in Ferrara in the 1440s, see E. H. Kantorowicz, "The Este Portrait by Roger Van Der Weyden," 367-80. Art historians continue to recite the traditional view that the Flemish master spent some time in Ferrara, but there is no firm evidence to support this belief.

[17] A. Venturi, "L'Arte a Ferrara nel periodo di Borso d'Este," *R.S.I.*, ii (1885), 689-750, esp. 717.

of arms, and that more celebrated painters were also used for the decoration of such utilitarian objects. Art and life were less distinctly separated than it is easy for us to imagine.[18] The beginnings of a serious and sustained interest in the visual arts certainly occur during Leonello's rule. But it was during the reigns of Borso and Ercole I that Ferrarese art became a substantial and identifiable movement, transcending immediate functional and decorative needs, and involving a larger group of distinct masters.

In some ways, the reign of Leonello's brother Borso stands in striking contrast to that of his predecessor. Personally, the two could have hardly have been more different. Leonello, graceful and sensitive, loved the company of poets and scholars, cultivated a very acceptable if not quite distinguished Latin style, corresponded with humanists and received works dedicated to him by such notables as George of Trebizond, Giovanni Aurispa, Pier Candido Decembrio, Tommaso Cambiatore, and Leon Battista Alberti, as well as many others.[19] Borso, stocky and robust, preferred the active life. An expert and devoted hunter and fisherman, Borso was a great lover of horses, dogs, and falcons, a splendid figure who reveled in the physical perquisites of power—ostentation and opulence in dress and surroundings, a showy magnanimity, frequent and ceremonious presence at public functions. He patronized the learned more for policy than passion, never bothered even to learn to read Latin, and preferred the company of shrewd statesmen with casual intellectual concerns to that of accomplished rhetoricians with untested political acumen. Still, these are dif-

---

[18] In addition to the studies of Venturi already cited, see "Le arti minori a Ferrara alla fine del secolo XV," *L'Arte,* xii (1909), 147-48, 380, 447-55; "L'Arte ferrarese del rinascimento," *L'Arte,* xxviii (1925), 89-109; and the articles by G. Campori dealing with these subjects (above, p. 50).

[19] See above, pp. 103-104.

ferences in degree, for Leonello occasionally delighted in the hunt—that noble, elegant, expensive, and thus eminently civilized and acceptable, substitute for warfare—and Borso loved art.

With Leonello, Borso shared an interest in books. But where Leonello had been drawn chiefly to their contents, what attracted Borso was their physical beauty. Consequently he not only continued, but increased, the patronage of miniaturists and illuminators that had made slight beginnings under Niccolò III and had grown considerably under Leonello. The court workshop in these years came to include both highly paid masters and mere technicians. Though many of these artists were local, some had to be recruited from Florence, and even from Germany, Flanders, and northern Italian cities. Giorgio de Alemagna, who worked under both princes, was one example; another was Borso's treasurer, an impressive polymath named Carlo di San Giorgio, who has sometimes been confused with another scribe who used the pseudonym Polismagna.[20] The records of Borso's *camera* reflect quite closely the seriousness with which this art form was taken.

Ferrarese illumination, like all book decoration, is essentially ornamental and illustrative. More often than not, it is ornamental without attempting to be illustrative, i.e., to bear a specific relationship to the text. Hundreds of codices from Ferrara survive—mainly in the Biblioteca Estense in Modena, and the Vatican Library, but also in libraries in Ferrara, Florence, Venice, London, New York, and elsewhere—and I have cast a historian's (not an art historian's) eye on most of them.[21] In general, I find a remarkable

[20] G. Bertoni, *La biblioteca Estense,* has dealt extensively with book illuminations and related subjects. See also M. Salmi, *Pittura e miniatura a Ferrara nel primo rinascimento* (Milan, 1961); and the same author's article "Ecchi della pittura nella miniatura ferrarese," *Commentari* (Apr.-June, 1958), 88-98.

[21] The major part of these materials have been studied by D. Fava and

difference between the illuminators when they are making the traditional decorative borders, and when they are presenting genuine miniature paintings that bear a relation with the text. In the first instance, the painting seems highly conventional, though often supremely elegant. In elaborate configurations of branches, leaves, or simply abstract, intertwined linear forms live a marvelous variety of real and symbolic animals and birds—apes, unicorns, leopards, frogs, finches, parrots, storks, ducks. In the greatest of these works —such as the famous Bible of Borso d'Este, on which Taddeo Crivelli worked for nearly ten years with up to twenty assistants at a time—the ratio of fauna to flora becomes very high, and the quality of the borders, though not uniform, ranges between technical excellence and sublime realization, over nearly a thousand folio pages. In less lavish works, the botanical and geometric patterns are more dominant. Invariably, of course, there is a high incidence of Estensi coats of arms, and emblems of the family or an individual.[22]

To encounter illustrative paintings within these texts, however, is to discover works of greater intellectual, and sometimes historical, significance. Here, the artist is forced to be relevant, to make a painting that is to be experienced in the context of a verbal message. An interesting example is the frontispiece of *Astronomical Tables* of the previously cited manuscript by Menghius Bianchinus, based on Sacrobosco's *De Sphaera,* in which the author is depicted in the act of presenting the manuscript to the Emperor, in the presence of Borso d'Este and some courtiers.[23] The stylized,

M. Salmi, *I manoscritti miniati della Biblioteca Estense in Modena* (Florence, 1950). Others may be approached through the catalogues—both printed and manuscript—of particular libraries, and now best of all through the researches of P. O. Kristeller, *Iter Italicum,* i-ii (Leiden, 1963-67).

[22] For the *Bibbia di Borso d'Este,* in addition to the comments by Longhi, *Officina Ferrarese,* 17, the materials cited above, pp. 169-70.

[23] L. Thorndyke, *A History of Magic and Experimental Science* (New York, 1934-52), iv, 254, 454.

almost Gothic elegance of the figures in a harmonious, composed, yet complex courtly setting prefigures much that is to come in larger-scale Ferrarese painting of the *Quattrocento.*

In fact, one of the most obvious characteristics of much Ferrarese painting before the Dossi to the student of Ferrarese miniatures is that it looks like miniatures writ large. Not only is the scale often indistinguishable from that of a work designed to fit in a very small space, but the burnished, enamel-like qualities of the surfaces (still evident in some panel paintings, though naturally long gone from the few remaining frescoes) closely resemble the high color of the miniatures. It is almost as though a painter like Tura could not bring himself to imagine that a wall painting would never be encompassed at a distance of inches, like the miniature ascribed to him in the great Cornazzano manuscript in the Pierpont Morgan Library (Fig. 14). To compare that diminutive masterpiece with the sizable central panel of the Roverella altarpiece in the National Gallery in London (Fig. 15) is to see the relative imbalance between size and scale in Tura's art, and this carries over completely to Cossa and Roberti. These painters, as well as some of their contemporaries in other centers, were instilled with the precious exactitude of the miniaturist. Even the mastery of the techniques of mathematical perspective, and of a modest measure of Florentine monumentality and ponderosity in some examples by Cossa, never canceled out the effects of the miniature tradition.

I believe that this typically Ferrarese inability to suppress detail for the sake of a gain in dramatic intensity, coherence, or human plausibility reflected not only the early training and values of the important local artists bred in the miniature tradition, but the tastes and preferences of the Estensi patrons as well. Some commentators on the magnificent frescoes in the Schifanoia Palace, done by Francesco del

Cossa, Ercole de' Roberti, and assistants (possibly under the overall supervision of Cosimo Tura) in the early 1470s have compared these works to tapestries, and suggested the presence of Flemish or Burgundian influences on the style of the court painters and patrons.[24] I now think, though neither view can be proven, that the main influence is to be found in the *botteghe* of the illuminators.[25] There is little evidence that the Estensi liked or admired the visual effects of northern tapestries. Leonello regarded them as confused and distracting in appearance. Although the Estensi occasionally purchased wall hangings, and at one point even tried to start a local industry in the field, there is nothing to suggest that they ever aroused much enthusiasm in the court.[26] None the less, they were familiar objects, in some rooms probably necessary to keep out the cold, and it is certainly possible that artists drew on their example in Ferrara.

Even if that were the case, the borrowings would have to be regarded as superficial. The Schifanoia frescoes are organized, both thematically and spatially, in a manner totally divergent from any known cycle of tapestries from the later middle ages. Indeed, there are really only three possible points of comparison. First, they cover the whole wall, which, however undeniable, hardly demonstrates influence. Second, they present an elaborate view of daily

[24] There can be no doubt that northern European art played a formative, if not dominant, role in northern Italian court painting in the early part of the fifteenth century. The precise nature of the influences and the sources from which they derived are much more difficult to establish with confidence. But Berenson's judgment that "without Florence, . . . painting in Northern Italy might have differed but slightly from contemporary painting in the Low Countries or in Germany," (*Italian Painters of the Renaissance*, 146), cannot be lightly dismissed.

[25] Cf. Longhi, *Officina Ferrarese*, 16 .

[26] G. Campori, "L'Arazzeria Estense," *AMP,* vii (1876, 415-455; also Gruyer, *L'Art ferrarais*, ii, 453-80.

life at Borso's court, the somewhat archaizing style of which reminds many observers of the Burgundian court, an association which, while not unjustified, has little to do with the question of sources. Finally, the presence in the frescoes of much naturalistic detail, a conscious delight in nature and its creatures, as well as other forms of elaborate detail has suggested the parallel. But considering the local tradition of book illumination, and its immediate bearing on the training and discipline of painters, this point really militates against the purported influence of the tapisseur's art.

In trying to explain why the work of miniaturists had so formative an impact on late fifteenth-century Ferrarese painters, there is yet another obstacle to be overcome: the fact that another artistic center, Florence, possessed a great tradition of manuscript illumination and a distinguished array of painters who were totally independent of that tradition. Indeed Masaccio, Castagno, Pollaiuolo, and later Michelangelo paint figures that are in an almost literal sense monumental. They seem to concern themselves with the technical problem of creating a three-dimensional image on a two-dimensional surface, and endowing that image with the properties of weight, physical solidity, and textural reality that it would have if it actually existed, or if it were a sculpture. One reason for this approach is unquestionably to be found in the more empirically-grounded tastes of the patrons for whom these works were created, representatives of a mercantile oligarchy governed according to republican forms, and determined to view themselves as the guardians of a tradition of solid republican liberty based on Roman examples, with the gravity and austerity that implies.[27]

[27] H. Baron, *The Crisis of the Early Italian Renaissance,* rev. ed. (Princeton, 1966), 200-205, has some interesting suggestions. See also A. Hauser, *The Social History of Art* (New York, 1957), II (paperback ed.), 16-52, where the author elaborates a distinction between middle-class

But there is another reason for these distinct stylistic differences, which I take to be equally important. It is the absence, in Ferrara, of serious competition from sculptors, a circumstance which had two distinct but related aspects. In Florence, painters and sculptors competed in the same general market for commissions of works of art on a relatively large scale. Thus, not only would the physical presence of a significant amount of monumental, three-dimensional art play an immediate and traceable role on the development of style in painting because of its natural interest to classicizing artists; but, equally, at least some painters would follow an unconscious, market-oriented impulse to monumentalize their styles, so as to compete more effectively with sculptors. The dramatic influence of Donatello's bronze panels, not to mention Ghiberti's, on Florentine painters may stand in support of this contention. The kind of artistic cross-fertilization that existed in Florence between painters and sculptors occurred in Ferrara between miniaturists and painters on a grander scale. Ferrarese painting did not have to prove itself in the market-place with a vigorous sculptural tradition. And the taste of Ferrarese patrons, nurtured in the tradition of book illumination and cultivated by humanist professors and courtiers, focused on painting throughout the *Quattrocento*. Indeed, it was not until the time of that fascinating figure, Cardinal Hippolito II d'Este, that sculpture became an essential element in the surroundings of an important member of the family; but he had left Ferrara as a boy, and the Villa d'Este is an entirely Roman phenomenon.

Sculpture may have never been important enough in Ferrara to exert a major influence or control on the develop-

---

and courtly art in the *Quattrocento*. Much of Hauser's argument is overdrawn and overstated, especially when differing artistic styles are explained entirely on the basis of the different social origins of patrons, but his eye for regional differences is acute.

ment of style in painting, but that is not to say that it did not exist. The Estensi interest in medals has already been cited, and it may be noteworthy that there were at least twenty medalists active in Ferrara between 1430 and 1500.[28] They functioned not only as sculptors in this miniature medium, but also in some cases as designers of Ferrarese coinage, which in this period was a minor art form in itself. It served not only as a medium of exchange, but also, in the manner of Roman imperial coinage, as an instrument of ducal propaganda. The medalists executed portraits of an impressive array of Ferrarese gentlemen, by no means all of them members of the Este family, and even a few ladies. Among those honored in this fashion we find, in addition to the princes themselves, Guarino da Verona, Leon Battista Alberti, Giovanni Tavelli, Lorenzo Strozzi, Pietro Bono Avogadro, Sigismondo d'Este, Bartolommeo Pendaglia, Pellegrino Prisciani, Bartolommeo della Rovere, Niccolò da Correggio, Iacopo Trotti, Antonio Sarzanella, Tito Vespasiano Strozzi, and Lodovico Carbone.[29] To be the subject of a medal was a form of recognition apparently reserved for the most esteemed dignitaries of the ducal circle.

What is true with regard to medals is even truer when applied to sculpture. With no convenient local source of suitable stone, Ferrara here confronted a natural obstacle. It could not have been easy to attract distinguished sculptors to the city for any length of time, and there is no evidence that there ever were any. The closest Ferrara came to having a resident sculptor of major ability was when Leonello hired the Florentine Niccolò Baroncelli to make

[28] G. Gruyer, i, 583-710. For surviving examples of Ferrarese sculpture, see G. Medri, *La scultura a Ferrara, AF,* n.s. xviii (1957).

[29] For a list of Ferrarese medals and their subjects, see Gruyer, ii, 604-605. Gruyer lists over 110 subjects, but this includes the entire sixteenth century. On Sarzanella, there is an interesting study by E. Gualandi, *Antonio Sarzanella di Manfredi, AF,* n.s. xxvii (1963).

some angels for the Church of Santa Maria degli Angeli.

This competent but not exceptional pupil of Donatello collaborated, with Antonio da Cristoforo, who had been trained in the same workshop, on the equestrian statue of Niccolò III that had been commissioned by the twelve *savi,* and of which what purports to be a copy may still be seen facing the façade of the *duomo*. Baroncelli was also given the commission for a statue of Borso enthroned, but died in the initial stages of the work, in 1453. It was finished by his son Giovanni and a number of assistants, and was erected in December, 1454, in front of the Palazzo della Ragione, facing the southern flank of the *duomo*. This statue, which was moved a few years later and placed near that of Niccolò III, was to honor Borso on his receipt of the ducal title from Frederick III, as an inscription written by Tito Strozzi indicated. Both of these works, cast in bronze and mounted on handsome corinthian columns, were smashed to pieces by a mob when the city was "liberated"—not from the Estensi but from the Vatican—in 1796.

In addition to these examples of monumental sculpture designed for public places, there are records of other commissions of sculpture for more private use, as well as for the adornment of churches and the decoration of palaces. A small amount of this type of work from the Renaissance still survives in Ferrara, and predictably confirms the dominance of Florentine artists in this medium. There is, for example, the remarkable doorway of the Palazzo Prosperi-Sacrati, with its decorative patterns reminiscent of Desiderio da Settignano.[30] It is possible that a good deal of work of this general type was also done for family chapels in the city's many churches and was simply replaced during the Counter-Reformation, and especially in the seventeenth-century, when Ferrara's churches were uniformly converted

---

[30] See esp. Zevi, *Biagio Rossetti,* 278-79.

to a Baroque style that is truly provincial in every sense of the word.

Painting, like sculpture, had as its prime patrons in Ferrara the Estensi, though the commune, the various churches, and lesser families of wealth also provided employment for painters. Owing to the tendency to regard artists as executors of plans made by men of knowledge, to their low social position reinforced by the weakness of the guild structure, and to what might be called the life style of the Estensi, the most important works for the court were frescoes scattered around a large number of palaces and country places, which are generally referred to in the literature as "luoghi di delizie," or simply as "delizie," and without consideration of which no discussion of Ferrarese life or art can be complete. The archives reveal that Leonello, Borso, and Ercole all spent by far the greater part of their time in residence at, and traveling between, these houses, and a relatively small part of the year in their central palace across from the cathedral in Ferrara. In the fifteenth century, they stayed in the famous *castello* only during periods of grave political or military crisis.

In fact the peripatetic and countrified life style of these *signori* suggests some of the most essential characteristics of their rule. It reflects, for one thing, the solidity and reliability of their own central administrative system, which carried on affairs of family and state effectively and discreetly in their absence. It reveals also the stability of the relationship between court and commune, formally distinct but practically subservient. It shows their great wealth, their lack of public accountability for the expenditure of funds, their love of the lordly and symbolically significant pursuits of hunting and fishing. It also demonstrates, to an extent that it has not been possible to appreciate adequately before, and will never be able to be comprehended fully, their taste and style as patrons.

In a study published in 1933, Gianna Pazzi described these houses and their uses, relying almost exclusively on allusions to and descriptions of them in the *Orlando Furioso*. Pazzi deals with nineteen "luoghi di delizia" scattered about the Ferrarese.[31] In the absence of appreciable data concerning their physical appearance, she concentrates on an attempt to re-evoke the activities of the court. Where the sources or actual remains allow, she describes works of art, such as the fountain at Belvedere, bearing the images of the great ladies of the house of Este. Only two of these houses remain substantially intact—Schifanoia and Mesola—and the present interior of Mesola is late. Schifanoia owes its survival to having been within the city walls, hence useful. Its frescoes were plastered over and discovered only in the 1820s. Some of the other structures are known in general terms from contemporary or early seventeenth-century descriptions, but until now there has been very little in the way of detailed evidence about them.

It is now possible to add substantially to what has previously been known not only about the Este palace and the *castello* in Ferrara, but also about the two greatest Este *delizie* of Belfiore and Belriguardo, through a manuscript that I have had the good fortune to find in the Vatican Library's Fondo Rossiano. A most unlikely source for such descriptions, it is a lengthy panegyrical treatise presented to Ercole I by the well known Bolognese humanist Giovanni Sabadino degli Arienti. Never published, and not listed in the literature on Sabadino, the treatise bears the title *De triumphis religionis* but is really a disquisition on all of the princely virtues, with chapters not only on religion, but also dealing with magnanimity, fortitude, liberality, magnificence, faith, justice, prudence, patience, and fortune. Clearly a presentation copy, bearing the Este coat of arms on the

[31] *Le 'Delizie Estensi' e l'Ariosto: Fasti e piaceri a Ferrara nella Rinascenza* (Pescara, 1933).

illuminated frontispiece, it can be dated internally to the year 1497.[32] Here, it will be possible only to touch on some of the principal contributions of the text, which bear directly on the views I am developing.

The passages of special interest in the context of Ferrarese art are to be found in the fifth book of the work, "Libro Quinto del Triumpho e dignita della Magnificentia: In cui si recorda le Nuptie ducale: et la gloria de li edificati Templi e de li palaci, Zardini: e acrescimento de la bella cita di Ferrara." [33] Following the procedure used throughout, Sabadino first offers a definition of the particular quality under

[32] Hereafter *DTR*. For full bibliographical references, see above, p. 185. For the definitive dating of the MS., see f. 90 rº: ". . . Retrovandomi questo Anno de Salute MCCCCXCVII a tanto spectaculo sancto. . . ." Bertoni, *La Biblioteca Estense*, gives a few notes on Arienti, and lists his *novelle* in the inventory of Ercole's library, as well as works dedicated to Giovanni Bentivoglio and Messer Egano Lambertino, an unspecified work in *volgare*, and a piece on the death of Madona Anna. But Ercole's inventory dates from 1495, and so none of the works listed there could have been this one. V. Rossi, *Il Quattrocento*, 204-206, lists and briefly discusses Sabadino's main works. The humanist is best known for *Le Porretane*, a series of *facezie* based on Boccaccio's *Decameron*. For the life and work of Sabadino, see above all U. Dallari, "Della vita e degli scritti di Gio. Sabadino degli Arienti," *AMR, Ser.* III, VI (1888), 173-218, which includes sixteen pages of documents; also S. B. Chandler, "Appunti su Giovanni Sabadino degli Arienti," *GSLI,* LXXX (1953), 346-50; and the article, with full bibliography, G. Ghinassi, in *Dizionario Biografico degli Italiani* (Rome, 1967), IV, 154-56. The work has appeared in print, as *Art and Life at the Court of Ercole I d'Este: The 'De triumphis religionis' of Giovanni Sabadino degli Arienti,* ed. W. L. Gundersheimer (Geneva, Droz, 1972). For another treatise in the same genre, also dedicated to Ercole I, cf. Andreas Pannonius, *Ad D. Herculem Ducem Civitatis Ferrariensis. . . . De Laudibus clarissimae Domus Estensis ac praesertim Herculis ducis,* BEM MS. Alpha Q, 9, 12 (Lat. 108), the presentation copy of a moral and religious work. Pannonius writes a treatise on the virtues, in the guise of a descriptive essay; Sabadino does precisely the reverse. The latter thus achieves a liveliness and relevance absent from the work of Pannonius.

[33] *DTR,* ff. 34-71.

discussion. For him, magnificence "consists of sumptuous, sublime and grand things," of "largesse and amplitude in spending gold and silver." Ercole is said to possess this virtue, like all the others, in ample measure. He reveals it not only in his personal appearance, which is always elegant without ostentation, but also in the surroundings that he has arranged for himself. Having established this connection between Ercole's personal style and that of the ducal buildings, the author begins to describe some of their notable features, with special attention to Ercole's own additions to them. He begins with some of the more recent constructions in the ducal palace in Ferrara, citing twenty-five new columns of "very magnificent" white marble. The erection of similar columns elsewhere is then cited. It is clear that both for Ercole and Sabadino, this is a major addition to the city's beauty. Some of these are Corinthian columns with portrait busts of Roman emperors mounted on top. Significantly, they are placed outside a row of shops in the piazza, as a stirring monument to the power and antiquity of princely rule.[34] On entering the palace from this square, according to Sabadino, one is confronted by similar magnificence. Here, too, columns of white marble were used in the construction of two handsome new loggias, under one of which there was a caged lion. Other features of this courtyard included mural representations of Este insignias and coats of arms. Ercole's personal *imprese* in green, white, and red marble, a "most dignified *sacello*" dedicated to the Virgin Mary with a vaulted ceiling done in terra cotta, and an "egregious" floor of white and red marble. From the courtyard, one ascended to the main floor of the palace by a magnificent staircase of forty-seven steps, in the middle

---

[34] *Ibid.*, f. 35 v°; where Sabadino speaks of "diece colomne ma quadre de simil marmo con cornice de fronde e capi de li antiqui principi Romani sculpti existendoli sotto boteche belle de varii exerctij honorevoli cose cha a la ducal piaça donano illustre ornamento."

of which was a splendid covered and colonnaded landing, the ensemble "worthy of being ascended by all the princes and kings in the world." (Fig. 16) [35] The ensemble gives an image of brightness and festive elegance of which nothing remains in contemporary Ferrara. The ducal palace at Urbino perhaps gives us some idea of what this must have been like.[36]

Sabadino goes on to describe parts of the *castello* which, surprisingly enough, had an elaborate garden described as "heavenly," and compared by the author to the apocryphal garden of Susanna.[37] In it, there is a pavilion with a lead roof supported by marble columns, sheltering a fine statue of Hercules, and several fountains. Other pavilions have beautifully inlaid floors, jasmine-trellised covers, charming

[35] *Ibid.,* f. 36, r⁰-v⁰.

[36] K. Clark, *Civilisation* (New York, 1969), 108-109, 111, in discussing republican and despotic cultural styles, states that "in the last quarter of the century the Renaissance owed almost as much to the small courts of Northern Italy—Ferrara, Mantua, and above all, Urbino. . . ." Clark does not even discuss Ferrara, and obviously ranks it well below the other two (p. 111): "There is no doubt that the court of Urbino, under both Federigo and Guidobaldo, was a high point in the history of civilisation. The same is true, in a lesser degree, of the court of Mantua." The court of Ferrara is not even mentioned in this evaluation, although for Castiglione it can offer Boiardo, Ariosto, and Tasso; in place of Mantegna, it has Tura, Cossa, Roberti, and the masters of the Belfiore and Belriguardo cycles; and to match the splendor of the ducal palace at Urbino, it had in Belfiore, Belvedere, Belriguardo, and the Castel Nuovo—leaving aside Schifanoia, the Palazzo Estense, the Palazzo dei Diamanti, *et al.*—four of the most beautiful and imposing signorial residences in Italy, and all within a radius of seven miles. It is true that Urbino today best evokes the lustrous grandeur of a Renaissance court. But after Milan, Naples, and the Vatican, Ferrara was the grandest of them all.

[37] *DTR,* f. 37 r⁰: "Ma alquanto del Iocundissimo Zardino de questo Castello nararemo: perche certo pare luoco celeste. Quando dentro in quello entrai subito a la mia mente me corse la vera fama del bel Zardino de Iohachino de babilonia prestantissimo citadino." See the Vulgate Daniel, 13.

sculptures, and the like. Various species of exotic trees fill the garden, and flowers are everywhere. Off to one side, there is a small garden for growing rare plants and herbs. On another side, there is a little fish pond "where with delight one sometimes see many beautiful fish turning around, one after another." This garden is always cool and shady, and Sabadino states that it was always a great favorite of the Duchess Eleanora's. She and her ladies would assemble there on hot days, with their tight sleeves rolled up and their veils lifted, to sit either under the trees, on the grass, or within the pavilion. It was also used sometimes for concerts of lovesongs under the stars.[38] Here we have glimpses of court life which are at the same time less idealized, more personal, and more realistically informative than those offered by Castiglione. For Sabadino was writing for readers who were intimately familiar with the scenes being described. They would be prepared for some measure of exaggeration, perhaps, but not pure invention. He gives them a *giardino d'amore,* founded on reality.

Returning to the *castello* itself, Sabadino continues his description of its beautiful windows, towers, and fortifications, its glorious views over the city, the port, and a great stretch of the Po. He then thanks the officials who allowed him to tour the castle, and who showed him around it.[39]

[38] *DTR,* ff. 39 v⁰-40: "La tua serenissima Madama giuncta questo Zardino molto honora adgiustando la sua felicitate con le sue donne e donzelle al caldo tempo che, disolte le strette maniche elevati de capo li candidissimi veli sedendo or sotto li Arborselli et or in altro loco sopra lherbe, Et or sotto il bel paviglione prendeva la recente Aura. In questo tempo anchora molta Audentia dava che certo era una beatitudine. . . . A le nocte in solacio per volunta tanta madonna li sonavano lieti instrumenti e laere sempiva de Amorosi canti sino che sopraveniva la nocte mostrando le stelle la loro luce."

[39] *Ibid.,* f. 41 v⁰: The description of the *castello* extends from f. 36 v⁰ to f. 42 r⁰.

Having completed this section, he announces his intention to describe the glories of Belriguardo.

Belriguardo was the most important of the Este *delizie,* and it is the one about which we know least. It was begun in 1435, and an ancient tradition attributes the original plans to the architect Giovanni da Siena, and holds that it was designed as a fortified castle. There are references to particular rooms in various works, so that we know that there were "green rooms," a "room of diamonds," and the "room of the Sybils." Tasso makes a fleeting reference to a painting depicting Psyche. Tura is known to have painted the chapel. Beyond this, there are some records of payments to various architects, painters, and sculptors for enlargements and decorations undertaken throughout the century. Several sixteenth-century writers give brief descriptions. Eventually, during the *Quattrocento,* Belriguardo grew to be an enormous establishment, large enough to hold several princes and their entire retinues at the same time. The palace, only nine miles from Ferrara, was a favorite of all the dukes. Leonello died there, Borso received the news of his election there, and it was at Belriguardo that Ercole was staying when he learned of Niccolò di Leonello's attempted coup. Despite the central role it played in Estense life and art, one must agree with Pazzi's judgment that surviving information has been simply too fragmentary to provide a clear conception of the place.[40]

Happily, Sabadino's lengthy, sustained, and uniquely precise description now makes a clear conception possible

[40] Pazzi, Le *'Delizie Estensi,'* p. 166. There is a brief description of Belriguardo in the *Discorsi* of Annibale Romei, first published in 1586, the most recent edition of which is that published by A. Solerti, *Ferrara e la corte Estense nella seconda meta del secolo decimosesto* (Città di Castello, 1891). Olivi, in his *Annali della Città di Ferrara,* states that Ercole made Belriguardo into "la più bella delizia d'Italia che avesse" (Pazzi, Le *'Delizie Estensi,'* 167). Some additional notices are given by Gruyer, I, 477-83.

to a degree never anticipated. After a reference to the "mountain of gold" spent on the place, Sabadino acknowledges the courtesy of the courtiers who gave him the tour of Belriguardo. He then praises the physical setting of the palace, located on a fertile plain with good roads leading in all directions. Then, after stating that the splendors of Belriguardo make Ercole's ducal magnificence known throughout the entire world, he begins his description.[41]

Outside the palace, with its great walls and merlons (the length of which he puts at 383 steps), there is a wide road, alongside of which lies an enormous fish pond bordered by poplars (Fig. 17). A bridge across the pond gives access to a long road through the meadows of Gambalaga. In the opposite direction stands the great gate of the palace, sheltered by a terra cotta roof mounted on four columns, two of white marble, two of terra cotta. Over the gate, but under the roof, Ercole's ducal insignia; over the roof, Estensi coats of arms in marble. One enters through a beautiful crenellated tower containing two rooms with columns and decorated ceilings. Thence into a courtyard as big as a meadow, through which runs a brick paved road. To the left, wine cellars and the *cancelleria;* to the right, an ample kitchen, barber shop, treasury, and dispensary. Beneath a loggia, possibly along the far side, there are seven suites with servants' quarters attached to each. Continuing, one proceeds into a "splendidissimo claustro," in which are two ceremonial staircases. Having climbed the one on the right one enters a room 31 paces long and 21 paces wide.[42]

The description continues in this vein, and the reader

---

[41] *DTR,* ff. 42-43: "Se suole dire che la presentia de le cose laudate diminuiscono de quella e la fama. Non voglio dire quella diminuisca per la presentia, ma ben scrivo che non e da maravigliare, se del splendore de tanto palazo a la foresta ad gloria de la tua ducal Magnificentia ne parla tutto el Mondo."

[42] *DTR,* ff. 43 r⁰-44 v⁰.

soon loses his bearings in the maze of enormous decorated rooms. Perhaps a skilled architect could make a plan based on Sabadino's description, for it is replete with measurements and directions. But our concern is with the narrative as it reveals Estensi styles of patronage and tastes in art. In general, it can be said that everywhere there are columns of brick or marble, and that in the many courtyards that characterize this decentralized and sprawling establishment, even the most utilitarian objects are transformed into works of beauty and interest. But what of the frescoed rooms?

At one point, not far from the kitchen, one passes through a large anteroom into a "room painted with [portraits of] wise men, with brief and singular moral sentences, and with the image of the ancient Hercules on a green field." This room, probably painted during Ercole's reign, placed his mythological namesake among the moral philosophers of antiquity. The flattering symbolism could not have been lost on anyone. It appears that on the left hand wall of the same room, in ancient letters that give the illusion of a carved inscription, was painted a plaque to the effect that the Duke of Milan and the Bentivoglio ruler of Bologna met and were lodged here in 1493.[43] From this room, Sabadino passed through a number of other large rooms, several secret rooms and secret gardens, and then returned to his starting point at the first staircase. He is then led through a great many additional rooms, stopping to admire (though without detailed comment) columns, windows, fireplaces and painted ceilings almost everywhere.[44] Occasionally he mentions inscriptions. Almost invariably, distances are given

[43] *Ibid.*, f. 45: "Et la sinistra mano lessi in antiche lettere in la pariete colorata de verde facte credo con una puncta de coltello da qualche uno per maraviglia de tanto Magnifico e commodato alhogiamento, come lo illustrissimo Duca de Milano tuo figlio genero et il Fortunatis imo principe Bentivoglio con alquanti suoi generosi citadini bolognesi quivi del Mille CCCCXCIII erano cum tua Excellentia alhogiati."

[44] *Ibid.*, ff. 46-47 v°.

in paces. Passing through a number of other splendid halls, he enters another frescoed room, in which is depicted "Your Excellency represented happily, relaxed and natural with all of your courtiers. One recognizes them by their images; and also by their names, which are inscribed in Roman letters, along with their crests, at their feet. All of which is delightful to see.[45] The description of a relaxed, natural assemblage of Ercole and his court reminds one immediately of the Mantegna frescoes of the Gonzaga court at Mantua, which date from approximately the same period. The use of inscriptions in the Roman style, and of ceremonial coats of arms, here noted by Sabadino, suggests artistic links between Mantegna and the court artists of Ferrara which have perhaps been suspected, but for which evidence has been vague.

At length he enters the room of the Sibyls, which may have been painted in 1448 by Niccolò Panigato. According to Sabadino, each of the ancient sibyls was depicted, together with the prophetic message with which she was identified.[46] This room, described as an antechamber, gave access to another hall in which the author saw what appears to have been a very lifelike equestrian fresco of Ercole in the company of his brothers and members of the court. Ercole's entourage in this triumphal scene, itself a nice example of *magnificentia,* included his "most loving" brothers Sigismondo and Alberto, Scipione d'Este, Francesco da Ortonomaro, who is identified as a Neapolitan baron, the noble Ferrarese courtiers Iacopo Trotti, Bonifacio Bevilacqua,

[45] *Ibid.,* f. 48 r⁰.

[46] *Ibid.,* f. 48 r⁰: "E a la sinistra entramo in una Anticamera in alto vaga in cui sono depincte le sybille con loro scripte prophecie: et con alto et aregio capocielo copra el lecto elaborato e pincto." From this room he passed into another in which there was the equestrian fresco of Ercole, with his brothers and members of the court. See Pazzi, 168; Gruyer, I, 476-80, who uses the information discovered by G. Campori, "I pittori degli Estensi nel secolo XV," *AMP,* Ser. III, vol. III (1885-86), 525-603.

Tomasso Caraccio, and Alberto Tolomei, Lodovico Carri, who is described as Ercole's physician, and one Magone Albaresano, an unknown figure mentioned here as a favored companion.[47] From this room, which obviously was part of Ercole's answer to Borso's frescoes at Schifanoia, Sabadino entered another interesting chamber containing a portrait of Ercole d'Este, "naturalmente depincta," and with a very rich jewel on his chest, a huge oriental pearl on his hat, and on his left leg a small jeweled belt called "impresa," given him by the King of England. This was almost certainly the Order of the Garter, which he received in the Spring of 1480. In this work, probably also a fresco, Ercole is again surrounded by courtiers, whom Sabadino does not identify.[48]

The next major stop in this lengthy itinerary is yet another secret garden, probably like a small cloister, the walls of which were frescoed with the story of Psyche. That this myth was in some way represented at Belriguardo we know from a passage in Tasso's sonnet "A Belriguardo," but Sabadino proves a more helpful guide: [49]

[47] *DTR*, f. 48 r°-v°:

[48] *Ibid.*, f. 49 r°.

[49] *Ibid.*, ff. 49 v°-53 v°. The full description of the Psyche frescoes appears here, and may be consulted in full in the text of the edition in the *Travaux d'Humanisme et Renaissance*. Longhi, *Officina Ferrarese*, 64, states that these frescoes were done in 1502 by the "greculo" Grimaldi. Our evidence shows, *per contra,* that this cycle was done before 1497. It is conceivable that Grimaldi may have been paid for some additions or repairs in 1502. As Sabadino's description indicates, this cycle was regarded in his time as the greatest of the remarkable decorations of this sumptuous palace. The circumstances of its creation—in connection with the previously mentioned poem on the Psyche myth by Niccolò da Correggio—strongly suggests that it was executed by an important Ferrarese master, and not by the mediocre Reggian painter Grimaldi. The Estensi incidentally had no compunctions about having alterations made on completed frescoes, as we know from the documentary evidence on the repainting of numerous heads in the Schifanoia cycle by Baldassare d'Este.

Tasso's poem does little more than evoke the mood:

On the walls one sees, with singular morality under a poetical veil, most delightfully painted, the story of Psyche, a heavenly nymph, the daughter of an ancient King of Ionia, so beautiful that Venus became jealous of her, and conspired to send her son Cupid to make a *vendetta* against her. One sees the worried father, having consulted the Milesian oracle, placing his daughter with funeral pomp on a dangerous mountain-top whence Zephyr lifts her from earth and bears her to grassy places and shady woods, where there is a palace like this one of marvelous beauty. Cupid, obeying his mother's instructions, flies there and is smitten with love for the beautiful Psyche. And [one sees] how, in their nuptial union, she is served by the nymphs, being honored by the chorus of singers of the sacred Muses, and then the nymphs around the conjugal bed, with the winged Cupid having left his arms at the foot of the bed comforting her [by telling her] not to be afraid of the oracle. . . . It shows how she gets up in the morning, and how the Nymphs bring food to her table on the walls, and how Zephyr brings her sisters, who envy her happiness and piously persuade her not to remain with her lover, who according to the oracle of Apollo is a serpent who one day will devour her. It shows how she keeps a knife in her hand, to protect herself against this danger, and a lamp, to cut off its head [sic]. . . .[50]

The description continues in immense detail, and the reader must conclude that this is an account of one of the major fresco cycles of the Renaissance, perhaps one of the

Reale albergo, il lungo tempo oscura
le immagini diverse e l'opre antiche
onde col vago suo dipinta Psiche
talor non si discerne e raffigura. . . .

See Tasso's *Opere*, ed. B. Maier (Milan, 1963), I, 947 (no. 1053).

[50] *DTR*, ff. 49 v°-50 r°.

most elaborate and detailed representations of a classical myth ever created in European art. After his remarkably detailed account of this phenomenally complex work, Sabadino concludes:

> These events and deeds of moral love, full of singular sentiments are depicted with such felicity that they equal Zeuxis. . . . They seem to be by his hands, not that of the best Ferrarese painter who painted this moral thing according to your ducal instruction, my dear most ingenious Prince. And this beautiful thing Nicolò da Correggio too has painted in light and sweet maternal verse, according to what Apuleius, an outstanding author, wrote.[51]

Niccolò da Correggio's important vernacular poem, the *Innamoramento di Cupido e di Psyche,* was dedicated to Isabella d'Este and contains autobiographical elements concerning this important condottiere, courtier, and versifier (Fig. 18).[52] It is safe to assume that Niccolò helped to de-

[51] *Ibid.,* ff. 53 rº-vº. Gruyer, I, 471, also credits Lazzaro Grimaldi with the painting of the Psyche room, and puts the date at 1496. If this dating is correct, it would help to explain Sabadino's enthusiasm for the cycle, which would have been the most recent, as well as one of the most ambitious undertakings at Belriguardo. However, Grimaldi (Gruyer, I, 110) was a Reggian, and therefore would not have been considered a native Ferrarese painter. But Sabadino specifies that the artist was an "optimo pictore ferrariense" (f. 53). A further inconsistency in Gruyer's view is that he claims that the cycle was painted for Belfiore, rather than Belriguardo. On the basis of the evidence available, I cannot even hazard a guess as to the identity of the artist, but Lorenzo Costa would be high on my list of possible candidates.

[52] For brief notes on the life and works of this intriguing nephew of Ercole, who was not only a poet, playwright, and translator, but also an accomplished diplomat and courtier, see V. Rossi, *Il Quattrocento,* rev. ed. (Milan, 1945), 532-33; more complete information is supplied by A. Luzio and R. Renier, "Niccolò da Correggio," *GSLI,* XXI (1893), 205 ff.; XXII (1894), 65 ff.; XXXV (1900), 283 ff.; also the monograph by A. Arata,

vise the plan for these frescoes, and that they date from about the same time as his poem, written in 1491. Filippo Beroaldo's allegorizing account of the myth could perhaps also have been a source, though all have a common *locus classicus* in Apuleius. The virtually simultaneous creation of both figurative and literary representations of a single pagan myth in late *Quattrocento* Ferrara suggests a consolidating, synthesizing thrust to Estensi patronage, and helps to explain the sense of a harmonious, interacting relationship between the arts that is a characteristic of this milieu.

At this point in the tour, Sabadino begins to show signs of fatigue, and states that he cannot describe all of the remaining splendors of the place. He does mention one room, not previously known, which depicts the Triumphs of Hymenaeus, the nuptial god. The flagrantly erotic paganism of these two rooms comes as something of a surprise, given Ercole's reputation for a chaste religiosity, and his known patronage of religious and eleemosynary institutions. It is evident that the *Quattrocento* dukes were easily able to maintain a workable distinction between their religious and secular concerns.

It is a remarkable feature of Sabadino's account that he does not even mention the chapel, with its paintings by Cosimo Tura. These were commissioned by Borso, who took a great interest in the progress of the work, as cameral documents suggest. What we have been left, for lack of other evidence, to regard as one of the major elements in the decoration of Belriguardo seems not to have been worth mentioning to its *Quattrocento* Baedeker.

The account concludes with a brief tour of the environs. The gardens, fields, and surrounding regions are surveyed, the stables (for 500 horses) are mentioned, and the great

Niccolò da Correggio nella vita letteraria e politica del tempo suo (Bologna, 1934).

attractions of the place to traveling foreigners are cited. Sabadino clearly believed Belriguardo to be one of the marvels of his civilization, and his description has made it possible for us to agree.

After touching briefly upon the comforts and delights of the hunting and fishing lodge at Commachio, Sabadino turns to the important Este residence of Belfiore, a magnificent estate just outside the northern walls of Ferrara, started by Alberto d'Este at the end of the *Trecento*.[53] Here, he describes an impressive fresco cycle depicting Alberto d'Este and his court at their various pursuits. This cycle bears a more than coincidental relationship with the content of the Borsian panels at Schifanoia, as well as with the Herculean scenes at Belriguardo.[54] Though historians of art have had slightly less scanty data on this palace, owing to the reports of Ciriaco d'Ancona and Bartolommeo Facio and the oration on its celebrated park by the Ferrarese humanist Ludovico Carbone, this significant room has not to my knowledge appeared in the literature. Nor has an adjacent room, in which Sabadino saw an impressive fresco of men and ladies hunting on horseback near the sea, nor the nearby courtyards, "painted in various ways with moral and amorous

[53] Sabadino's description of Belfiore is to be found on ff. 57-62.

[54] *DTR*, ff. 57-58: "Se li vede effigiata la illustre memoria del prelibato principe Alberto estense con molti gentilhomini e dame a cavallo ad venatione con pardi. E veltri e lepore e caprioli e cervi et ad ursi dove se li vede la fiera preda de li Caciati animali. . . ." Another scene in this cycle shows ". . . in sedia il principe Alberto vestito di brocato doro havendo in capo una Dama. . . ." Perhaps this testimony may help to modify our image of Alberto as an ascetic scholarly figure, the Gothic saint who stands guard over the façade of the *duomo*. Indeed he seems to have enjoyed if he did not initiate in Ferrara the noble pursuits and pastimes that the Estensi shared with such monarchs of the Middle Ages as Edward I of England (cf. F. M. Powicke, "King Edward I in Fact and Fiction," in D. J. Gordon ed., *Fritz Saxl, 1890-1948: A Volume of Memorial Essays from his friends in England* (London, 1957), 120-35).

exempli." [55] Beyond this courtyard, which also had a sculptured figure of Jealousy on a marble column, he entered a large hall with yet another set of paintings of men and women hunting. More recent aspects of the decor include a sculpture of an elephant, done after the live specimen brought to Ercole by Cypriot merchants, a painted scene of Ercole's pilgrimage to Santiago de Compostela, a room decorated with paintings of panthers, another with lions.[56] Another room not far from the warm baths was decorated with "certe virgine," each one leading a wild animal on a leash. This was the first part of a great cycle of frescoes showing both the old and new parts of Ferrara, the palace gardens and, as nearly as I can determine, a small zoological garden containing a panther, a tame wolf, and a giraffe.[57] There follow scenes from the hunt, including Eleanora d'Este and members of her entourage, and of the life of

[55] *DTR*, f. 58: "Laltro salotto e pincto de homini et Dame andanti ad cacia sopra legiadri cavalli a la marina vulnerando con optimi e forti acti or questo or quello animale con le saete da le belle Donne. Poi in uno Triumphal Carro tanta nobile compagnia si vede, che sia felicie cosa."

[56] *Ibid.*, f. 58 v°: "Se li vede presso uno gentil paviglione sopra sei colomne de Marmo copertato de piombo, che naturale simiglia effigiato lo Elephante, che ad te fue menato de li Mercanti Cypriani, che fano molti e molti Anni che in Italia Elephanti furono giamai veduti. Se li vede anchora seriosamente quando la tua Excellentia exitte fuori de la cita di Ferrara per andare in Hyspagna ad venerare il Templo dello Apostolo Iacobo con splendidissima compagnia. . . ." The date of these scenes would therefore be placed around 1486 or 1487. It is somewhat puzzling that Ercole's departure for Spain was considered worthy of such commemoration, even though he never reached his destination. Yet this is not the least significant event recorded in mural form in a Herculean palace (cf. f. 59 r°). Indeed the decorations and Belriguardo and Belfiore might have been conceived at least in part as a kind of visual chronicle of Ercole's reign.

[57] *Ibid.*, f. 60: ". . . si vede la vagheza del prato pieno delli varij et diversi Arbori fructifferi ad sexto e ad misura: e quasi tutta la prisca e nova citate. Dal capo verso lantiqua citate li e una panthera e uno lupo . . . che uno legiadro giovane e una venusta donzella li tengono con lassi al collo: Se li vede una Girapha col capo altissimo. . . ."

the court. It included musicians, dancers, a splendid feast. There was a section recording Eleanora's arrival as a young fiancée in Ferrara, with her prospective husband, and another showing the matrimonial celebrations. From Sabadino's relatively schematic description, the impression emerges that this room was dedicated to Ercole's duchess, perhaps a unique artistic tribute to a lady of the Renaissance, though it is also worth noting how prominently women appear to have figured as full participants in virtually all of the scenes Sabadino records.[58]

The next room is given over to scenes of hunting with falcons, and also shows famous people—men and women—at this activity. The following room is painted with a scene of the court disembarking for the hunt from the ducal bucentaur. They are going after boar, and they use huge dogs. There are very graphic scenes of the party killing these ferocious animals. The next two rooms are given over to wolves and bears, respectively. At this point, Sabadino comments on the general opulence of the palace;

> All the rooms of this palace take light from glassed windows. The joy of seeing the ornaments of the delicate and splendid beds, and coverings, makes this habitation appear like an earthly paradise. From which, curtailing my remarks, this palace should no longer be called Belfiore, but because of your magnificent works deserves being called "Iocundo Sole."[59]

Belfiore stood within the so-called "Herculean Addition,"

[58] *Ibid.*, ff. 60-62. See Appendix III for some extended excerpts from this description.

[59] *DTR*, f .62: ". . . e tute le stantie de questo palacio prendeno lume per vitriate finestre presso la felicita del vedere li loro ornamenti de li dilicati e splendidi lecti & Tapezarie che pare una Abitatione de uno terestre paradiso Diche perstringendo el nostro dire, Questo palazo non piu Belfiore, ma in laude delle tue magnifice opere Iocundo sole merita essere chiamato."

the vast new quarter added to old Ferrara according to the design of the architect Biagio Rossetti in the 1490s. This addition, one of the first examples of deliberate urban planning, tripled the area within the city walls and provided needed land for the growing population of the city, and the residential needs of its patriciate. Sabadino comments on the addition quite specifically, but without adding appreciably to what is already known.[60] The same is true for his description of the new city walls, and for the important Dominican Church of Sta. Maria degli Angeli, also designed by Biagio Rossetti. Sabadino also mentions Ercole's benefactions to the church of Sant' Agostino, and others. The word "templo" is invariably used in the description of these Ferrarese churches. In concluding his description of the city, Sabadino compares Ercole to Augustus, on account of his great public works:

> Just as he found Rome in brick and left it in marble, so too will your Celsitude, by virtue of your *Magnificentia,* be recognized by posterity with very great glory. For you found a Ferrara of painted brick, and you will have left it . . . carved in adamantine marble, as a result of which one can already make this judgment: that this your city, gleaming more than oriental *lapillo,* will be among the wonderful cities of the world.[61]

[60] *Ibid.,* ff. 62-68.

[61] *Ibid.,* f. 66: ["Ma con quale divino preconio Ingeniosissimo principe se puo la virtu della tua Magnificantia celebrare per lo Argumento grande et illustre, che hai facto con tanto mirabile ordine a la tua prestantissima cita de Ferrara cum cio sia se potra meritamente dire:] come di se stesso Cesare augusto disse—che havea trovata Roma di terra et alla lassarebbe di marmo. Cosi la tua celsitudine per virtu di Magnificentia sera perconizata a la posterita con grandissima gloria, che Ferrara de terra pincta trovasti, & di marmo de Adamanti sculpta [tua indomita divisia] haverai lassata. Per il che gia Iudicare se puote, che questa tua cita splende piu che orientale lapillo sera delle mirabile cita del mondo."

This statement illustrates the hazards of prognostication. It may even provide an implicit warning, if one were necessary, of the humanist tendency toward hyperbole. But there is enough solid factual description in Sabadino's account to convince me, at least, that our image of Estensi patronage in the *Quattrocento* has to change. It must begin to take account of the fact that there was clearly much more fresco painting in Ferrara than has ever been suspected. It must recognize that virtually the entire extent of this vast, missing, anonymous *œuvre* was totally secular in its iconography, and dealt with either pagan mythologies or depictions of courtly pursuits. It should begin to acknowledge not only the decorative but also the political function of this art. It was not only an adornment of life, an ingredient in the establishment and maintenance of a particular cultural tone, but also a manifestation of *Magnificentia,* the kind of elegant sumptuousness that connotes power and premanence, and that therefore relates quite directly to the main business of a prince. This latter suggestion may require some amplification.

I noted earlier that Sabadino chose to introduce the entire discussion of the artistic surroundings of the Estensi in the context of the topic *Magnificentia.* It would have been possible also to have done so under the rubric *Liberalità,* had the author in any way wished to stress patronage of the arts. But he does not do so.[62] Nor does he do so in the entirely conventional book on *Magnanimità,* which could also have provided him with a suitable occasion.[63] Instead

[62] In the fourth book, on *Liberalità* (ff. 27-34), Sabadino treats Ercole's generosity to the Church, endowments to poor virgins and other impecunious people, and similar sorts of philanthropic works, all in extremely general terms, and citing ancient models.

[63] The book on "Maganimity," ff. 12 v°-16 r° considers Ercole's generosity in dealing with enemies, and with real or supposed insults or slights. On f. 14 r° there is this interesting observation: ". . . la Magnanimita in li principi debbe essere virtu peculiare & opportuna senza laquale de

of viewing the art of the court primarily as a product of princely generosity, enlightenment, or concern for culture, he sees it as the major element in Ercole's magnificence, that is, the physical realization and exemplification of his power and majesty. To take the argument a step further, one could mention in passing the other subjects Sabadino treats in the book on magnificence. They are family weddings, the spectacular nature of which is evoked in the author's description; theatrical performances, jousts, and tournaments, which are specifically described as offered to please the populace, and at great expense; and then such lesser but impressive manifestations as gold and silver cloth, and other elements of royal pomp.

Magnificentia then, for Sabadino, is a quality that is embodied in physical objects or events. It is the product of lavish spending, and it adds pleasure and delight to life. But it also symbolizes and represents power and authority. It is an essential ingredient in the recipe for ruling successfully, and the Estensi have brought it to a high state. Their search for magnificence through the visual arts—both in their own palaces and in the temples, walls, and streets of Ferrara—is the overriding concern of Sabadino's discussion.

It should now be evident that Sabadino's account, though it gives us nothing new to look at, greatly expands and specifies our knowledge of *Quattrocento* painting in Ferrara. It also offers useful evidence to the cultural historian of the social role of the visual arts in the view of the fifteenth-century observer.

---

stati non sono degni essere chiamati signori, se non Tyranni. Ma negare non si puo che tu non sij vero principe e signore per la tua usata Magnanimita, e con Mansuetudine sempre grande." It is, then, magnanimity which reinforces legitimacy in a ruler. This simplistic assertion is helpful, because it strikingly corroborates the concept I have been trying to develop here of a kind of implicit social contract between the *signori* and their subjects.

Sabadino brings us a long way from the manuscripts, playing cards, and little medals of the court of Leonello and the early Borso. He reveals painting and patronage on an immense scale under Ercole, offering a useful clue to the nature and content of the undoubtedly enormous missing *œuvre* of Francesco del Cossa, Ercole de' Roberti, and their students. In describing the content of a vast panoply of court art, he bears witness to both its achievements and limitations, human and intellectual. The great frescoes at Schifanoia may no longer be viewed as a unique outpouring of classicizing creative energies by painters generally occupied with altarpieces and the like, but rather as a perfectly representative example of Estense patronage of Ferrarese painters, and as the only extant link in a chain of cycles designed to represent ducal magnificence. Sabadino also reveals that sculpture played a somewhat more important role in Ferrarese art than has traditionally been supposed, although this role tended to be more functional and decorative than aesthetically ambitious. But there is no question that the visual beauty and political utility of Ferrarese painting was rivaled among the arts only by architecture and urban planning. These subjects have been fully studied by others, most notably Bruno Zevi, but it will be useful to outline briefly the general ways in which they relate to this inquiry.

In the late fifteenth century, Ferrara came to be transformed from a little medieval town to a large Renaissance city. The process by which this happened was not the familiar modern method of new construction on the sites of previously demolished structures. Rather, it was achieved by adding to the *urbs* what had previously been undeveloped surburban land. Medieval Ferrara, which one can still sample today in the picturesque alleys around the Via delle Volte, was a hodge podge of small, narrow houses squeezed together along cramped, sometimes winding streets. The

Herculean Addition, also called "terra nova," was a large spacious region of broad, straight avenues, comfortable houses, elegant palaces, extensive parks and gardens, and monumental religious houses. Yet the new section was designed to coexist with an inter-relate to the old, as the deployment of north-south streets clearly indicates (Fig. 19).[64]

The expansion of the city was a vast project. While Sabadino degli Arienti's comparison of Ercole to Augustus may seem fanciful (though less so than my comparison of Borso to Caesar), it could be said that in some ways it is not inept. None of his predecessors and none of his successors did as much to shape the city. It is no accident that during the later part of Ercole's reign there appeared an ever-increasing volume of literary allusions and even entire works devoted to the praise of Ferrara's beauty.[65] To contemporaries, it came to be regarded as an object of wonder, a city designed for pleasure and civilized pursuits, but at the same time well-fortified against the harsh realities of the world outside. To Ariosto it represented a perfect synthesis of arms and learning, *Ars et Mars,* an "exquisite fortress." [66] Sabadino, in a more elaborate and much more detailed passage in his book *Iustitia,* stresses *Ars* without neglecting *Mars.* A host

[64] See esp. B. Zevi, *Biagio Rossetti;* and the recent book of maps and plans published by F. Bonasera, *Forma veteris urbis Ferrariae* (Florence, 1965).

[65] Most of the many poems and epigrams in praise of Ferrara are unpublished, and may be approached through the index to Kristeller's *Iter.* Naturally these documents cannot be accepted uncritically, but after having made all the necessary allowances it remains evident that the city made a formidable impression on contemporary observers, from about the time of Borso d'Este onward. In the late sixteenth century, so sensitive and critical an observer as Montaigne wrote: "We were all that day at Ferrara [including an audience with the Duke] and there saw many beautiful churches, gardens, private houses, and everything that they told us was remarkable." For this document, and problems of its authorship, see D. F. Frame, *The Complete Works of Montaigne* (Stanford, 1948), 861-63, 925.

[66] *Orlando Furioso,* Canto VI, 22 (cited by Pazzi, *Le Delizie,* 21).

of court poets and visitors to the city echo these themes, which appear even in such trans-Alpine sources as Hartmann Schedel's *Nürnberg Chronicle.*[67]

Ercole's success in his ambitious building projects must be attributed in large measure to the work of the court architect, Biagio Rossetti. Together with this local genius, Ercole worked singlemindedly at the new additions, especially the new walls, and often refused to attend to other business. The Venetian War had taught him a grim lesson in civil defense. To realize their common vision for Ferrara, Ercole was willing to make extraordinary demands of his subjects. New taxes were levied, forced labor brought in from the *contado,* budgets ruthlessly cut in court and university. As the walls rose, the new streets were paved in brick, and wealthy nobles and citizens were urged to build in the new quarter. In the space of a decade, twenty palaces and a dozen churches went up in the addition.[68]

The speed with which all this happened, its planning and execution by a single individual, albeit helped by numerous assistants, the presence of a planned model for urban growth —all of these elements help to explain the harmony and elegance of the "esquisita fortezza" that Ferrara became during the decade when Sabadino wrote. But alongside all of these looms the controlling interest of the Duke, and perhaps the Duchess, acting and planning out of the complex, intertwined motives of self- and dynastic-aggrandizement, expansion and beautification of the city, and the desire to use modern, rational techniques of design and fortifica-

[67] Hartmann Schedel's *Nürnberg Chronicle* (Nürnberg, 1493) describes some of Ferrara's glories, but uses the same stylized woodcut to illustrate them as for Naples and other cities.

[68] It would be pointless to duplicate here the essential work of B. Zevi, *Biagio Rossetti,* which offers an extensive analysis of the Herculean Addition. For a brief but competent summary, based on Zevi and other sources, see E. A. Gutkind, *Urban Development in Southern Europe,* Vol. IV [Italy] (New York, 1969), 300-309.

tion to eliminate the dangers and errors of the past. When the Estensi decided to take advantage of their despotic powers, they did so shamelessly and effectively. The art and architecture of Ferrara thus reflect the evolving priorities of successive rulers, revealing powerful elements both of continuity and change.

VIII   The Style of a
Renaissance Despotism

ON MARCH 1, 1480, Ercole wrote to his orator at Milan, Cesare Valentini,

> Messere Cesare: We learn from your letter of the death of your wife, which gives us much displeasure, both on account of your loss and of ours. However there is always the public good to be placed against the private, and one must have patience and not break up, because the thing cannot be tolerated with grief and lamentations. Comfort yourself as a strong man, lacking neither arms nor horses. You will find yourself another one, and you will have a new dowry and younger flesh. Don't on account of this put aside our affairs even for the shortest interval, . . . and give no thought to your own particular trials.[1]

As a letter of condolence on the death of a wife, Ercole's statement has no classical models. But it does help to bring home a few important points about Ercole's despotic style, and it does so in an unguarded way. There is a total, and rapid, acceptance of reality. There is a tough, categorical demand for service and obedience. There is an insistence on the maintenance of control over the emotional and religious aspects of a human problem. And above all, there is an emphasis on the primary and overriding obligation of the

---

[1] ASM, ASE, Cancelleria, Estero, Milano, Busta 2: "Messere Cesare. Intendendo per la nostra lettera de la morte de la donna vostra, ne havemo recevuto dispiacere assai et per lo incommodo vostro et per lo nostro. Tutavia l'è sempre da anteponere il bene publico al privato, e'l si bisogna havere patientia et non vi rompere, perchè suscitare la non si pò cum dolori et lamenti. Confortative [*sic*] che a valenthomo non manchò mai ni arme ni cavalli; voi ne trovareti un' altra, et hareti dota nova et carne più fresca. Non mettiti per questo li facti nostri in alcuno minimo intervallo . . . sichè non guardati a vostre tribulatione particulare." I owe this reference to Professor Nicolai Rubinstein.

public man. "Il bene publico" is not precisely the phrase that one would expect to find in the private communication of a Renaissance duke to one of his subordinates. And yet, as I have shown, a deep and lasting concern for the commonweal was one of the constant characteristics of Estense rule in the fifteenth century. Within the standards of their time and place, and together with many other interests and concerns, each of the rulers considered here was devoted to an ideal of governing well and attempted to implement that ideal in some form.

There were large areas of continuity in the ways that Niccolò, Leonello, Borso, and Ercole sought to improve the lot of the citizens of Ferrara, and thereby maintain their own powers and privileges. In fact, each of these princes, when he made administrative, bureaucratic, or fiscal changes, seemed to have been adapting or refining a generally acceptable, traditional practice in the light of new conditions. As early as the fourteenth century the Marquess of Este succeeded in establishing an unusually thoroughgoing despotism within the framework of Ferrarese statutory law, and with the almost unvarying support of the people. Originally, this absolutism represented an escape route from magnate disorder and popular unrest. Its general effectiveness in maintaining public order and avoiding civil war led in the fourteenth century to the expansion of the Este state to include a vast portion of the southern Po Valley. To control and govern this region, with the important cities it contained, the Estensi were obliged to develop a substantial diplomatic and administrative bureaucracy, which evolved gradually and more or less continuously over two centuries. Marchesal institutions were superimposed on the magistracies and other formal governmental arrangements of the medieval commune. Here the Estensi appear less as innovators than as followers of the example of the Visconti in Milan, even though they were in many ways clients of the

Venetians. Unlike the Visconti, however, the Estensi ruled in a small city, which enabled them to exercise their power more personally and directly. Though they occasionally used consultative mechanisms and committees, these were generally either conceived as, or degenerated into, mere fictions while the prince preserved all decision-making powers for himself. Typical here is the popular *parlamento,* convoked to elect a new *signore* all through the fifteenth century even though the practice had long been abandoned elsewhere. At the same time, the Estensi were careful not to subvert the forms of other communal institutions. Instead, they skillfully redefined the functions and the accountability of the communal magistracies, so as to have absolute power over them. Thus the *podestà* became in effect a hand-picked administrator of signorial policies, the *savi* a governing board of trusted subordinates, the chief financial officers courtiers from loyal families.

The Estensi could offer substantial rewards to those who served them, including attractive grants of arable land in the Ferrarese and other regions, where reclamation gradually added to an already abundant supply. These lands in turn became sources of agricultural wealth, and therefore produced new fiscal revenues. The very small number of non-noble citizens who managed to enrich themselves through commerce could generally be induced to take a place in this hierarchy, and to share in the rural and courtly pursuits of what had never ceased in fact to be a feudal class. Indeed, by repressing the guilds in the late thirteenth century, the Estensi set the direction for Ferrara's economic development as a rural and agrarian rather than an urban and commercial state. This in turn led to a situation in which a small enough number of men of new wealth arose so that they could be accommodated comfortably within the ruling group. Thus, the absence of noble birth never became a serious impediment to preferment or advancement at court.

Perhaps it even served as an asset, by revealing the openness of what otherwise might have come to be resented as a closed ruling élite. By the same token, the increasingly common sale of offices and titles became a source of needed revenue to the expanding court, while serving to firm up stronger loyalties to the dynasts.

While the Estensi were careful to reward their faithful servitors with emoluments of all kinds, they were also vigilant and quick to react against any real or suspected threat to their rule. The elaborate, articulated chain of command which the *signori* established through their bureaucracy made it possible for them to protect themselves against being personally identified as evildoers or exploiters on the few occasions when popular uprisings threatened the stability of their regime. The rare outbreaks of disloyalty or treason by members of the court or rivals within the family were invariably met with severe reprisals. In fact, the Estensi reveal a degree of canniness in their use of rewards and punishments which could scarcely be improved upon by modern rulers familiar with the insights of behavioral group psychology. Moreover, they appear also to have shown concern for and mastery of other psychological techniques of government. We have called attention to the use of the *castello* not only as a means of physical protection, but also as an instrument of intimidation, and to the self-conscious and continuous use of magnificence, display, and various forms of ritual behavior.

One of the major results of this absolutist style was the emergence of a stable social order. Crime, while always a major social problem throughout the period, occurred on the level of individuals, not of mass movements. The only events which might at all be considered revolutionary do not involve mass popular support, and are the work of disgruntled rivals within the family. Indeed, the *popolo* functions (and is utilized) as a conservative force in all such cases. It seems evident that such stability is not merely the product of coercion and intimidation, nor even of less blatant kinds of repressive force. It also reflects consistent and increasing efforts by the Estensi to achieve certain concrete goals within their state. In this connection, I have called attention to their concern for the food supply, their efforts in flood control, irrigation, and reclamation, their interest in the effective functioning of the judicial system, their religious and philanthropic works, and their use of pageantry and entertainment as forms of vicarious popular participation in the good life. The stability to which these practices contributed became in turn a precondition for the extraordinarily mobile and peripatetic style of life that characterized the reigns of Borso and Ercole in particular.

With a comparatively secure state and a reasonably competent administration, these princes could indulge themselves in cultivating what may be called a neo-feudal model of monarchy, that included all of the elaborate trappings of country life—hunting, fishing, falconry, jousting, and the attendant pleasures of the traditional feudal aristocracy. What emerges, then, is the somewhat paradoxical combination of a highly rationalized, effective, and up-to-date administration, fully conversant with the techniques and methods of the most successful governments of its kind, in the hands of a dynasty that consistently maintains the styles and manners of feudal monarchs in an almost atavistic way. But that is only part of the story. There is no denying that the Estensi clearly conceived of themselves in terms of northern European aristocratic ideals, notably those of Carolingian France. They found their own mythic past in the chivalric circle of the *Chanson de Roland*. Through the *Quattrocento,* they maintained ties with the Burgundian and French courts, and at the end of the period they received Charles VIII with enthusiasm while other Italians regarded his arrival as a catastrophe, a disgrace, and even a sign of

divine disfavor. The cultural affinity with northern traditions extended chronologically from the appearance of Pro-
vençal troubadours in Ferrara in the *Duecento* onward to
the end of the sixteenth century, and took such forms as
direct artistic influences, dynastic marriage, books and manuscripts, and the presence of composers and musicians beginning in the 1470s, or even earlier.

There is nothing uniquely Ferrarese about this Francophile tendency, nor was it a consistently dominant influence.
On the contrary, what seems to me crucial is the fact that
this northern aristocratic courtly tradition came in *Quattrocento* Ferrara to coexist with the most contemporary Italian
cultural, literary, and artistic concerns and influences, thus
producing a degree of intellectual cosmopolitanism quite
remarkable for a small Renaissance city. Leonello, for example, was not only acutely aware of, but also closely involved in, the work of some of the major Italian humanists
of his time. Borso continued the patronage of humanists
and by virtue perhaps of his own relative ignorance gave a
significant stimulus to the development of vernacular literature in Ferrara. Under Ercole, the new emphasis on Italian
as against Latinate culture blended with the traditional
Francophile values of the Estensi to stimulate an epic Italian
literature embroidered around Carolingian themes, and in-
corporating the dynastic and personal histories of the Estensi.
I refer of course to the major poems of Boiardo and Ariosto.
At the same time a cosmopolitan, secular art transformed
both the palaces of the Estensi and the physiognomy of
Ferrara. Humanistic and courtly themes in Ferrarese painting are presented in the art of Tura, Cossa, and Roberti in
styles that reflect not only the pervasive aristocratization of
painting in late *Quattrocento* Italy, but also in particular a
kind of elegance and precision that may owe almost as
much to French and Flemish masters as it does to Florentine and Paduan examples. In the arts and sciences, as in

all other areas of life in Ferrara, the *signori* played a dominant role in selecting the direction and extent of activities, both in court and university, and here their approach was anything but atavistic.

There is another aspect of the pervasive, consistent, and successful absolutism of the Estensi which should not escape our notice. It is the idea of the dynasty as a cause, in and of itself. Any family or group that succeeds in ruling a population over a period of centuries is bound to develop its own myths and ideologies. Commonly these myths in effect prefigure the terms in which such groups would like to have themselves seen by their contemporaries and later generations, and they often succeed in achieving that goal. Both Florentine and Venetian writers routinely produced such myths, as recent scholarship has shown.[2] Perhaps it is not quite so evident that the despots had a similar interest in managing their historical images, but this study of the Estensi has yielded much evidence to show that this was indeed the case. However, the dynastic-despotic myth is in

[2] See, for example, the recent article by D. Weinstein, "The Myth of Florence," *Florentine Studies: Politics and Society in Renaissance Florence,* ed. N. Rubinstein (London and Evanston, 1968), 15-42; and the same author's book *Savonarola and Florence: Prophecy and Patriotism in the Renaissance* (Princeton, 1970), where the theme is taken up in greater detail. Nicolai Rubinstein's articles have opened up this field for modern scholars. See esp. "The Beginnings of Political Thought in Florence," *JWCI,* v (1942), 198-227; "Some Ideas on Municipal Progress and Decline," *Fritz Saxl Memorial Volume,* 165-83. On the myth of Venice there are the articles by G. Fasoli, "Nascità di un mito," *Studi storici in onore di Gioacchino Volpe per il suo 80° compleanno* (Florence, 1958), I, 55-79; F. Gaeta, "Alcuni considerazioni sul mito di Venezia," *BHR,* xxiii (1961), 58-75. See also W. J. Bouwsma, *Venice and the Defense of Republican Liberty* (Berkeley, 1968). Interesting thoughts on historic myths of this type in general are in A. Dufour, "Le mythe de Genève au temps de Calvin," *Revue suisse d'histoire,* ix (1959), 489-518, and reprinted in his book *Histoire politique et psychologie historique* (Geneva, 1966), 9-35.

many ways fundamentally different from the republican myths, and in the formal sense it seems more complex.

The differences in the terms in which ruling élites account for their origins and justify their behavior and their prerogatives are of course reflections of differences in the states themselves. Republican myths, at least in the Italian Renaissance context, generally involve an account of origin, referring to foundations in Roman republican times. The new republic is often presented as the heir of the Roman progenitor. It stresses a kind of missionary function, in the sense of perpetuating or spreading the values and benefits of republican government to an entire region (by force of arms, if necessary). It emphasizes the role of the states concerned as guardians of republican liberty in general, and thereby underlines the defensive function of the state's military involvements. Finally, it often involves claims to a kind of destiny, a special role that the state has been created to play in history, because of its special values and achievements.

Despotic myths, on the other hand, though based on many of the same kinds of impulses, generally take a notably different form. Perhaps the key difference is that there has to be a distinction between the thing governed and the governors, a fact that requires in effect two different sets of myths.

On the one hand, the dynasty must have its own mythology. This requires an account of its origins, designed to manifest its nobility, antiquity, and its claims to political legitimacy; second, it requires emphasis on the traditional virtues fostered by the dynasty through a long line of rulers and other heroes; finally, at any particular moment it needs to be associated with an individual, the reigning prince of the moment. Here, particular qualities or abilities have to be dramatized, which is another way of saying that the propagandist has to build upon whatever virtues he can find in a particular ruler. If the ruler actually possesses such strengths, the task is greatly simplified.

The second aspect of despotic mythology is that of the state governed. It must be made to reflect the quality of the dynasty. Accordingly, the myth of the well-governed despotism tends to depend upon the demonstration of very tangible kinds of achievements, rather than the more abstract or even ideological values and traditions often incorporated into republican mythologies.

These distinctions are immediately evident in Ferrarese literature of many types. The fifteenth-century chroniclers, who take the despotism absolutely for granted, evaluate each prince in terms of his particular virtues and contributions. But a similar and more articulated pattern has been shown to emerge in the panegyrical writings of court orators and poets. Here, in the course of the fifteenth century, an entire genre of poetry and treatises in praise of Ferrara seems to appear. It stresses the physical beauty of the city, the works that have been done to improve it, its solicitude for social and economic justice, and its role as a center of the arts and learning. At the same time, many of the same authors also write in praise of the individual Este princes. They are presented as exemplars of their house and its traditional virtues, but also as individuals with particular strengths (not weaknesses). These tend toward love of peace, religion, justice, order, learning, and the arts. This is in a sense the literary analogue of the despotic, hierarchical, benevolent rule that we see idealized in the Schifanoia frescoes, and that must have been at least as dramatically presented in the other fresco cycles described by Giovanni Sabadino degli Arienti. That the Estensi themselves were conscious of the dynasty as an independent and self-evidently valuable cause emerges from their behavior. The example of Ercole d'Este providing full and honorable funeral services for his rebellious nephew Niccolò di Leonello, after first having had him decapitated and then having had his head sewn back on, is evidence of his recognition of the formal claim that membership in the family imposed, and there are other, less melodramatic instances of similar assumptions at work. In such acts as births and funerals, the erection of statues and monuments, and other public celebrations, a well-defined sense of family solidarity is often evident. This may have helped to reduce personal rivalries which, though infrequent, tended to be explosive, and have therefore often been overemphasized.

Each of the four *Quattrocento* princes reveals this sense of family identification. But at the same time, all of them felt free to give independent reign to their own interests and causes, while continuing in the basic signorial practices of their predecessors. Since the differences in the interests and commitments of these men were considerable, the changes produced in Ferrarese life and culture during the period are perhaps more dramatic than the normal internal dynamics of cultural change might have been expected to generate. In fact, one of the main developments that I have tried to explain in the course of this study is that of a transformation of Ferrara from a dank, strife-ridden, culturally retrograde region into an elegant, peaceful, well-ordered, cosmopolitan cultural center. I have also tried to show how this transformation, shaped during the reigns of Niccolò III and Leonello, is itself transformed through the changing energies and interests of Borso and Ercole. The era of general peace and stability that begins in the reign of Niccolò III may be regarded as an essential precondition for the extraordinary literary and artistic developments that begin then, and receive mature formulation in the reign of Leonello.

It was in Leonello's short term as *signore* that humanism made its deepest impact at Ferrara—that the city became an internationally celebrated crossroads for men of knowledge. The school of Guarino da Verona, though imitative in many ways of the early foundation of Vittorino da Feltre at Mantua, outstripped its predecessor in the intensity of its scholarly life and substantive contributions to the classical revival, and in its effects on the life of the court. Under Borso, what had been the limited, private cultural world of a small courtly circle continued, but without the princely enthusiasm that it had previously enjoyed. Therefore its leading figures began to find more congenial surroundings in the university, to which Borso made important financial contributions. At the court, a less Latinate, classicizing group surrounded the new *signore*. Many of these were worldly men trained in the law, who tended to come from noble families, men who served less as intellectual soulmates than as companions at the hunt, and as collaborators in Borso's plans for political and personal aggrandizement. Ludovico Casella may be considered the principal link between the political and cultural interests of the divine Borso. During these years, the prince acquires important new titles, and rules as a towering public figure, a benevolent, fatherly protector who dispenses justice, keeps the peace, and shows his face to the people. The Schifanoia frescoes mirror the benign despotism of Borso at the time that came to be regarded later as a golden age. Ercole, raised in the splendid setting of the Neapolitan court, brought new standards of magnificence to Ferrara. His program of enlarging, beautifying, and fortifying the city, the works he commissioned in the enlargement and decoration of his palaces, the scale of his generosity to the poor, the patterns of strategic marriages with other noble families, all of these indicate the exercise of princely prerogatives on a new scale. At the same time, there remained the persistent public piety, never absent from the lives of the Estensi rulers, and the traditional concern for the *bene publico,* which also (though sometimes just barely) managed to

justify the *signoria* in the minds of the people. The Herculean court was that of a true monarch, one who continued
to recognize traditional and legal obligations and constraints
on his power, but whose sense of legitimacy was unchal-
lengable.

During the continuing urbanization of Ferrara in the
fifteenth century, one finds a tendency toward an increasing
specialization and differentiation of functions, not only
within the court, but in society at large. In the Herculean
period, with its greatly expanded demands for public funds,
this tendency is intensified. Ercole, in trying to revivify the
guilds and the commercial life of Ferrara, revealed a constant need for new money. This led him not only to protect
Jewish bankers, pawn personal property, borrow from
Florentine houses such as the Gondi, and renege on his
vicarial dues, but also to resort to the sale of offices and
other emergency measures. His attempts to realign Ferrarese
diplomacy led to the disastrous war of 1482-84, an episode
which worsened the financial problems, and led to the
temporary imposition of certain kinds of austerities. Yet
through all the turmoil of the late *Quattrocento,* Ercole
endured. Alphonso, his firstborn, succeeded him peacefully,
having married Lucrezia Borgia, the daughter of Pope
Alexander VI. A younger son became a prelate of some
distinction. His daughters linked him by marriage with the
ruling houses of Gonzaga and Sforza, among others, and
Isabella's achievements at least were impressive.

The tendencies that we see emerging throughout the
fifteenth century continued in Ferrara during the next
hundred years. The administrative machinery of town and
court is further elaborated and bureaucratized. The statutes
are increasingly refined and subdivided. There comes to be
a more complete differentiation of functions between university and the culture of the court. The scientific and
legal faculties enter their most productive period, and

scholarly humanism gradually takes refuge in the literary academies of the erudite. Courtly culture, on the other hand, tends to continue in the direction of pageantry and entertainment established by Borso and Ercole. Music and the drama continue to thrive, and vernacular poetry composed by noble Ferrarese submerges the contributions of such neo-Latin authors as Tebaldeo, Bendedei, and Guarini. Religion continues as a major element in the Estensi public style. In painting, Venetian influence makes a powerful impact in Ferrara early in the century when Bellini and then Titian created their celebrated works for Alphonso I. Subsequently, few Ferrarese artists are entirely free of this influence.

The transformation I have traced, then, is essentially a cultural phenomenon, and one that reflects mainly the activities and interests of an aristocratic élite. Though this group consciously cultivated chivalric traditions and styles, it also contributed to and took part in much that was innovative and contemporary in the arts and sciences of Renaissance Italy. Though it exacted a high price from the citizenry in terms of liberty, representation, and political rights, it also succeeded in maintaining a stable political order for centuries. Though it glorified the rule of a dynasty and perpetuated an expensive and parasitical nobility, it also exacted standards of performance from these ruling groups which perhaps could not have been met on a sustained basis by any other available political form at that particular time and place. Even the Florentine republic, after having been subverted and reinstated time and again, eventually succumbed to the secure authoritarianism of a legitimized despot. Avoiding such vicissitudes, most Ferrarese would probably have preferred their native land where, as Abraham Lincoln wrote of Tsarist Russia, "they make no pretense of loving liberty . . . where despotism can be taken pure, and without the base alloy of hypocrisy."

APPENDIX I

The Administration of the Estensi

In many places throughout this study I have presented the administration of the Estensi as one characterized by increasing centralization and bureaucratic differentiation. Though the administrative history of Ferrara awaits extensive study, it may be useful here to summarize the principal features of the Este bureaucracy, which is perhaps simpler and more straightforward than might be assumed. I hope that the descriptions that follow—schematic and limited though they are—may serve, first, to arouse interest in more thorough and analytical treatment of this problem, and, second, to provide a reasonably sound basis for and justification of my even more general comments on Ferrarese administration, throughout the preceding chapters.

The source of what follows is the appointments list for the year 1476, as it appears in the manuscript chronicle of Ugo Caleffini, the distinguished Ferrarese notary who was both the most precise and the most perceptive of contemporary observers of the Estensi.[1] Caleffini generally gives good information concerning both court and state appointments at the beginning of each year of the chronicle, but 1476 offers a particularly complete listing, and was compiled in an obvious attempt to be systematic and comprehensive. Though I have used the 1476 list as the basis for this summary discussion, there is nothing in Caleffini's other lists to challenge the substantive content of this one, or to qualify the modest conclusions drawn from it.

The appointments may be divided basically into two categories: appointments to state offices, and court appointments.

[1] MS. Vat. Chig. I, I, 4, *Chronica facte et scripte per Ugo Caleffino* . . .

Formally and structurally, there was of course a clear distinction between "casa" and "stato," a distinction that is still preserved in the organization of the Este archives. State officials responded to a different set of superiors, were paid out of communal treasuries, and served in offices that were prescribed and circumscribed by statute. Appointees within the ducal household served at the pleasure of the duke, and regardless of their formal titles might be called upon to fill a wide range of functions. In a sense, of course, this is a distinction without a difference, because all of these offices were subject to ducal control, by virtue of the signorial power of appointment to communal offices, including the magistracy of the twelve *savi,* the highest magistracy, which incidentally was not subject to the limitation of a one-year term of office. Following the Ferrarese custom, I shall discuss state and court appointments separately.

I

In 1476, the state list included some 150 office-holders ranging from the exalted position of *podestà* of Ferrara, which heads the list, down to the captaincies of various small strongholds and border outposts throughout the territories of the Estean state.[2] The most important appointments in this broad category are the various judgeships, key notarial offices, supervisory positions related to agriculture and the taxation of agricultural and other products, local judicial and executive posts, such as the *podestà* of the various towns, and captaincies of important garrisons, especially those at the gates of Ferrara. No distinction is made or even implied between appointments of a civilian or primarily military char-

[2] Chig. I, I, 4, ff. 49-50 v, has the list headed "Distributiones officiorum anni 1476," on which this section is based. A less detailed list of the same offices is the index of a "Libro d'Officii del Stato di Ferrara al tempo del sig. Duca Borso," 1450-65. ASM, ASE, Cancelleria, Registri di Cancelleria, vol. A/6, listing 119 positions, but not including captaincies of garrisons.

acter, though some of these jobs would obviously have required the commanding of at least a small squadron of troops. The list as Caleffini gives it seems to be compiled in order of descending importance of the various positions. It begins with the *podestà* and the *sindaco* of the palace of Ferrara, by which is meant the *Palazzo della Ragione*. These are followed by a number of judgeships, defined both on the basis of geographical jurisdictions and particular areas of authority, such as the post of "iudex ad victualium," who in turn are given jurisdiction within a particular region. Yet another judicial office is entrusted with the wheat supply ("iudex bladorum ferrariae"). The term *iudex* should not be taken in its limited modern sense; it would seem to describe a position of executive responsibility, in which an official was responsible for the supervision and management of the matters under his jurisdiction. This would of course have involved strictly judicial (or, at least, law-enforcement) functions as well, since a large body of positive law surrounded all aspects of land tenure, grazing, agriculture, property rights, water use, and so forth. This group of officials includes a small number of notaries, some with specific functions, and such miscellaneous officials as the keeper of the clock of Ferrara.

The next group of appointees are the financial officials of the communes, led for Ferrara by two *factores generales*. Under them there served the *sindacus camerae Ferrariae,* an executive probably entrusted with the day-to-day management of the financial offices of the commune. The *camera* over which the *sindacus* cast his watchful eye included some eleven salaried officials, bearing such titles as *ratiocinator* (2), *exactor generalis, thesaurarius,* several notaries, custodial officials, and a keeper of the books (not a "bookkeeper," but a guard, charged with the physical safety of the documents, which were of course maintained by the notaries).

The executive, judicial, and financial bureaucracy, including some forty people, comprised the highest level of Ferrarese communal government, below the magistracy of the twelve *savi*. In the list for 1476 it is evident that Ercole had taken care to appoint some of his close associates to a number of these important positions. Some of the names in the list are familiar figures at court, and even major office-holders in the ducal household, not only during this period, but even in the same year. Such names as Severi, Sardi, Sandali, Villa, Ariosti, Barbalonga, Cestarelli, Machiavelli, Giglioli appear in both lists and are familiar as servants and beneficiaries of the dukes. But it is also worth noting that there are many names which are not so familiar, and many great families—Trotti, Contrari, Bevilacqua, Calcagnini, Gualengo, to mention a few—whose names do not appear on the state list. This may suggest a class distinction between the great, land-holding noble families, whose services tended to take more dignified or exalted forms, and a slightly less distinguished and more dependent group of noblemen and wealthy citizens for whom state service was important as a means of livelihood and advancement.[3]

After the principal Ferrarese officials, the next in order of prestige and importance are the judicial and executive officials of the other major towns in the territory. In general these towns filled their own offices by various traditional means, but there was always at least one higher figure appointed by the duke, and a military garrison as well. This category includes the *podestà* of such towns as Modena, Massa Fiscaglia, Codegoro, Massa Lombarda, Lendinara, and many others. Other towns lived under the surveillance of a "vicecomes" or "vicarius" or "capitanus." Some, such as

[3] Caleffini, ff. 39r and v, provides a list of the great families of Ferrara. There are 38 families of "zentilhomini antiqui" and 19 of "zentilhomini moderni," but the writer does not state his criteria in distinguishing between the two. A later hand has added some sixteenth-century families to the lists of "moderni."

Modena, had more than one governor, including such officials as treasurers and other fiscal administrators. It is clear from the list that there was no set of strictly uniform criteria for administering the provincial towns. The system left a good deal of scope for the play of local traditions and practices, which are of course reflected in the diverse statutes of individual towns. (These, like guild statutes, were subject to ducal confirmation.) The objectives of central administration seem to have been political fidelity, financial returns, and a reasonable adherence to and enforcement of the laws.

After the list of provincial governors and territorial officers, there follows a large group of financial administrators. Most of these bear the title merely of official, "officialis," and are entrusted with some particular function related to the collection of specific taxes, the supervising of books of account for particular crops, the supervision of collections in a particular region. At the head of this group of auditors and tax-collectors was an official called the *Superior gabellarum Ferrariae,* or chief tax-collector, who probably oversaw all of the specialized subordinates who gathered the revenues.

A final group of office-holders is that of captains of fortified places in Ferrara and its surroundings. This group includes the keepers of city and town gates and other sites throughout the region. The names of these men are generally unfamiliar to a reader of court records or chronicles, and it is probable that this last category of captains is a military group, unlike the captains mentioned previously, who are included among the *podestà* and viscounts, who probably had primarily political and semi-judicial functions, and who include in their number such court favorites as the poet Tito Strozzi.

II

The list of salaried officials in the ducal household published by Ercole on January 22, 1476, is much longer and more detailed than the list of state offices.[4] By giving the monthly salary of each of the appointees, expressed in *Lire Marchesane,* it offers some useful information as to their relative importance to their employer. At the head of the list is Ercole's brother Sigismondo, with a stipend of 2,375 Lire (hereafter "LM") per month. Next is a man described only as Messer Alberto Ramaldo, the recipient of 500 LM per month, for services that are not specified. He may well have been Sigismondo's main companion, or chief-of-staff. Three other members of the Este family follow: Alberto, Ercole's half-brother, at a stipend of 831 LM per month; Scipione, Alberto's nephew, at 120 LM; and Polidoro, another nephew, at only 15 LM per month.

After this small group of relatives and intimates, there comes the *Consiglio Segreto,* which might best be characterized as a group of close, trusted advisers to the Duke. Though there is a small *fondo* of correspondence to Borso and Ercole from his secret counsellors at the Archivio di Stato in Modena, it is evident (even from that correspondence) that the *consiglio* characteristically functioned as individuals, and not as a formal deliberative body, like its nominal counterpart in Milan.[5] In 1476, the counsel con-

---

[4] *Ibid.,* ff. 51-5.

[5] ASM, ASE, Consigli, Giunte, Consulte, Reggenze, Buste 1a, 1b. The documents do not entirely confirm Valenti's claim ("I consigli di governo," *art. cit.,* 31) that ". . . al Consiglio Segreto venivano sottoposti dal principe . . . i più spinosi e delicati problemi che sorgevano dalla quotidiana attività di governo." The *Consiglio Segreto* did on occasions meet as a body—sometimes jointly with the *Consiglio di Giustizia* (as on May 10, 1470, according to a letter to Borso in Busta 1b). It was occasionally called upon to act during the Duke's absence, or to consider some matter too trivial for the Duke's attention (see Busta Ia, letter from Borso to the Consiglio dated August 10, 1466, referring a matter because "Nuy non havemo tempo de audirlo, come era il nostro pensiero."). Many of the letters sent to the council by Borso and Niccolò di Leonello ask for advice or expertise relative to pending decisions, and others offer instructions and directives. These are rarely important matters of state; they have to

sisted of six members, at salaries ranging from 8 to 80 LM monthly. This body was followed, in order of precedence on the list, by the *Consiglio di Giustizia,* consisting of three doctors of law, all foreigners, and all receiving a stipend of 45 LM.[6] I have already suggested (p. 142) that this body was not a judicial organ as such, but rather an advisory council that helped the Duke in legal matters in which his interests were involved, or which required his decision.

Following these high-level advisory appointments, comes the chancellery, headed by Paolo Antonio Trotti, as "first secretary," a powerful position paying 50 LM per month. Ercole, unlike Borso, did not have a *referendarius,* but Trotti appears to have played an analogous role for many years, and is sometimes referred to as "referendarius" in the chronicle (see Caleffini, f. 38). Under Trotti there served two officials with the rank of secretary, and six additional appointees who also served as "cancelleri," drafting documents, and perhaps also serving merely as scribes. Their stipends range from 8 to 24 LM per month, the latter sum for a full-fledged secretary, who could therefore have lived quite comfortably. A small group of couriers and horsemen follow, and all of these were paid a regular stipend of 21 or 22 LM, though this may not have turned out to have been as generous as it perhaps seems, in the light of their heavy expenses for food, lodging, and maintenance.

Next on the list are the "oratori" or resident ambassadors. In 1476, there were only four of them. Bonfrancesco degli Arlotti, a physician from Reggio, served as ducal orator at the papal court, with a stipend of 28 LM. Alberto Cortese, a Modenese nobleman, was assigned to Venice at 40 LM. The

---

do, as Valenti rightly says, with day-to-day administration. It is this that distinguishes the Ferrarese from the Milanese *Consiglio Segreto* (Valenti, 32).

[6] For the year in question, these were Guglielmo Pincharo da Parma, Manfredo Maldente da Forli, Francesco Verlato, Cavaliere da Vicenza.

Reggian Niccolò dei Roberti held perhaps the most sensitive post as orator in Milan, at a huge salary of 83 LM. Finally the Ferrarese nobleman Niccolò Bendedio held the post in Florence, at 41 LM. It is interesting that at this period Ercole should not have had an ambassador in Naples, where he had such strong and recent marital ties. The reason may be that he had much less to fear from the more distant Aragonese than from the great powers that hemmed him in on all sides.

The section of the list that I have just described also includes a number of minor assistants to the various commissions, and also a few other personal assistants at relatively low salaries. For all of these stipendiaries, excluding only Sigismondo d'Este with his princely allowance, Ercole had to spend a total of 1884 LM per month.

The list then proceeds to the financial officials of the ducal *camera*. Interestingly enough, the same two men listed as *factori generali* of the communal *camera* are appointed to the same office in the ducal *camera*. Filippo Cestarelli and Iacomo Machiavelli both received 20 LM monthly for their services to the duke. It would require a substantial amount of additional research to learn whether such duplication, even in that office, was standard procedure, but there is nothing to indicate that this was regarded as irregular in any way. That these two accounts were not as separate as their structure might suggest has of course long been obvious, and fits in perfectly with the general pattern of ducal control of communal institutions. Given such overlapping, it becomes easier to understand how effectively this could be maintained. In addition to these *factori generali,* there are account managers, various types of notaries, accountants, and agricultural officials. Though some notaries are simply listed as such, many have special assignments. For example, Antonio Francesco de' Sardi is appointed "exactore generale de la camera." Bartommeo da Valenza is made "notaro de la exacteria." One Iacomo Lorenzo is entrusted with the *catas-*

tri, which means, I suppose, the *Catastri delle Investiture,* discussed previously (p. 136, n. 17). Giovanni Maria Girondo is made "governor of the books of the *camera.*" Simone da Milano becomes custodian of the "bolleta di salariati," or chief payroll officer. In all, there are perhaps forty officials in this group, which administered the ducal finances. But this large company is carried at a relatively low cost—340 LM per month.

This list is followed by another group of twenty-three men, the caretakers or *factori* of the various castles, palaces, and country houses. These men are paid very small salaries, ranging from 1 LM per month at places like Consandolo and Fossadalbero to 6 LM for the keeper of a large establishment such as Belriguardo. Twelve engineers and craftsmen round out this category, and at higher salaries. The builder Piero de Benigni receives 26 LM; Iacopo, the gardener at Belfiore, gets almost 9 LM.

Following this mundane collection of caretakers and functionaries come prestigious categories of "compagni," "zentilhomini," "medici," "camerlenghi," "seschalchi," and "scuderi," in that order. These are the courtiers, arranged in order of their descending rank, salary, and importance. There are five companions, led by the noble poet of courtiers himself, "Conte Mathio Maria Boiardo," who, along with Theophilo Calcagnino, and Bonifacio Bevilacqua, earned 70 LM per month. The "zentilhomini" too come mainly from important old families, such as the Assassini, Roverella, de la Sala, and Gualengo. "Antonio da Cornazano, poeta" is included in this group, and for the quality of his work and his social position, may perhaps be considered as a Type I humanist.[7] After the eleven gentlemen come four physicians, including Niccolò da Lonigo, the translator of Procopius.[8]

---

[7] See above, p. 221.

[8] BEM, MS. Alpha H 4,2 (Ital. 463), *Tradutione de Procopio de le Guerre de Gotti facta de Greco in Vulgare P. Maestro Nicolo da Lonigo*

The physicians are followed by fifteen chamberlains and two seneschals, one of whom was Francesco Ariosto, and twenty-nine "scuderi," or equerries, whose salaries varied between 22 and 30 LM per month.

Next on the list are the more clearly service-oriented employees—the court barber, porters, bakers, and the like. Separate categories include five butlers, four cooks, and several types of tailors. Then come the masters of the stalls, and the men charged with birding, falconry, and other kinds of game. This group includes *occelatori,* or birders, at salaries ranging from 8 to 28 LM. There are also some much more lowly hunters and birders listed as employed at some of the more remote palaces.

Of greater cultural interest is the long list of musicians which follows. The instrumentalists are divided into "musici," "trombeti," "piffari," and "tromboni." The highest paid member of the instrumental coterie is not, as one might suspect, the famous Pietrobono dal Chitarino, who earned 18 LM, but rather the piper Corado de Alemagna, at 26 LM. Salaries in this group averaged in the low teens, so that instrumentalists were priced at a slight discount under singers who, as we shall see, averaged in the high teens. The instrumentalists are followed by tailors, staff-bearers, archers, and muleteers. Small groups of wagoners, grooms, and chaplains follow. Bringing up the rear in Ercole's list are the ducal singers, of whom there are twenty, all at salaries ranging from 7 to 25 LM, with most of them in the 13 to 19 LM category. There are sopranos, tenors, basses, and many unclassified voices. They come from Flanders, Brabant, Cambrai, Holland, France, Paris, Mantua, and other unidentified places. These men must have comprised the choir which

---

a *Contemplazione de lo Illustrissimo Signore Misser Hercule Ducha di Ferrara.* . . . This is the presentation copy to Ercole, with miniatures and illuminations. Other Mss. are in BAV, Barb. Lat. 4085 (XLVI, 27); Biblioteca Marciana Ital. Vi, 222 (6040); see chapter V, n. 67.

Sabadino degli Arienti describes in the passage quoted on p. 194.

III

The list of singers concludes the *bolleta di salariati* for Ercole's account. According to Caleffini's total, the monthly expenditure for the salaries of the entire staff of the ducal household alone came to 9,328 LM per month for the year 1476. This of course includes only salary, and does not include the stipend of Eleanora d'Aragona, and her own personal household, which is budgeted separately. Including Eleanora's income of 700 LM per month, this separate account adds an additional 1,700 LM to the total of court salaries, for a grand total of 11,000 LM, in round figures.

Ercole's staff, including all appointees from the merest stable boy to the most distinguished noble companion, numbered close to 600 people, at an average stipend of about 15 LM per month. Leaving aside the artifically high incomes of several individuals, such as Sigismondo and Alberto d'Este, we obtain a more realistic average of approximately 12 LM per month. It is clear from the list that a man could live, though almost certainly very badly indeed, on less than 2 LM per month, though he would probably have had to do so without frequent recourse to the monetary economy, through bartering, handouts, and good luck. A stipend in excess of 25 LM was sufficient to keep an important gentleman in good style, and anything in excess of 40 LM, ranging to 85 or 90, was reserved for the great grandees of the court, and for extremely talented specialists from without, such as the jurists of the *Consiglio di Giustizia*. The extremes of wealth and poverty must have been as striking toward the end of the century as Gandini found they were during the time of Niccolò III.[9]

[9] See above, p. 88, n. 42.

Perhaps the most notable aspect of this comprehensive list is the relatively small number of people involved in significant political activity. Adding together the members of the *Consiglio Segreto,* the chancellors, orators, companions, and gentlemen, all of whom may be assumed to have been active in this area, we have a total of only about thirty people. Most of them were Ferrarese aristocrats, with some input from the great families of Modena and Reggio, and they received an average stipend of 45 LM per month, a generous salary indeed in an economy such as that which we have described. It is then perhaps not surprising that we can describe the Este bureaucracy as exceptionally able, efficient, and loyal. It was small enough to be effectively supervised, large enough to execute its function with dispatch. Above all, it offered very appreciable rewards in terms of salaries, opportunities for advancement, the intangible satisfaction of serving a great personage, and ultimately, the possibility of even greater gifts of land, titles, and other noble prerogatives.

APPENDIX II

The Preface of
Ludovico Carbone's Translation of Sallust

TRADUCTIONE DI SALLUSTIO HISTORIO-
GRAPHO PER LODOVICO CARBONE ALLO
ILLUST. ET GRATIOSO MISSERE ALBERTO
DA ESTE & PRIMA IL PROEMIO:

Ragionando pochi giorni inanti con Nicolo
Bendedio vostro fidele servitore & mio caro discipolo, lui me
hebbe a dire quanto volentiera la signoria v[ostra] legeva le
historie,[1] quanto piacere prendea depse in sapere la vita et
costumi di quelli antichi Romani che in ogni laude et
gentilezza fuorno tanto gloriosi. Dilaqual cosa non mi mara-
viglio niente, cognoscendo in voi lanimo valoroso & gentile
che in questo ben dimostrati a desiderare la notitia di coloro
che forno il fiore di virtute & darme. Et certo non e lectione
alcuna piu conveniente agli signori che quella delle historie,
dove insieme si ritrova gli acti virtuosi con gli suoi exempli,
dicendo il nostro Tullio la historia e un testimonio degli
tempi, luce della verita, conservatione della memoria, maes-
tra della vita nostra, nunciatrice della antichitate; & sopra
tutto intesi che molto vi gustava il parlar di Crispo Salustio
con quella sua gravissima brevitade. Et anche in questo
havite bon giudicio, peroché niuno altro auctore latino fu
mai, che in si poche parole comprendesse tante alte & pro-
funde sententie. In modo che ognuno ha che dire & stupire
di questa brevitade salustiana. Cosi volesse idio se ritrovassino

[1] This is the first evidence we have of a well-defined interest in history
on the part of Alberto. For Ercole's apparent interest in the past, see
above, p. 168.

lopre sue magiore dove tutta la Romana historia diligentissi-
mamente conscripse, come spesso vedemo allegarsi dalli
nostri prestanti grammatici. Ma gli tempi sinestri & le
calamita ditalia, la negligentia degli homini ce ha privati
dital gioia. Io, adonca, che sempre ve ho portato & continu-
amente porto singolare affectione, maxime da poi che ritor-
nassemo da este dove dal nostro sapientissimo Duca fosti
mandato io insieme con voi a celebrare & honorare le
exequie di Bertholdo [M, II, 219] vostro morto nella
morea in servitio de signori venetiani, in si laudibile expedi-
tione per la fede christiana.² Et io feci quella oratione funebre della quale ancora tuttil quegli montanari ne parlano.
Voi alhora in si facta maniera vi portasti á consolar la donna
& á confortare gli altri rimanenti, & á respondere con tanta
humanitade & gratia, che havesto inamorato un cor di pietra.
Da quel tempo in qua, me crescette nel animo un si
smesurato amor verso di voi che non e peso si duro & aspro,
che non mi paresse agevole & legerissimo pur che sentisse di
poter compiacere al mio M. Alberto. Et pero non e da pigli-
are admiratione se tanto site grato & caro al vostro illustrissimo fratello & suavissimo Duca nostro che non solamente
ve ame & reverisca come fratello, ma etiam ve habia electo
per sua fida compagnia, & indissolubile communione del
viver suo, tanto se dilecta nella digna presentia vostra, piena
di fede & di bontade.

Io adunca mi ho tolto questa piccola fatica in voler vul-
garizare quanto mi sara possibile, cosi bella & famosa historia
della coniuratione di Catalina, perche siando voi dati alli
exercitii signorili non havite havuto il tempo a poter im-
parare il senso litterale. Et noi, che per vostri beneficii
havemo acquistata la scientia delle lettere, semo obligati a
dover vene fare participi. De una cosa pero vi voglio
certificare Signor mio, che non si puo havere quella integra
& perfecta dolceza nel vulgare che provano & sentino i

---

² For the career of the *condottiere* Bertholdo d'Este, see *Ant. Est.* II, 219.

letterati, per la maiestade degli ornatissimi vocabuli, & per quelle galantissime clausule tanto aptamente serrate. Et se questo potesti chiaramente vedere, lassaresti ogni altro piacere & subito correristi alle schole nostre per impararle. Se bene in laltre cose site a noi superiori, in questo per certo habiamo avantagio da voi.[3]

Legeti vi prego benignamente loperetta mia, la quale se me accorgero che vi vada per la mente; abracciatò anche del altre magiore, benche alpunte sia occupato intradure due opere pellegrine composte da dui graeci, luna come debba essere facto il bono capitano, laltra de tutte le forme & modi de ordinare le schiere in campo. Et di queste due ne faccio un presente al vostro dolcissimo & amantissimo fratello M. hercule, alquale sempre chio viva sero grandemente obligato, per[che se non fosse stata] la sua liberalissima cortesia, [non

---

[3] This assertion of a literacy superior to that of the princes is not uncommon among Ferrarese humanists in the later *Quattrocento*. Their claim to expertise (and with it superior taste and knowledge) was perhaps not only calculated to enhance or advance their own status, but also perhaps to shame their patrons into taking them more seriously. In this preface, Carbone seems to be rather deftly combining flattery and condescension to achieve his ends. Cf. the remarks of Carlo da San Giorgio, the chronicler of the Pio conspiracy, who wrote in his Preface to Borso (published by A. Cappelli as "La congiura contro il Duca Borso d'Este," *AMP, Ser. i, vol. ii* [1865], 48): "La fortuna inimica de ogni virtuoso huomo non ha voluto a li altri tuoi singolari ornamenti adiungere l'ornamento de le littere, il quale è più excellente che l'huomo havere possa." He goes on to apologize for having committed the impropriety of first presenting the work "in latino et non nel nostro vulgara parlare." Yet in a way he seems to be reveling in Borso's ignorance and that of his associates as he goes on to say: "Et per volere ad te, unico et caro mio Signore, et a li altri tuoi fratelli et compagni, come è mio desiderio et debito, fare cossa che agradire vi debia, a ciò quello che per manchamento de littere gustae non poteti, cussì vulgarmente legendo qualche dilecto ne pigliati (benchè tanta differencia sia/da l'uno parlare a l'altro di dolceça et suavità, quanto de una dolce et delicato vino ad un altro bruscho et despiacevole che per sede bevere se conveni), questa mia opereta in vulgare ho reducto."

potressimo vivere.] [4] Peró non viscorde Signor mio con-
firmarme nel amore Del nostro gratiosissimo Duca, che una
volta intenda, & cognosca il mio nobile ingegno [non merit-
tasse di cadere in tanta bassezza,] anche allui novamente
compono un libro di facetie & piacevolezze.[5] Ma lasciamo
star li facti nostri & udiamo parlar il savio & polito Sallustio.

[4] This is probably a reference to some unspecifiable benefice, perhaps
one of Carbone's university appointments. It appears, from the reference
to "M. Hercule" and from the deferentially nameless allusions to the
"Duca," that Borso was still duke when this was written, but that it had
been Ercole who had supported or protected Carbone. For a sketch of
Carbone's life, see L. Frati, "Di Ludovico Carbone e delle sue opere," *AF*,
xx (1910), 55-80.

[5] This can only be Carbone's *Facezie*, which can be consulted in
A. Kader-Salza, ed., *Le Facezie di Ludovico Carbone ferrarese* (Livorno,
1900); see also the remarks by V. Rossi, *Il Quattrocento*, 2nd ed. (Milan,
1945), 209, 217.

INDEX

All persons mentioned in the text and notes are indexed by their surnames, with the exception of popes, kings, and a few other individuals known almost exclusively by their Christian names. Names of classical authors are given in the most familiar form, those of modern scholars are entered by surname and initials. In general, citations in the notes are indexed only if the reference is of interest not merely as documentation, but in relation to some substantive or theoretical issue. In addition to entries for particular subjects, the subheadings for the entries on the various Este rulers, the Este family, and Ferrara are designed to facilitate access to specific subjects treated in the various sections of the book.